PROFESSIONAL STUDIO TECHNIQUES

WEB DESIGN ESSENTIALS

MARIA GIUDICE WITH ANITA DENNIS

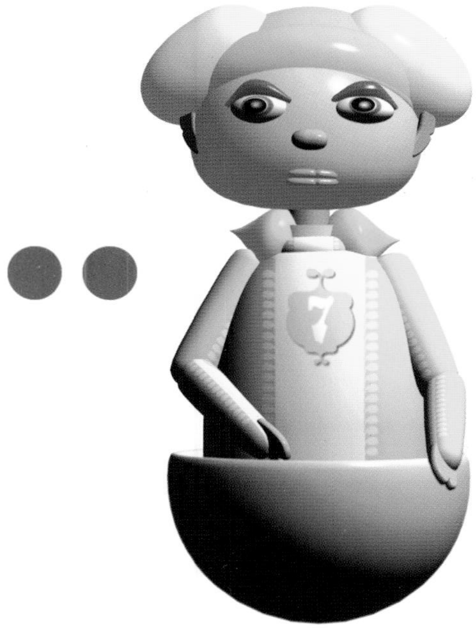

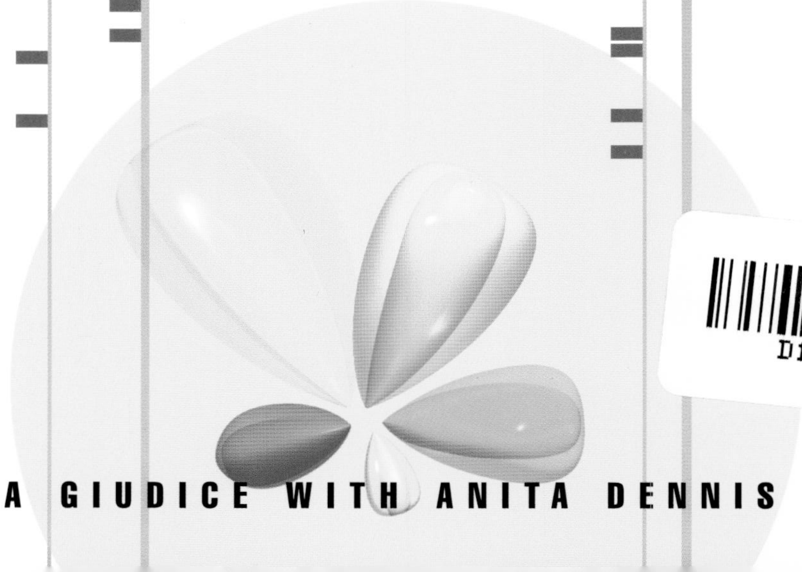

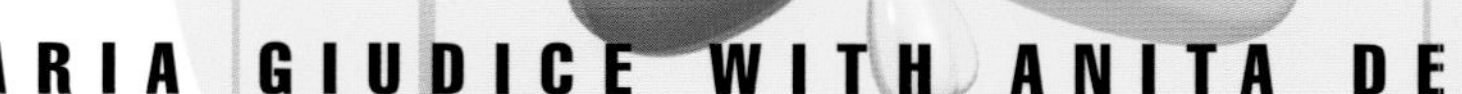

Web Design Essentials

Maria Giudice with Anita Dennis

This Adobe Press book is published by Peachpit Press.
For information on Adobe Press books, contact

Peachpit Press
1249 Eighth Street
Berkeley, CA 94710
800-283-9444
510-524-2178
510-524-2221 (fax)
http://www.peachpit.com

Peachpit Press is a division of Addison Wesley Longman

For the latest on Adobe Press books, go to
http://www.adobe.com/adobepress

ISBN 0-201-70011-5
9 8 7 6 5 4 3 2 1
Printed and bound in the United States of America

Introduction

Easy Intermediate Advanced

Web Design Essentials offers advice for all levels of users. At the beginning of each tip is a guide that indicates whether it is easy, intermediate, or advanced. If you're a beginner, you can start with the easy tips and work your way up to the more challenging techniques.

Today's Web designers face more challenges than ever.

It used to be that all you had to do—all you *could* do—was hand-code HTML in a text editor such as BBEdit, specify a few inline graphics, and put the pages on your server for the world to see. But in the last few years, myriad technologies have come along that bring Web pages to life: Cascading Style Sheets, animated GIFs, frames, and streaming video, to name a few.

The problem is that while these technologies let designers create ever-more sophisticated Web sites, mastering them remains a time-consuming and resource-draining task. No sooner do you grasp one technology than it's replaced by a more elegant, more trendy alternative.

And it's ironic that despite all of these changes and advances, we still have little control over how our pages appear in any given visitor's browser. There are just too many discrepancies in the features and fonts that different browsers and operating systems support. This makes our job all the harder.

Thankfully, Web software tools have matured to a point where they make our job a little easier. Applications, particularly those from Adobe Systems, are well integrated and let us seamlessly exchange files between both platforms and applications. And we can complete all phases of our designs in a graphical environment that uses consistent tools, palettes, and menus.

That's why we've compiled an assortment of step-by-step tips that can help you take full advantage of all that Adobe's software has to offer. All good software offers multiple ways of executing the same task; Adobe products are no exception. But we think that the best advice comes from real-world designers who know the software first-hand and have developed personalized, tried-and-true methods for performing typical production tasks.

Thankfully, Web software tools have matured to a point where they make our job a little easier.

So that's exactly what we've collected. The techniques described in these pages will not only make your everyday design and production workflows easier but also make your Web sites more stylish.

We think these tips will pay off in other important ways, too, both professional and personal. You'll please clients by producing sites with fast-loading and well-placed graphics, cohesive color and typography across platforms and browsers, and a clear and consistent navigational interface. Plus you'll have the satisfaction of successfully tackling the most exciting technological and design challenges to come along in decades.

Although *Web Design Essentials* covers the current versions of Adobe software for both the Macintosh and Windows—including Photoshop 5.5, ImageReady 2.0, Illustrator 8.0, and GoLive 4.0—you can accomplish many of these techniques in older versions of the applications. One of the biggest differences between Photoshop 5.0 and 5.5, for example, is the addition of the Save for Web feature. If you're still using Photoshop 5.0, save your GIF graphics for the Web by changing the image mode to Indexed Color, specifying your preferred palette, and then exporting your file as GIF89a.

Wherever possible, our instructions are written in platform-neutral language, but occasional keyboard shortcuts are presented in red with the Macintosh key command first and the Windows equivalent in parentheses.

Acknowledgements

Web Design Essentials *came together thanks to the team at HOT.*

We greatly appreciate Renee Anderson's tireless and efficient project management, which included everything from recruiting contributors and tips to managing content and workflow. Renee kept *Web Design Essentials* on track and on time. Noreen Santini was equally dedicated and critical to the success of the book: As the project's lead designer, she spearheaded the design and production of the pages. We're also grateful to the other members of the HOT team— Hyland Baron, Florian Fangohr, Julia Hummelt, and Gregory Ramsperger—for working so diligently and for providing many of the useful tips and techniques in these pages.

We'd also like to thank our other contributors for sharing their time and their talent: Jeremy Tai Abbett, Tom Bray, Geoffrey Brown, Casey Caston, Anne-Marie Concepción, Melissa Crowley, Katrin Eismann, Michael Everitt, Sandra Kelch, Frank Kolodziej, Jason Kottke, Steve McGuire, Joachim Müller-Lancé, Macky Pamintuan, Steve Piasecki, Ben Seibel, and André Sjøberg.

Finally, many thanks to Amy Franceschini for her cover artwork and editorial contributions; to Nancy Ruenzel, Kate Reber, and Nancy Davis at Peachpit Press for supporting us throughout the project; to David Herman, Susan Horovitz, and Irv Kanode at Adobe Systems for their technical review; and to Antony Bolante, Tema Goodwin, Andrea Dudrow, Victor Gavenda, Cheryl Landes, and Rebecca Plunkett for their editorial assistance.

Table of Contents

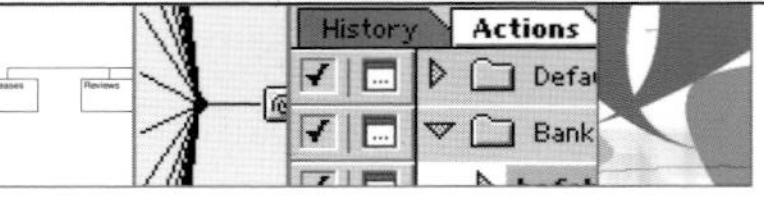

4

HTML, Tables, and Frames

5

Animation and Rollovers

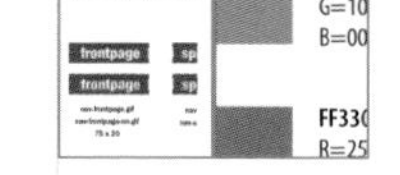

6

Appendices

Chapter 1

Planning Production

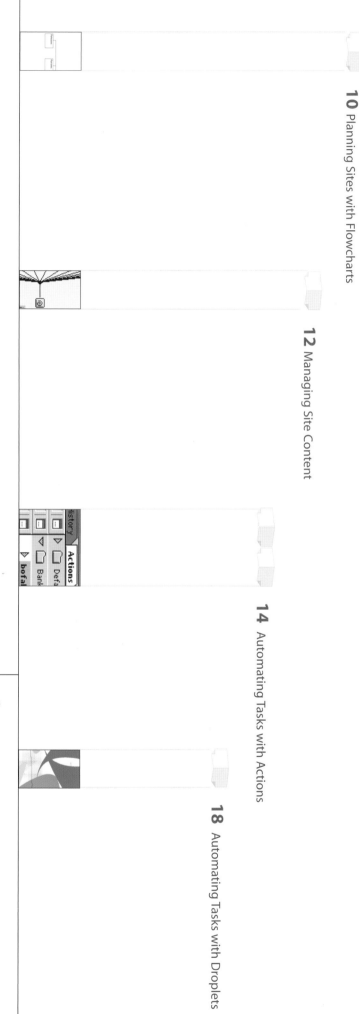

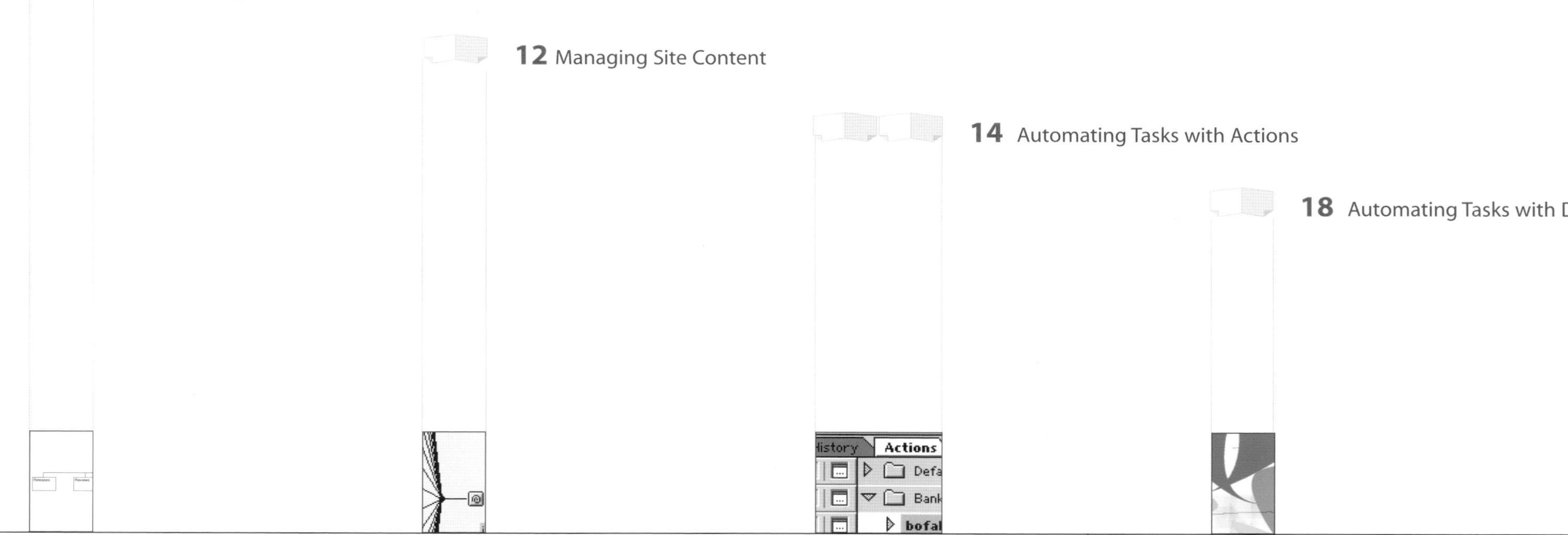

André Sjøberg
Razorfish–Norway
www.razorfish.com

Planning Sites with Flowcharts

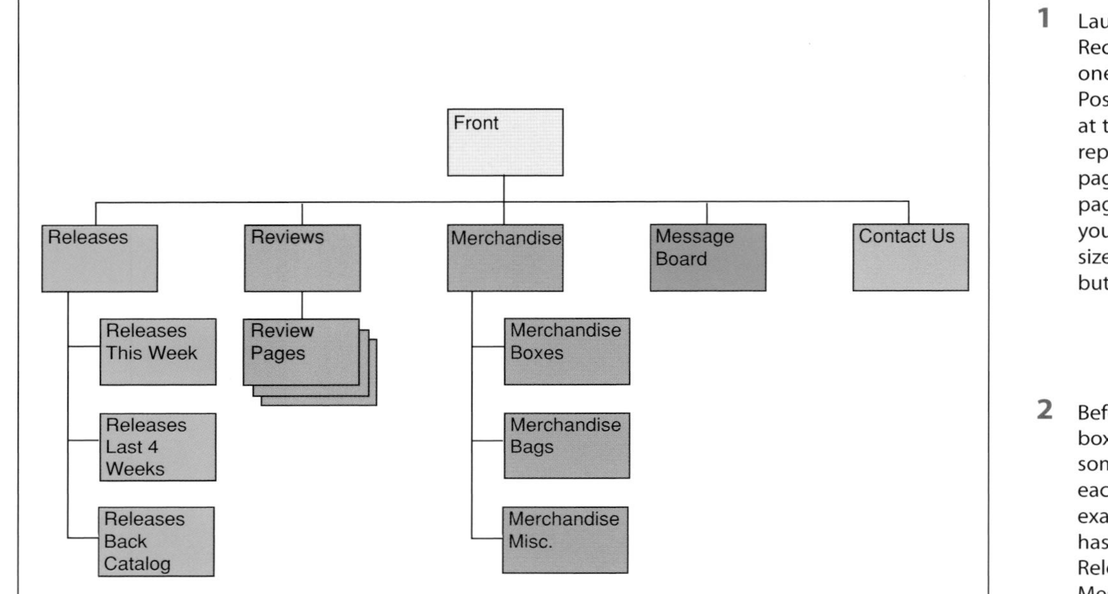

One of the first steps in designing a Web site is creating a flowchart that shows how the site will be organized. A flowchart also gives you a visual sense of what pages and sections need to be filled, and it helps you plan navigational elements. Finally, a flowchart lets you establish an optimal structure for the developers and designers who actually produce the site. Here's how to use Adobe Illustrator to create efficient flowcharts.

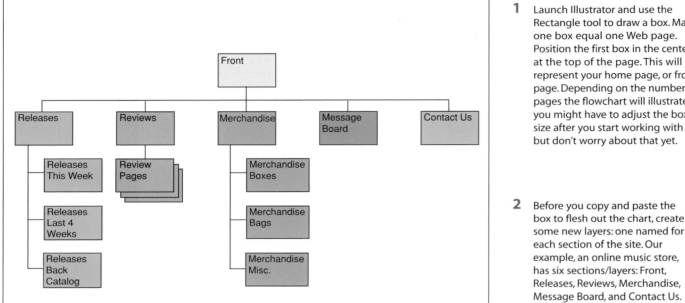

1 Launch Illustrator and use the Rectangle tool to draw a box. Make one box equal one Web page. Position the first box in the center, at the top of the page. This will represent your home page, or front page. Depending on the number of pages the flowchart will illustrate, you might have to adjust the box size after you start working with it, but don't worry about that yet.

2 Before you copy and paste the box to flesh out the chart, create some new layers: one named for each section of the site. Our example, an online music store, has six sections/layers: Front, Releases, Reviews, Merchandise, Message Board, and Contact Us.

3 Now copy the box you drew for the front page and paste one on each section layer, positioning the new boxes one tier down from the front page and spreading them evenly and horizontally across the page. By giving each section of your site its own layer, it's easy to move, add, or edit individual sections.

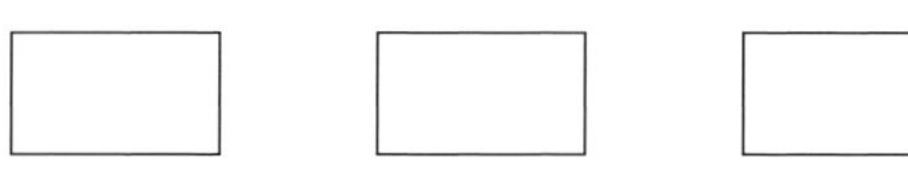

4 Identify each box with the name of the section so that design sketches or other documents used to plan content can be easily paired with their relevant box and page. For large Web sites with hundreds of pages, you might want to use a systematic naming convention, such as "Section01_Subsection02_Page05." Put all the text in a separate layer called Text and make it black, so it will be readable after you color-code your boxes.

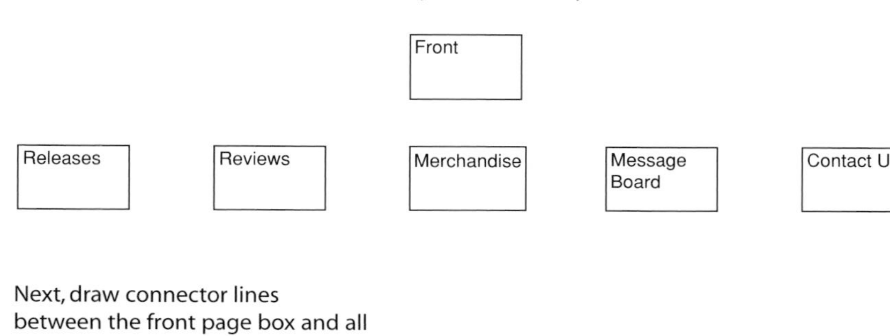

5 Next, draw connector lines between the front page box and all the main section boxes, putting them in a separate layer called Lines. This makes it easy to redraw the lines if boxes are moved.

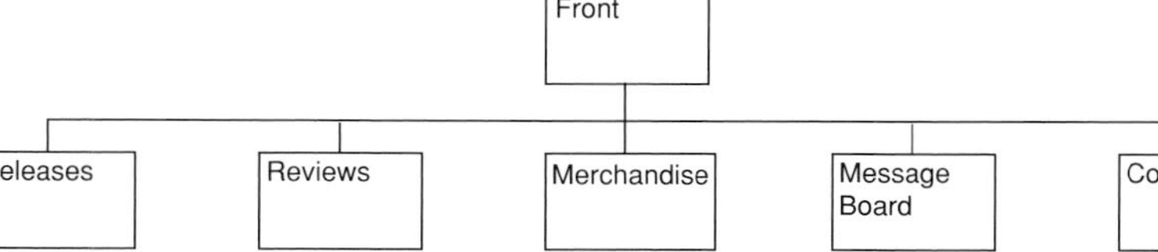

6 As you add content, paste new boxes into the appropriate layer, naming them and adding connector lines as you go. Our Releases section has links to three other pages, for example: releases from the past week, releases from the last four weeks, and the entire back catalog. The stacked pages in our Reviews section represent templated content that will automatically be generated from a database.

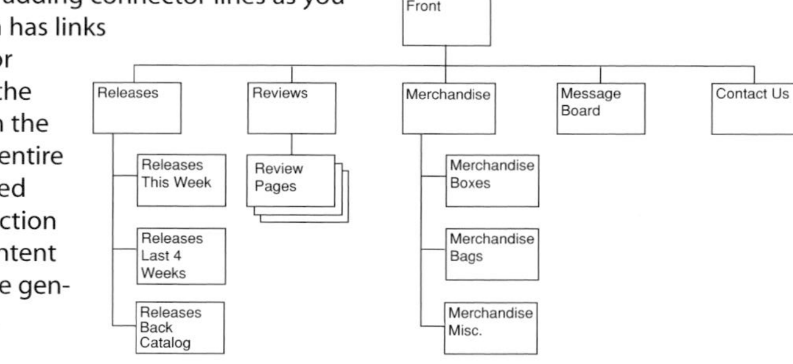

7 Finally, color-code your boxes so that you can easily recognize each section and see which ones need to be developed, which are too full, and so on. Toggle off all layers but one by clicking the eye icons next to the layer names in the Layers palette. Select all of the boxes on that layer, and give them a fill color, such as blue for our Releases section. Repeat the procedure using a different color for each section.

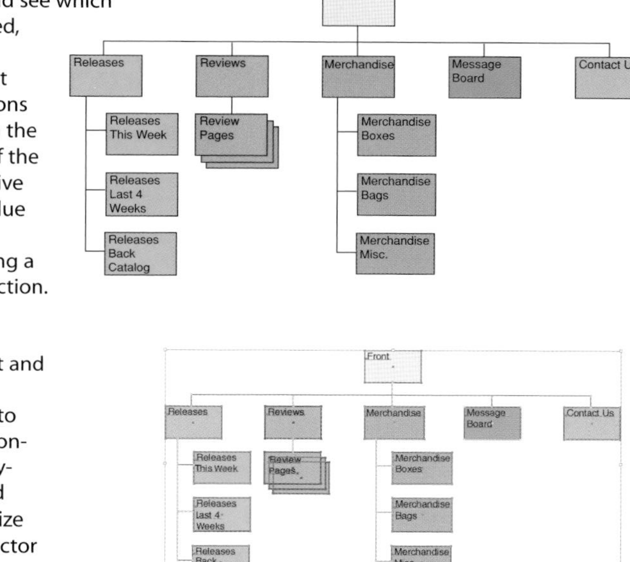

8 If you move a box, select it and its text so that they flow together. And if you have to shrink boxes as you add content, perhaps so that everything fits onto one printed page, you can globally resize the boxes, text, and connector lines by selecting all and pressing the Shift key as you click and drag with the Scale tool (to keep all objects in proportion).

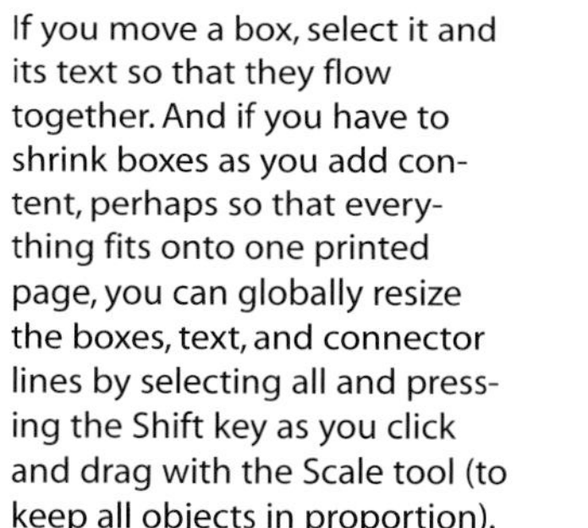

Julia Hummelt
HOT
www.hotstudio.com

Managing Site Content

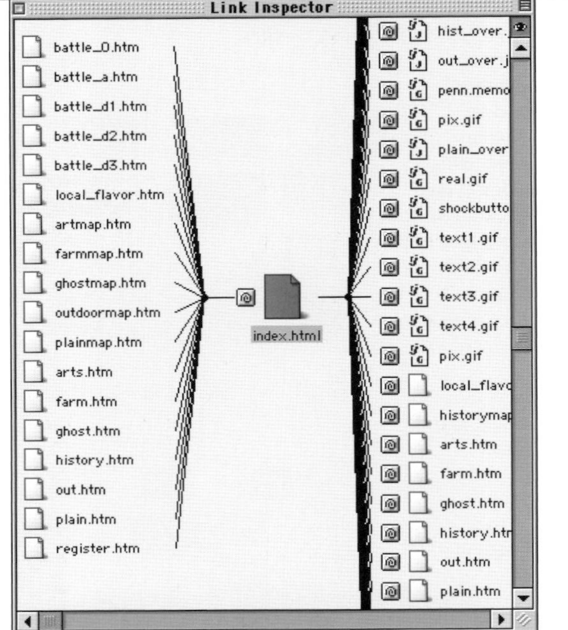

Sometimes it's impossible to plan a site's structure separately from developing the content. In those cases, GoLive might be a more useful planning tool. You can not only design flowcharts and automatically manage page hierarchies but also track and manage files, links, and pages as you create them. GoLive stores the content for a site in one folder and lets you manage those files through the site window, the File Inspector, and other tools. Here's a quick tour of the program's site-management features.

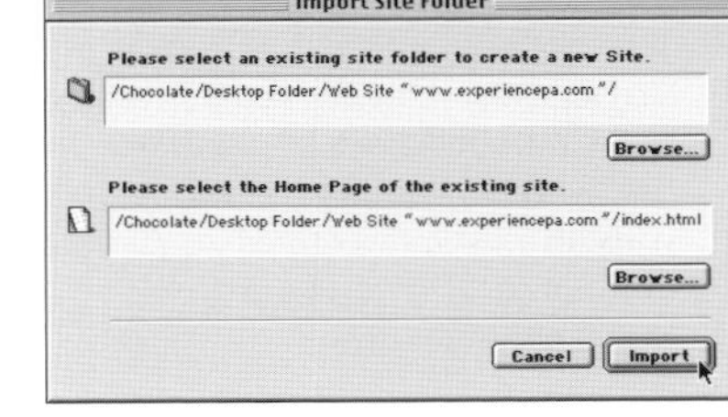

1 To create a site in GoLive, choose New Site from the File menu and select Blank. Specify where you want to place the site in your directory and name the site. GoLive opens a site window with a blank index page and displays the File Inspector. You can also import sites by choosing Import from Folder from the New Site menu item and browsing to find your folder.

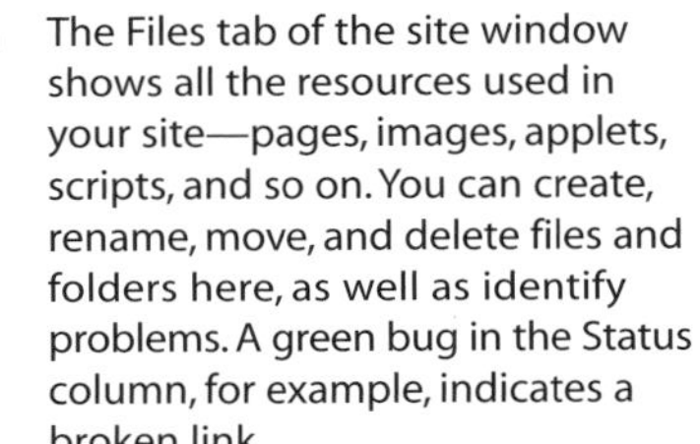

2 The Files tab of the site window shows all the resources used in your site—pages, images, applets, scripts, and so on. You can create, rename, move, and delete files and folders here, as well as identify problems. A green bug in the Status column, for example, indicates a broken link.

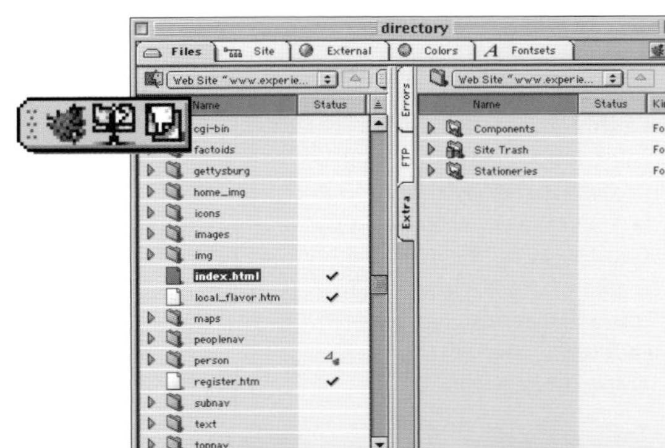

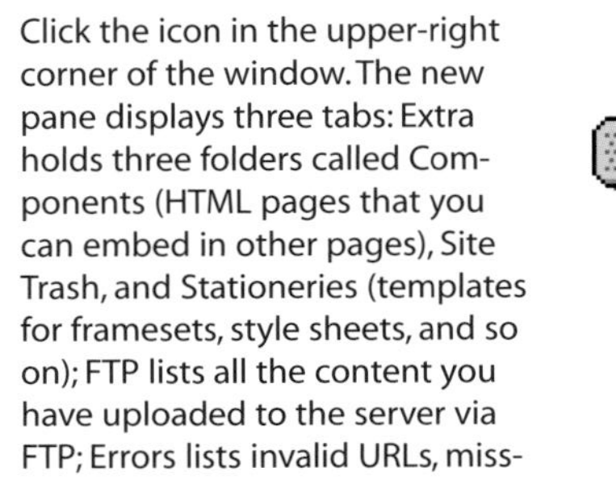

3 Click the icon in the upper-right corner of the window. The new pane displays three tabs: Extra holds three folders called Components (HTML pages that you can embed in other pages), Site Trash, and Stationeries (templates for framesets, style sheets, and so on); FTP lists all the content you have uploaded to the server via FTP; Errors lists invalid URLs, missing files, and orphan pages.

4 The context-sensitive File Inspector also lets you manage file properties and contents. Select a GIF in the site window, for example, and you can view a thumbnail in the Content tab. This is a good way to search for images.

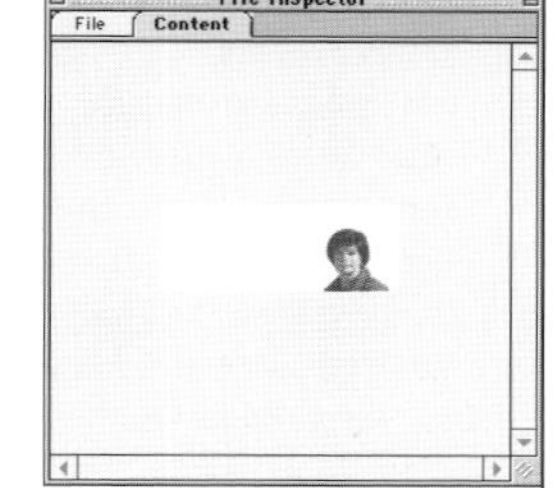

5 Move files or folders by dragging and dropping in the File tab of the site window or by using the Point & Shoot Navigation button. Create new folders by clicking the New Folder button in the toolbar. Add content to a folder by choosing Add Files from the Site menu. Rename files or folders in the site window or in the File Inspector. GoLive updates all links as you go.

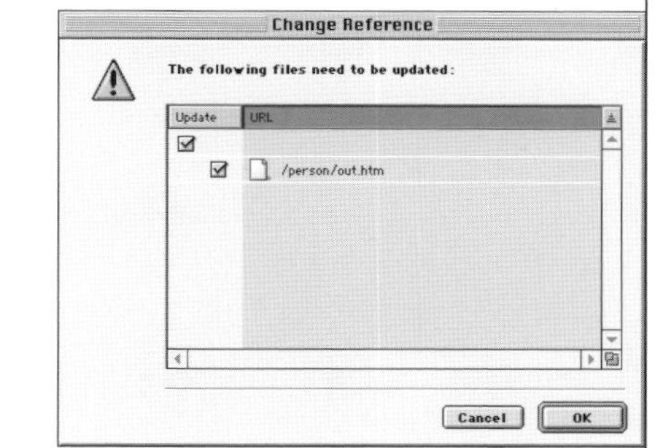

6 The Site tab of the site window gives a graphical view of the structure of your site. The Navigation Hierarchy view shows parent/child/sibling relationships between pages; you can dynamically add pages in this view or click the Link Hierarchy button in the toolbar or in the Arrange tab of the Site View Controller Inspector to make the view read only.

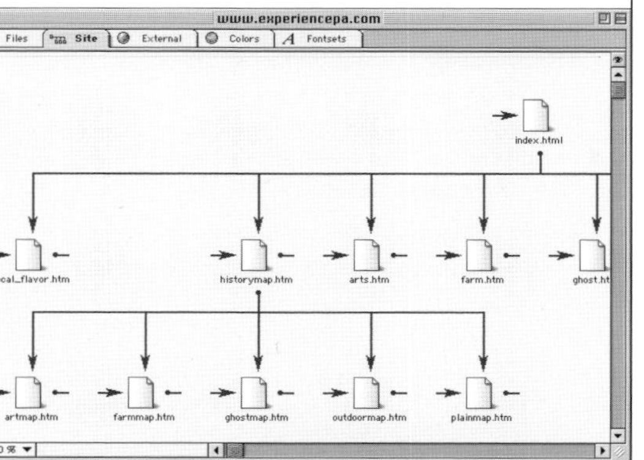

7 To add pages in Navigation Hierarchy view, check the Use "Create New Page" Live Button box in the Site View Controller Inspector. Move the mouse cursor near a page icon, and click to position a new page above, below, or to the side of the page. To actually link the pages, double-click the parent page, select the element that you want to link, and hold Command (Control) while dragging to the new page in the site window.

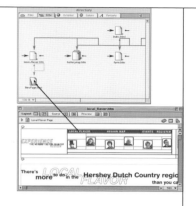

8 Click the Open Site Navigator button in the toolbar to help you interactively navigate a site view that is too large to fit on your monitor's screen. Click and drag, or draw a marquee to change the viewing area.

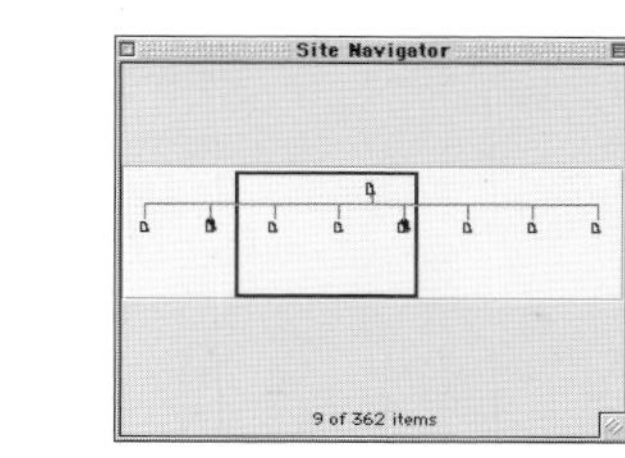

9 Click one of the link indicators (or the Open Link Inspector button in the toolbar) to open the Link Inspector, where you can view, create, redirect, and repair broken links. Click the eye icon in the upper-right corner of the Inspector to access the Link View Controller, where you can specify what you want to view in the Inspector.

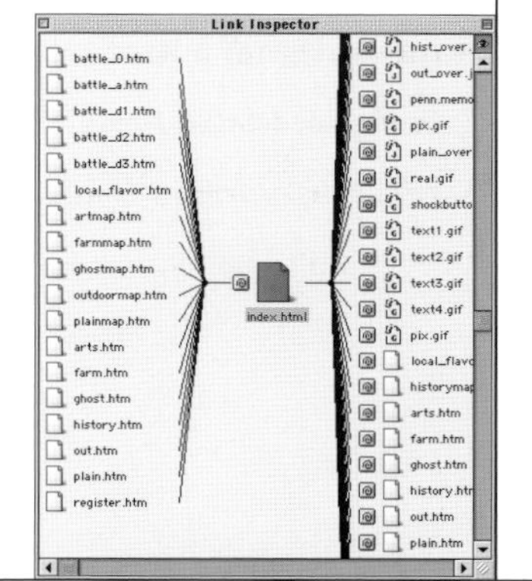

Renee Anderson
HOT
www.hotstudio.com

Automating Tasks with Actions

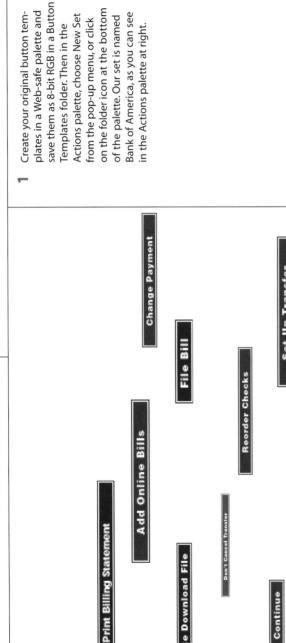

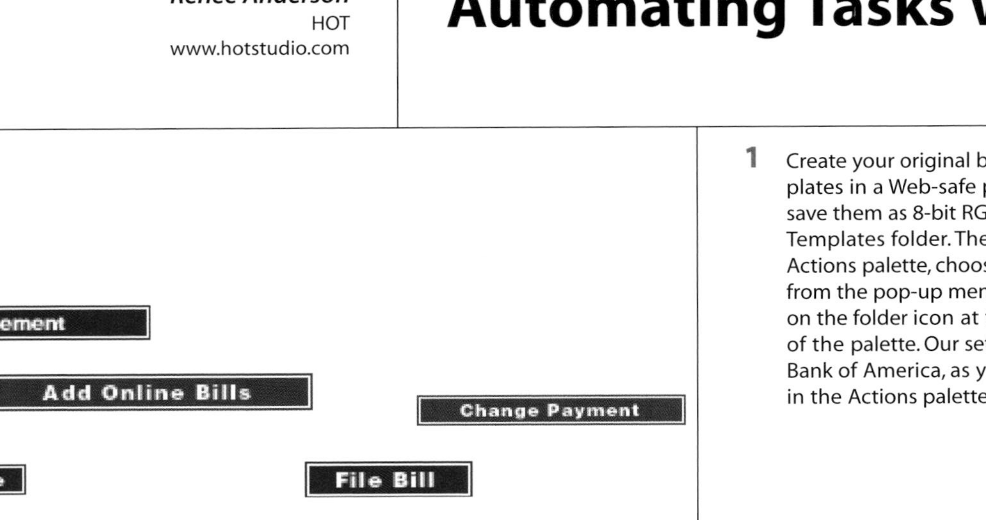

Photoshop lets you group a series of commands into what it calls *actions*, which can be a tremendous help in automating routine production tasks. In Web design, actions are particularly useful for applying text or effects to a series of navigational buttons, for example. The following action was created by HOT designer Renee Anderson for naming and saving the navigation buttons for a prototype online-banking site for Bank of America.

1 Create your original button templates in a Web-safe palette and save them as 8-bit RGB in a Button Templates folder. Then in the Actions palette, choose New Set from the pop-up menu, or click on the folder icon at the bottom of the palette. Our set is named Bank of America, as you can see in the Actions palette at right.

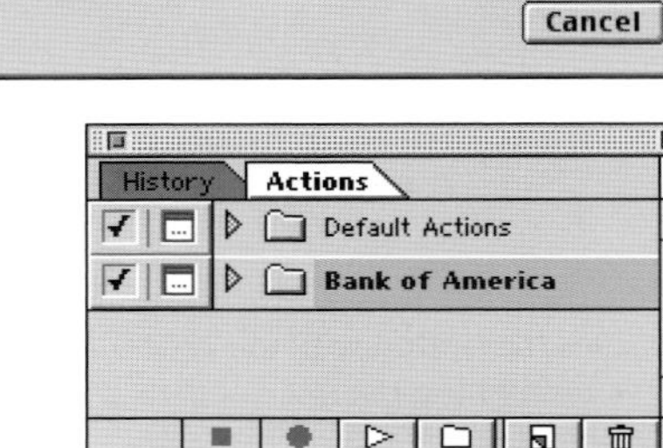

2 Now choose New Action from the pop-up menu and give the action a logical name, such as "bofabutton-action." Assign a function key if you like. The action appears in your set in the palette; click the Record button to begin recording the steps of the task you want to automate.

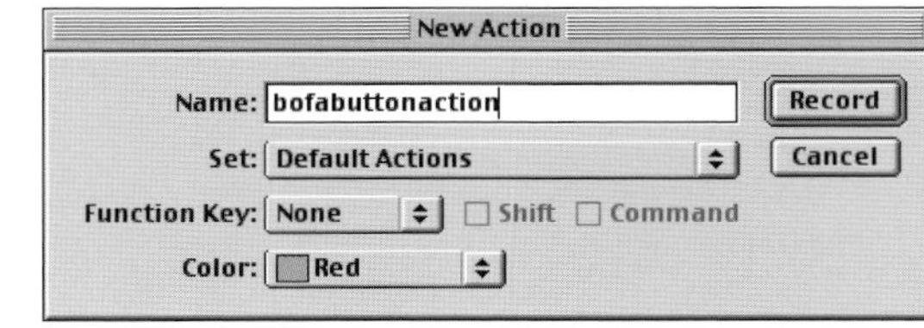

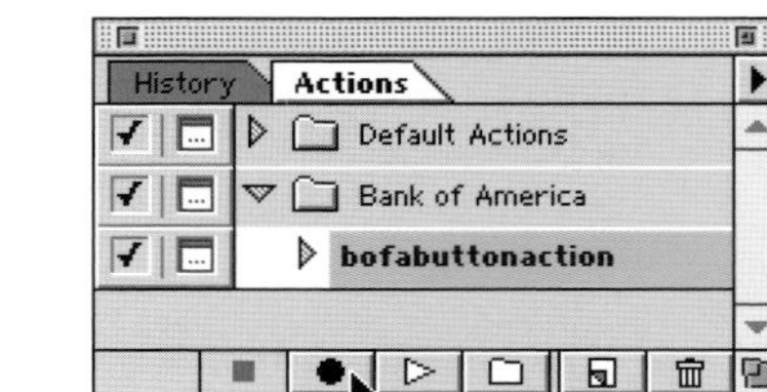

3 Open your first button file and double-click on the layer name in the Layers palette to name the layer "button." This will appear as your first step in the Actions palette.

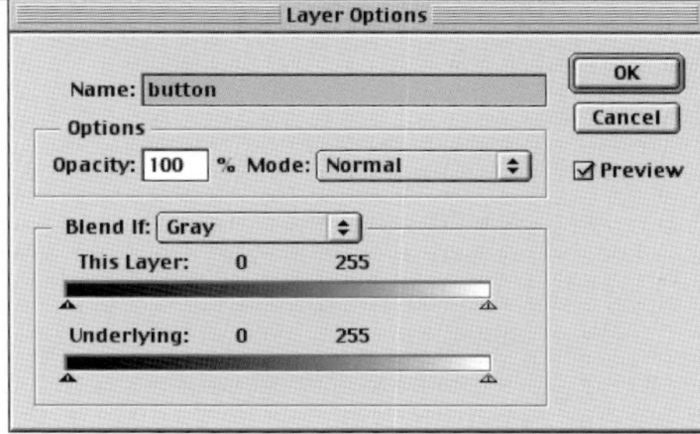

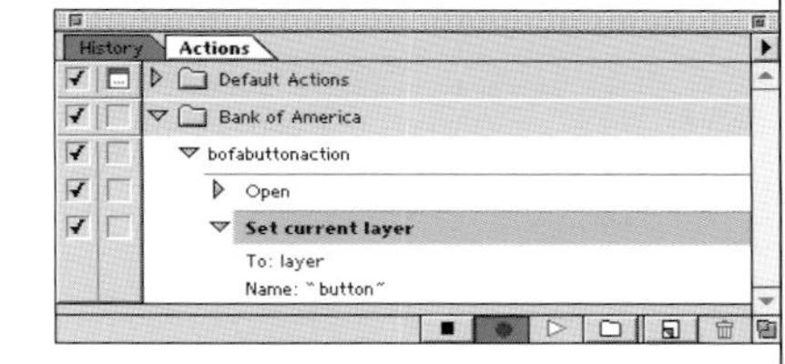

4 Click the button with the Type tool and enter the text you want for the button in the Type Tool dialog box.

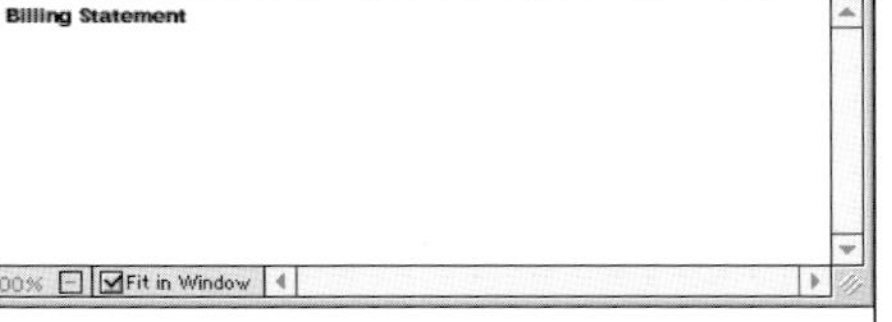

5 Photoshop automatically puts the text on its own layer, whose name is the text itself, "Print Billing Statement," in our example. Choose Layer Options from the palette's pop-up menu to change the name of the layer to "text." The change is reflected in the Layers palette as well as in the Actions palette, where your steps are being recorded.

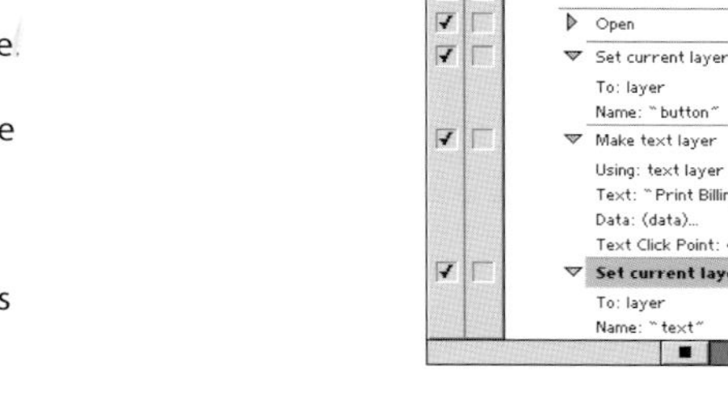

6 To center the text on the button, select the button layer and click the box between the eye icon and the layer name to link the text layer to it. Then choose Align Linked from the Layer menu and choose Vertical Center. Repeat the Align Linked command, this time choosing Horizontal Center.

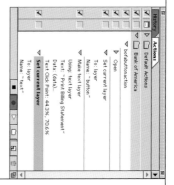

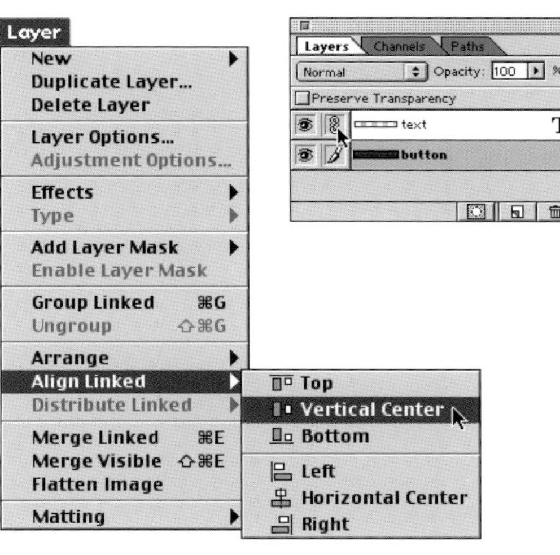

Renee Anderson
HOT
www.hotstudio.com

CONTINUED...

Automating Tasks with Actions

7 If the type doesn't look perfectly centered, you may have to nudge it a bit. Unlink the layers, and then select just the text layer. With the Move tool, use the arrow keys to refine the text's position in the center of the button.

8 When you're satisfied with the button, make it a GIF: Choose Save for Web from the File menu. Use an Adaptive palette, no interlacing, and reduce the number of colors in the file to just a few—say, 16. Experiment with the 2-Up and 4-Up tabs to see what looks good. You can make the file nice and small because you designed the template with just a few Web-safe colors. Click OK, and then create a folder to hold your new GIFs, name your finished button, and save it.

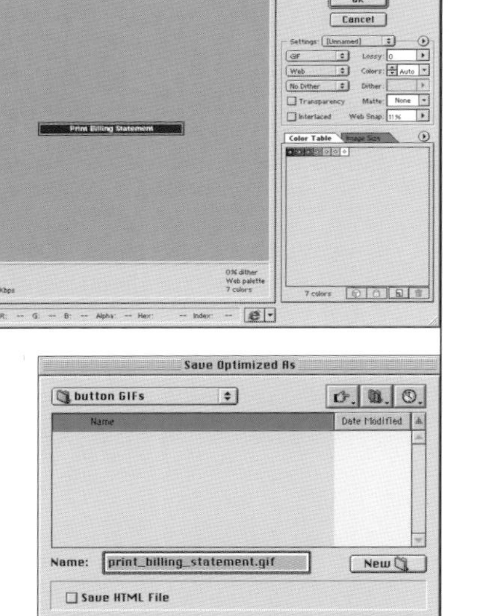

9 Close the image and choose Don't Save in the warning box, because you'll use this button template again. This is the last step in your action, and you can click the Stop Recording button (the one with the black dot at the bottom of the Actions palette).

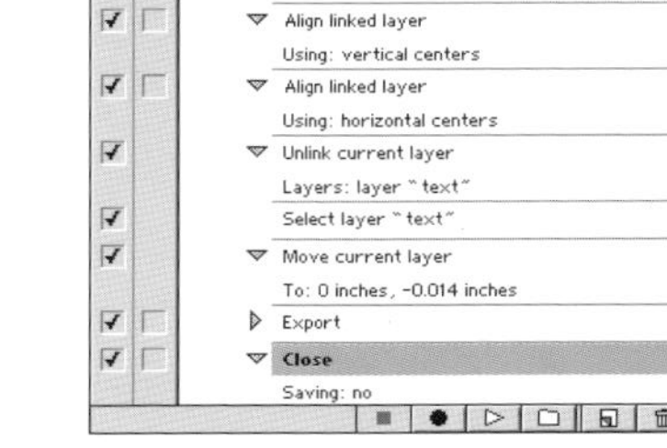

10 But you're not done yet: This action will open the same button, type the same text, and save a GIF with the same name, so you'll need to select the "Toggle dialog on/off" icon in the Actions palette to automatically open certain dialog boxes as you play the action.

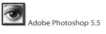

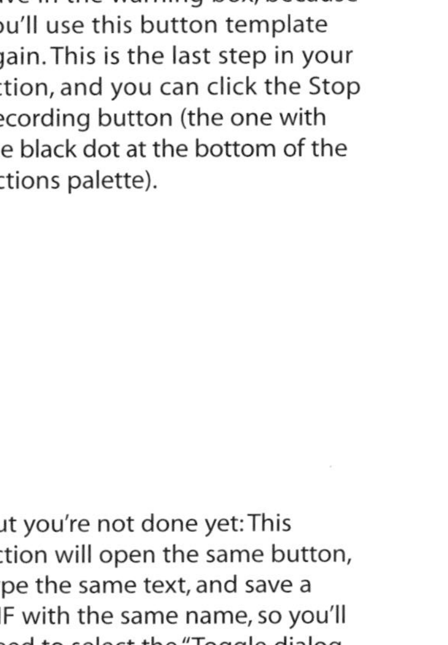

11 Toggle on the following dialog boxes: Open, so you can select a button; Type Tool, so you can enter the name of the button; and Save for Web, so you can save your final button with a new name. In our case, the nudging we performed for the first button looked good on all of our buttons, but you can also toggle that step on and manually nudge the text for each button.

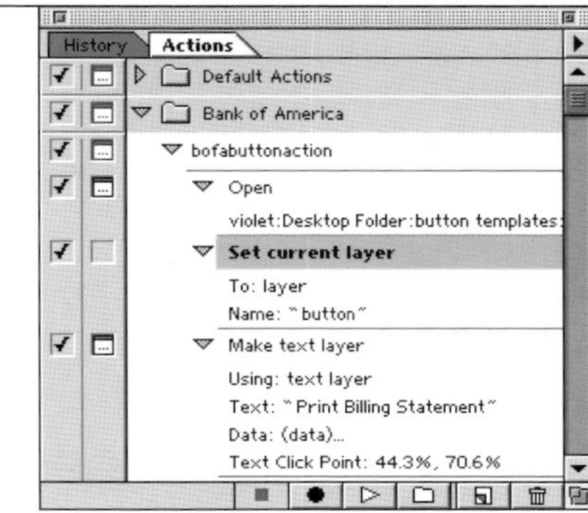

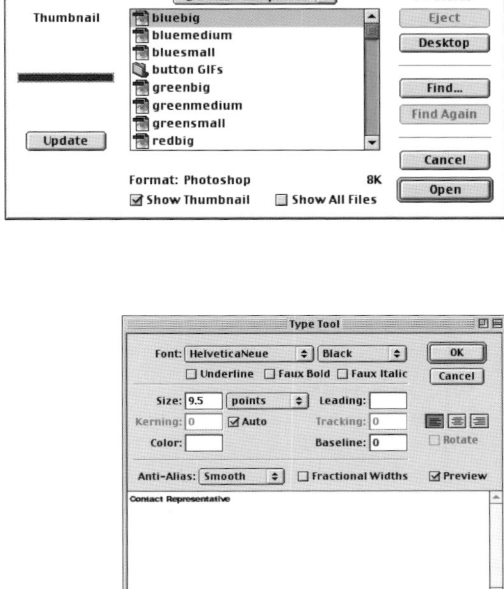

12 To execute the action, select it in the Actions palette and then click the play button (the right-pointing triangle) at the bottom of the palette. Photoshop prompts you to open the next button file so that it can perform the tasks you recorded.

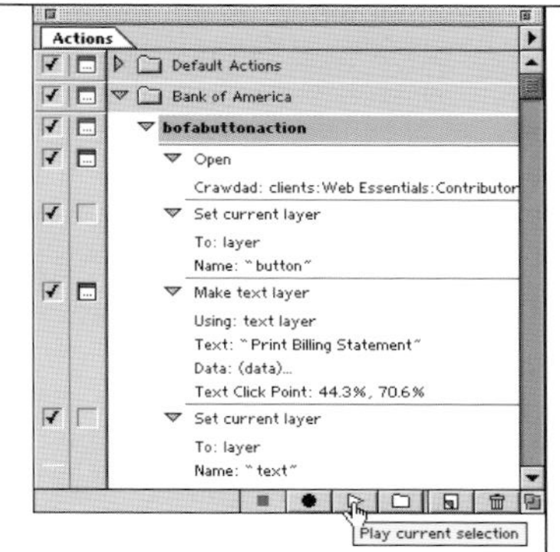

13 Here are your new files, which you can place in the appropriate HTML page.

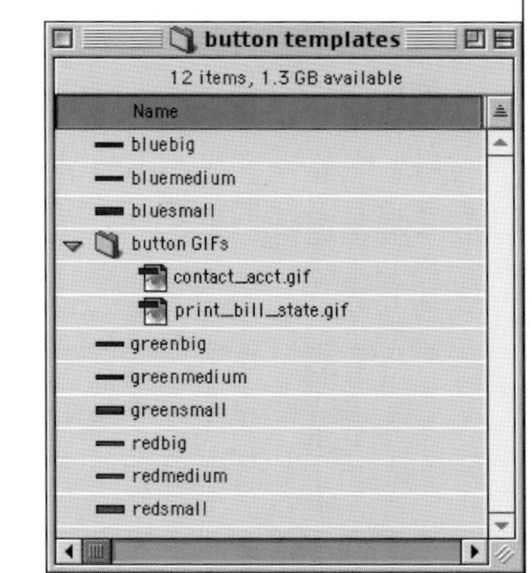

Florian Fangohr
HOT
www.hotstudio.com

Automating Tasks with Droplets

Photoshop isn't the only software you'll use in Web production; ImageReady was designed from the ground up to automate the processing of images published to the Web. Adobe built in a feature called *droplets*, which allow you to batch-process images by dragging and dropping them onto an icon. First you create an action, and then you save the steps as an executable droplet, which automatically launches ImageReady and performs the specified steps. This is a great way, for example, to ensure consistency and speed the creation of navigational graphics for a Web site. Or say you've made dozens or even hundreds of style guides for clients in PDF format, and you want to show the cover of each on your Web site, uniformly sized. Here's how to automate the process in ImageReady using actions and droplets.

1 Open one of the PDFs in ImageReady and use it to define your droplet. Don't create a new image because an empty document won't let you see if your scaling works properly. Click OK in the Generic Parser and Rasterization Options dialog boxes, and ImageReady will open the first page of your PDF document, sized properly.

2 Choose New Action from the Actions palette pop-up menu (or click the button at the bottom of the palette), and then click the Begin Recording button.

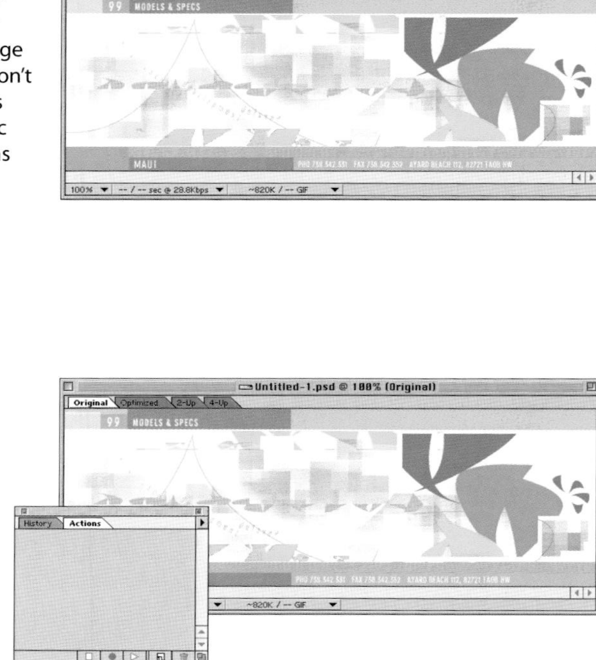

3 Choose Image Size from the Image menu and specify your desired maximum width—300 pixels in our example, which is the space allotted in the HTML table we'll be using. Since the height of the PDF brochures may vary, we only constrain proportions by width, and we select Do Not Enlarge because we don't want the quality of the art to be compromised by being enlarged too much.

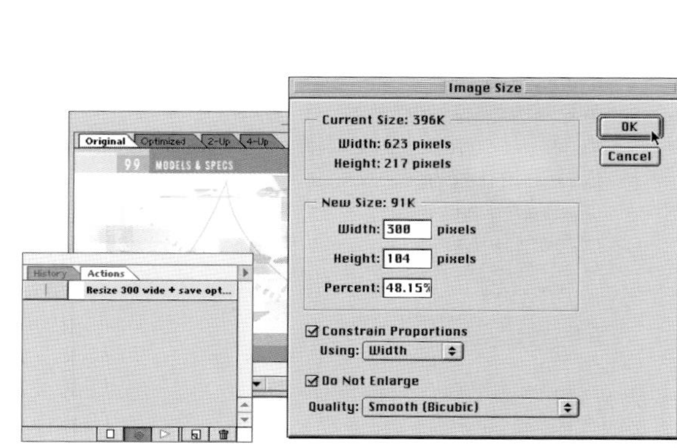

4 Optimize the PDF page as a GIF using an Adaptive palette with many colors, because the PDFs probably won't use only Web-safe colors and each will have its own style.

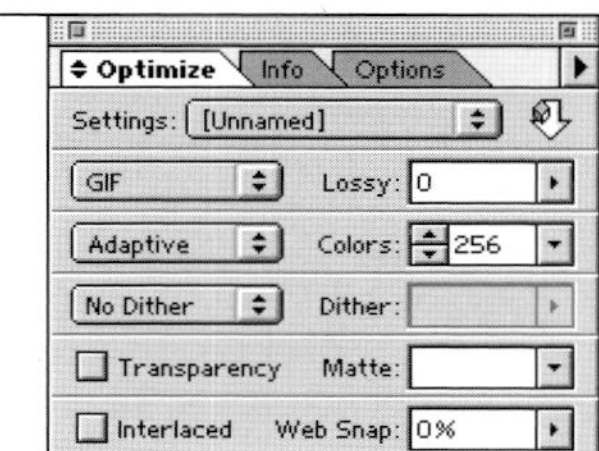

5 From the File menu, choose Save Optimized As and check Save Images. Click the Save button, and then click the Stop Recording button at the bottom of the Actions palette.

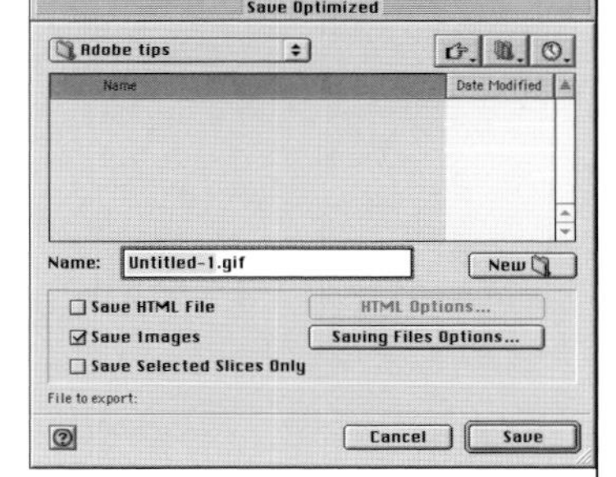

6 Drag the action to the desktop to save it as an executable droplet, or chose Create Droplet from the Actions palette pop-up menu. Now you can drag each subsequent PDF document onto the droplet and the first page gets automatically resized and saved as a GIF—you don't have to open, edit, and close each file.

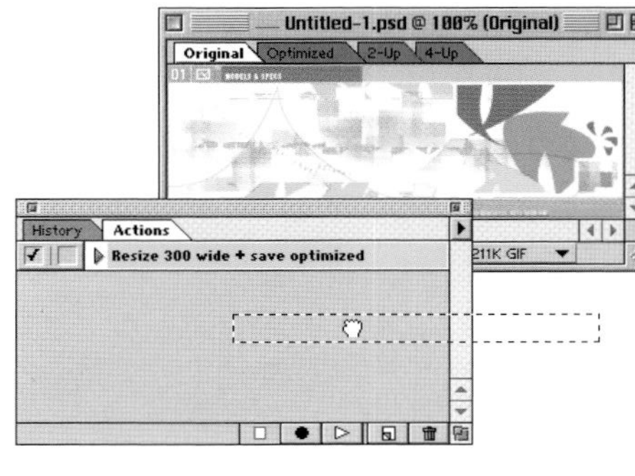

7 To take this one step further, say you also want to post a screenshot of 50 or so QuickTime movies: Drag a QuickTime file onto the droplet, and in the Open Movie dialog box that appears, click Selected Range Only, choose the frame you want to import by adjusting the slider, and click OK.

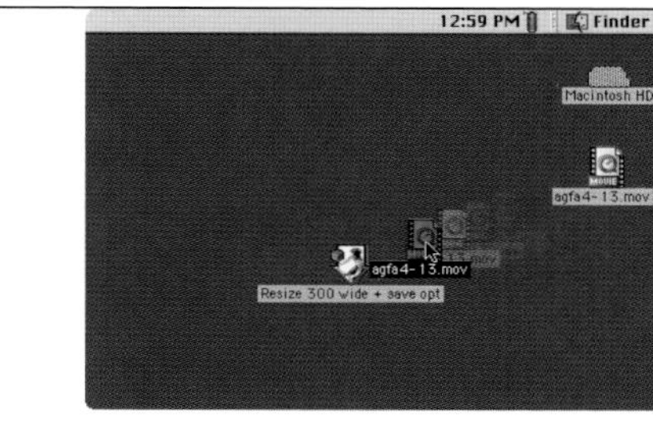

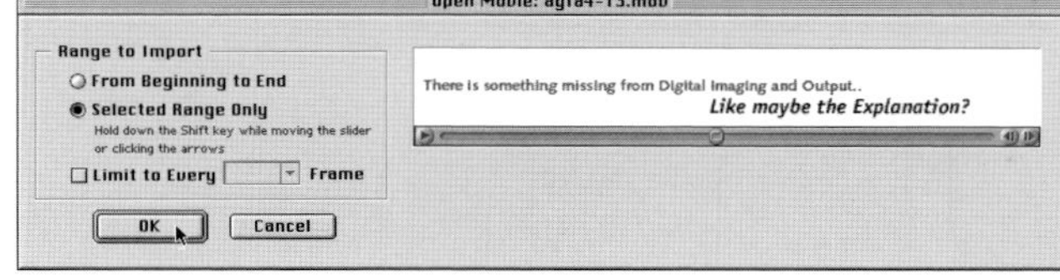

8 If you simply want to streamline your optimization process for a series of graphic files, use the Create Droplet icon in the Optimize palette. Without any images open, specify the palette, colors, dithering, transparency, and other settings that you want to use, and then click the downward-arrow icon to save the settings as a droplet. Then drag images onto the droplet to automatically optimize them.

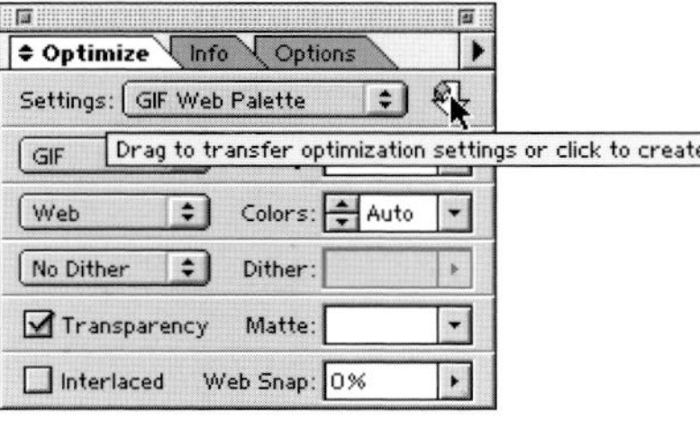

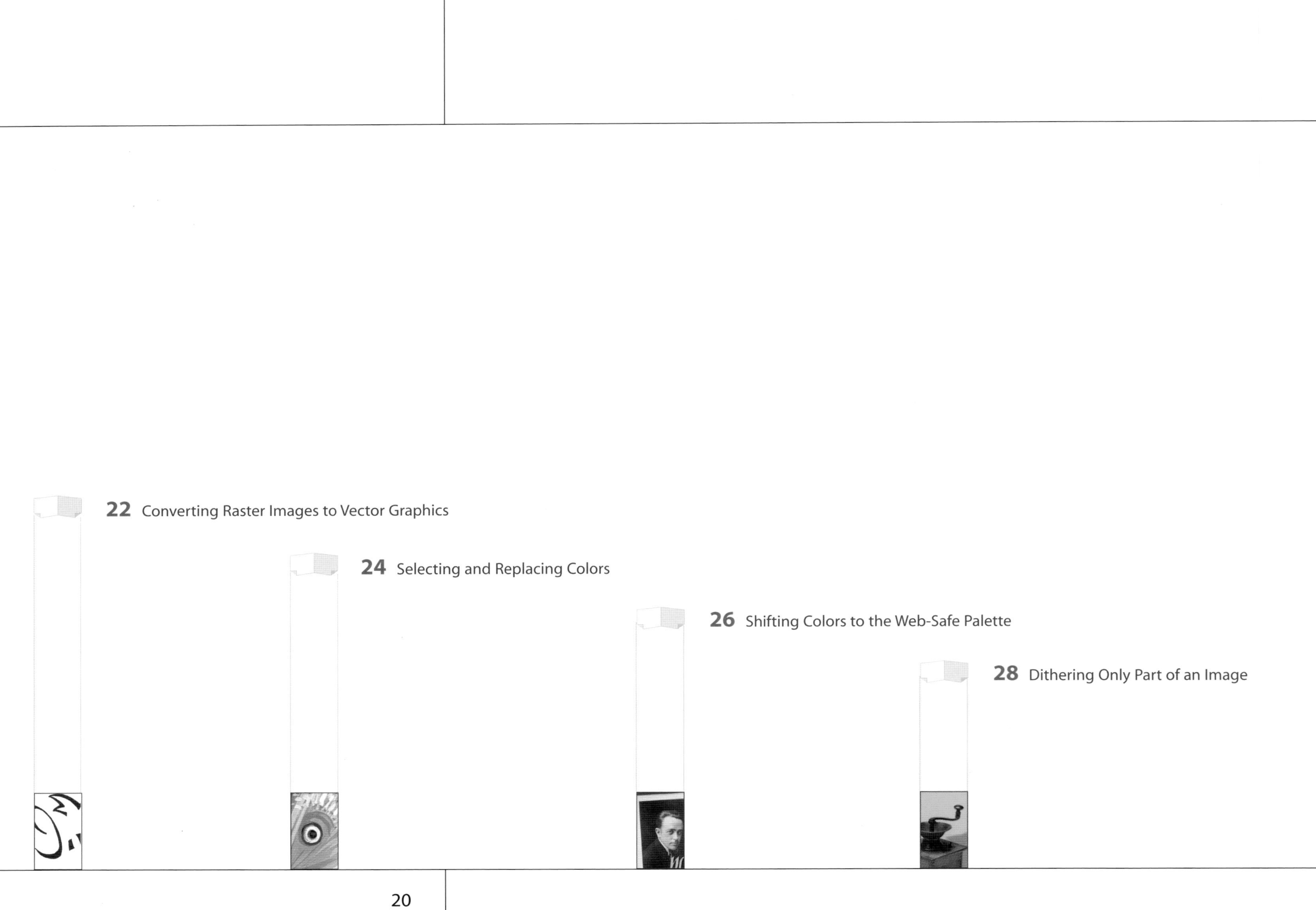

Chapter 2

Preparing Graphics

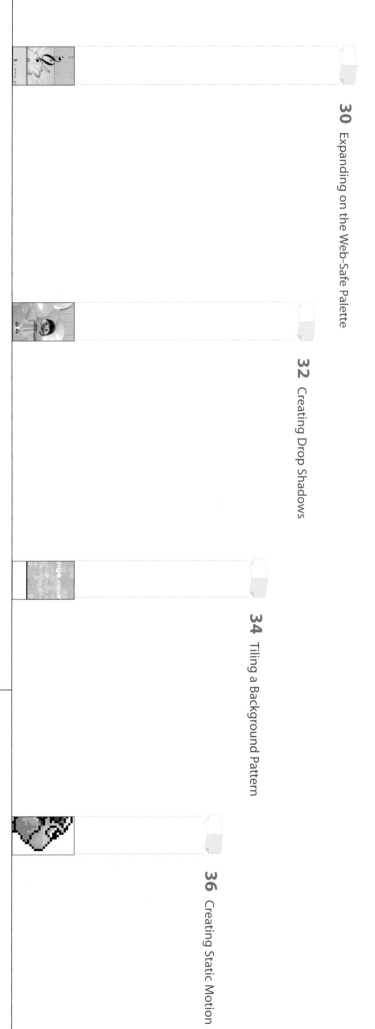

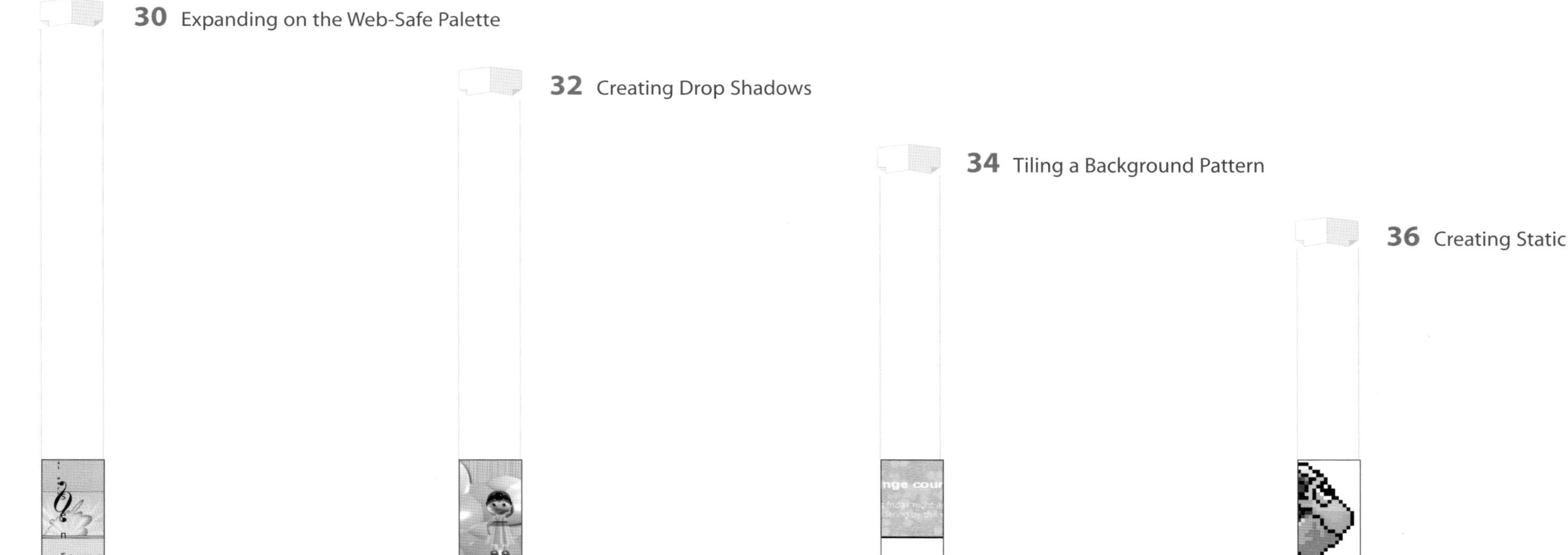

Hyland Baron
HOT
www.hotstudio.com
logo design: ***Macky Pamintuan***

Converting Raster Images to Vector Graphics

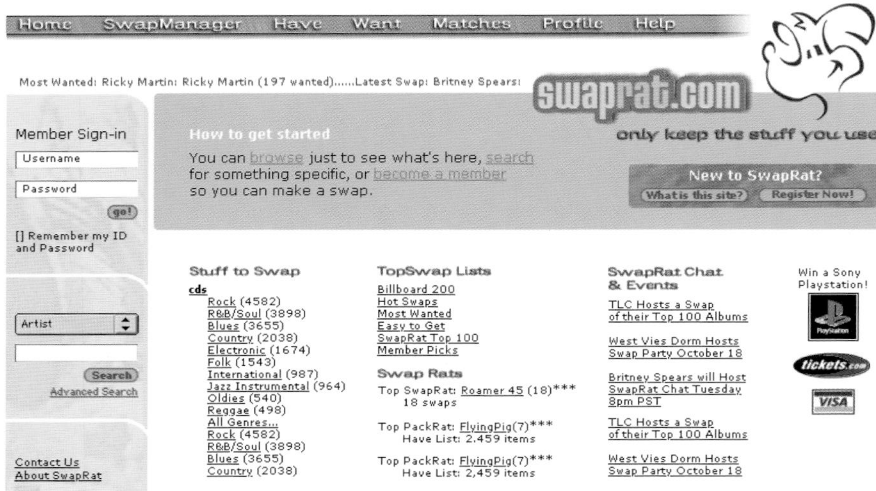

Converting raster images to vector graphics (sometimes called *autotracing*) is an essential technique in Web publishing. You often need to autotrace when a client can provide only a hard copy of a piece of artwork, which you must bring into the digital workflow by scanning. The problem is that scanning renders raster images, which are substantially larger in file size and often times more difficult to edit than vector graphics. Simple artwork such as logos or icons in particular are easier to manipulate in an illustration program before you optimize them as GIF in Photoshop or ImageReady. Streamline is made to help you convert raster images to vector artwork; HOT designer Hyland Baron shows how to use the software to convert a scanned inked drawing into a vector format.

1 Scan your artwork at 100 percent and at a high resolution—between 300 dpi and 600 dpi. The more detailed the artwork, the higher resolution you need to use.

2 Open the raster artwork in Streamline. Choose Settings from the Options menu for a scrolling list of standard conversion options such as Hand Drawn Sketches, Inked Drawings, and Technical Illustration.

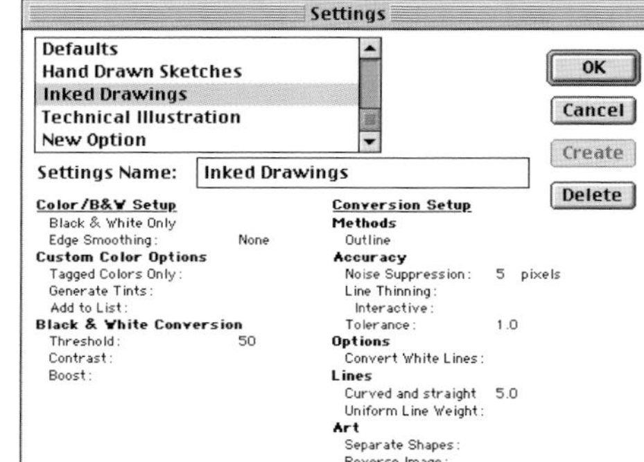

3 Select the most appropriate option for your raster artwork. For better results, customize your settings by choosing Conversion Setup from the Options menu.

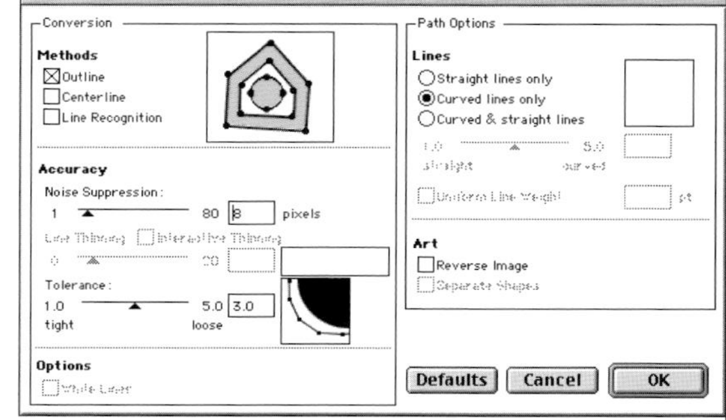

Adobe Streamline 4.0

4 Although Streamline will let you choose more than one conversion method, it's best to choose only one at a time when you're experimenting with settings. For this logo, we selected Outline.

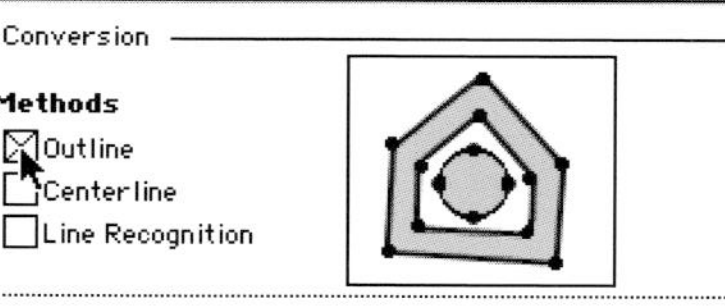

5 When converting to outline, you can adjust the Noise Suppression slider, which lets you eliminate stray pixels that might have been introduced in the scanning process. The Tolerance slider specifies how closely Streamline traces curved and straight edges in an image. A looser tolerance yields longer line segments and fewer anchor points.

Accuracy
Noise Suppression:
1 80 30 pixels
Tolerance:
1.0 5.0 4.0
tight loose

6 In the Path Options section of the Conversion Setup dialog box, specify whether you want your vector artwork to contain straight, curved, or curved and straight lines.

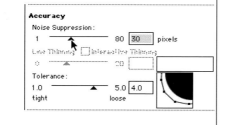

Path Options
Lines
Straight lines only
Curved lines only
Curved & straight lines

7 When you're satisfied with your settings click OK, and then choose Convert from the File menu. A progress bar indicates the status of the conversion.

Progress
Outlining – 1 path
Stop

8 Check the quality of Streamline's paths and anchor points by choosing Artwork from the pop-up menu. If you opted to convert to curved and straight lines, the curved lines will appear in red and the straight lines will appear in green.

9 Now you can edit the art in Streamline or Illustrator, tweaking paths and colors to suit your needs. When you're satisfied, optimize the file as a GIF in ImageReady or Photoshop.

Sandra Kelch
www.theispot.com

Selecting and Replacing Colors

Most Web designers these days prefer GIF graphics over JPEG when they want complete control over color in their graphics. With GIF, you can choose an indexed color palette and the specific number of colors you want to use, which lets you balance the use of color with the size of each file. You can even select specific colors and shift them into and out of the Web-safe spectrum in both Photoshop and ImageReady. But to take full advantage of this pixel-level control, you need to know the best ways to select colors in Photoshop. Illustrator Sandra Kelch shows how to find and change colors in a scanned gouache painting with many areas of flat color.

1 The Magic Wand tool is ideal for selecting a consistently colored area of an image without having to outline it. In the Options palette, start with a Tolerance of about 40. Select Anti-aliased if you want soft edges for the selection; Contiguous if you want only adjacent pixels; and Use All Layers if you want to capture pixels on layers other than the one that's active.

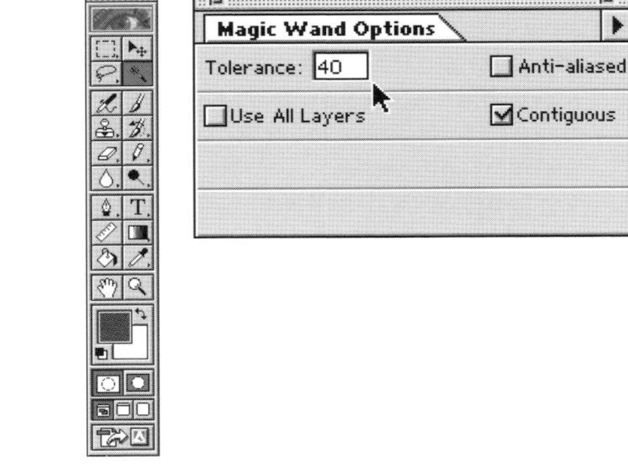

2 Click an area of color that you want to change in your RGB image; we started with the plate in the upper-left corner. You may need to adjust the Tolerance if the tool doesn't capture all the right pixels. Choose Similar from the Select menu to add all the other pixels of that color to your selection; press Shift and click to add specific areas to the selection or press Option (Alt) and click to delete them.

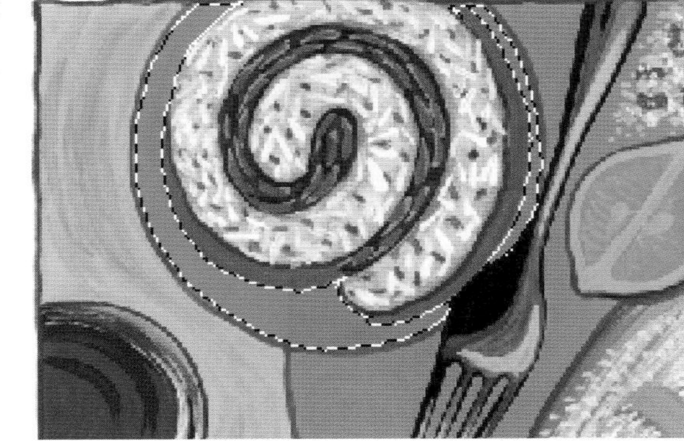

3 To choose a replacement color, use the Color palette, toggling on Web Color Sliders in the palette's pop-up menu.

4 You can also use the Color Picker, which gives a good sense of where a color falls in the spectrum. Click the foreground color swatch in the toolbox to open the Color Picker. Check the Only Web Colors box so that you view only Web-safe colors. Notice that the RGB breakdown for each color is a multiple of 51: 0, 51, 102, 153, 204, or 255.

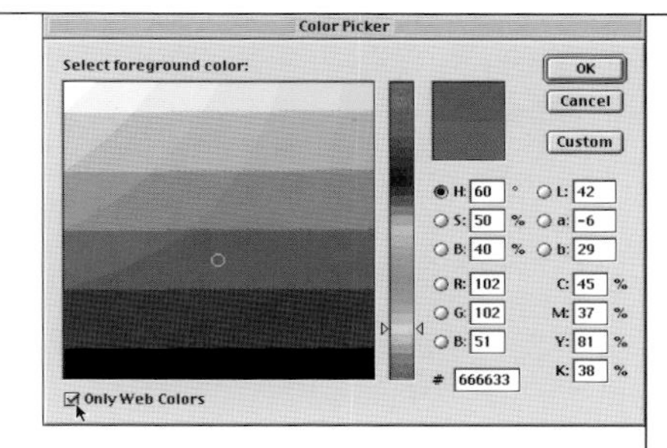

5 Choose Fill from the Edit menu, and use the foreground color for your Contents. If you apply a blending mode, be aware that you will probably add colors to the file that are not Web safe.

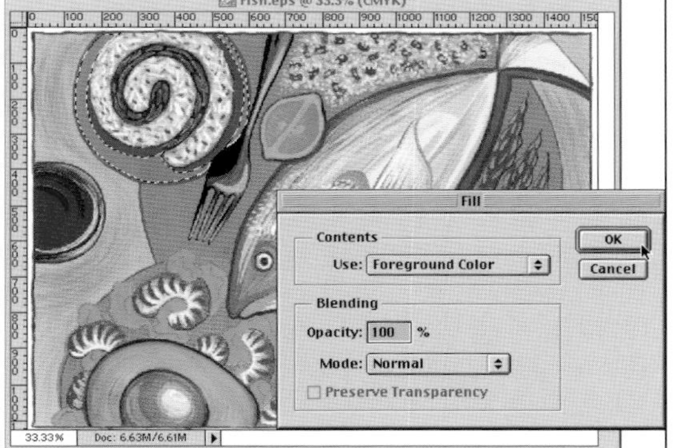

6 You can also replace colors using the Paint Bucket tool. That's how we filled the background with red 102, green 51, blue 51, 80 percent opacity.

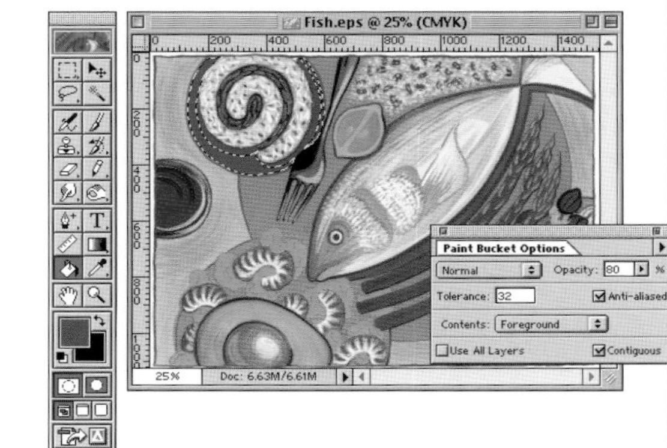

7 Another way to capture all the pixels of a given color is to choose Color Range from the Select menu. Choose Sampled Colors from the pop-up menu and click a given area, such as the lime, with the Eyedropper. Adjust the Fuzziness slider until you include all appropriate pixels in your selection.

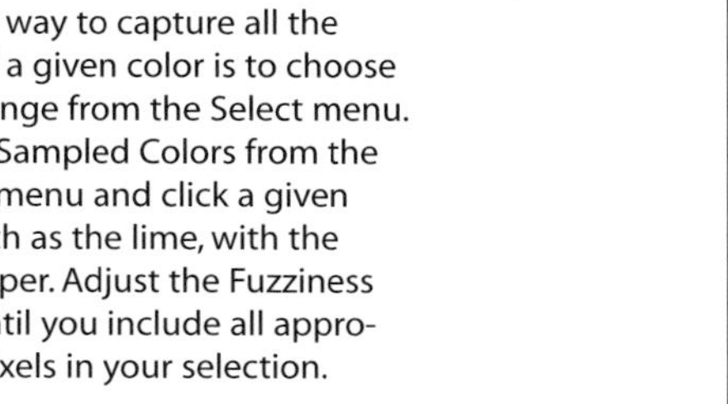

8 Click the Selection radio button and choose White Matte from the Selection Preview pop-up menu. Tweak your selection and review the results in this window and in the image window, and click OK when you're satisfied. Then replace pixels with a new color by pressing Option-Delete (Alt-Delete).

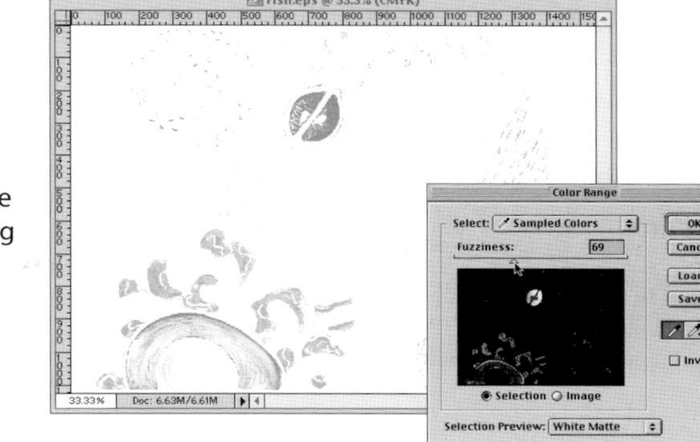

9 When you're finished, choose Save for Web from the File menu, and then define your palette and edit your color table before saving an optimized GIF.

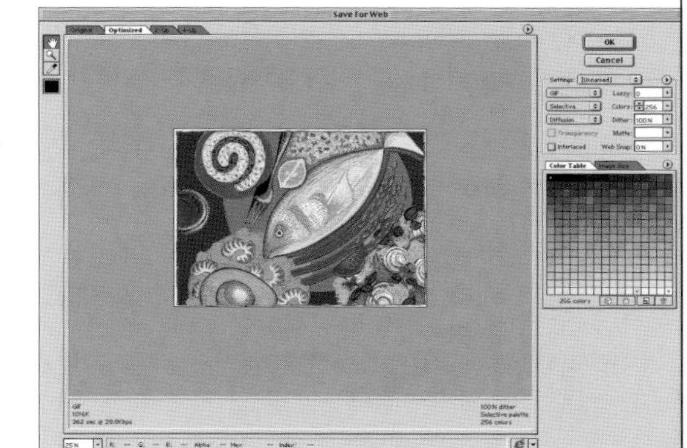

Casey Caston
CNET
www.cnet.com

Shifting Colors to the Web-Safe Palette

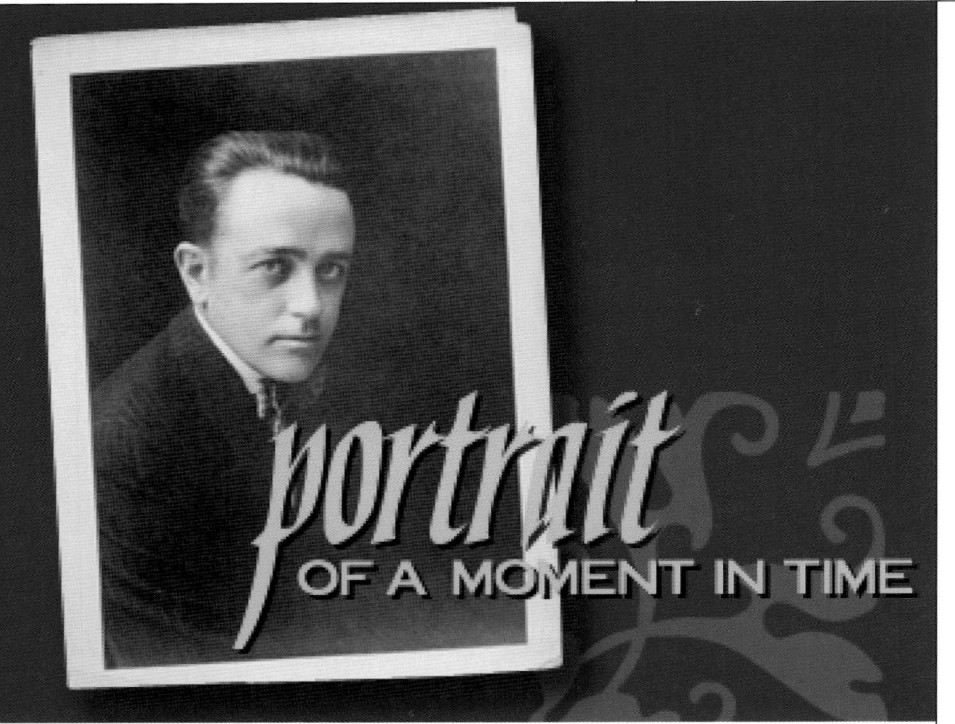

Many Web graphics, particularly those with subtle gradations such as skin tones, are ruined when the Web-safe palette is forced onto them. Either the images appear unclear and the file is made unnecessarily large by dithering, or the colors are ruined by banding if you don't dither. Although there's little you can do to stop dithering in photographic images on 256-color monitors, you have greater control over any area of solid color whose exact shade isn't critical. In those cases, you can specify the solid color as Web safe so that it won't dither on displays that only support 256 colors. Here's how.

1 Open your image in ImageReady and change it to GIF in the Optimize palette, setting the method to Perceptual. (This option does a better job than Adaptive at maintaining Web-safe colors.) Specify the number of colors at 256, the Web Snap at 11% (adjust down if needed), and specify no dithering.

2 Click on the Optimized tab of the image window to see your changes take effect. The Web-safe colors in the image appear in the Color Table palette as a swatch with a dot in the center.

3 To make a particular color Web safe, such as text or a background, select its swatch in the table and choose Web Shift-Unshift Selected Colors from the palette's pop-up menu. This shouldn't affect the image's overall appearance unless the image has a very small number of colors (generally 32 or fewer).

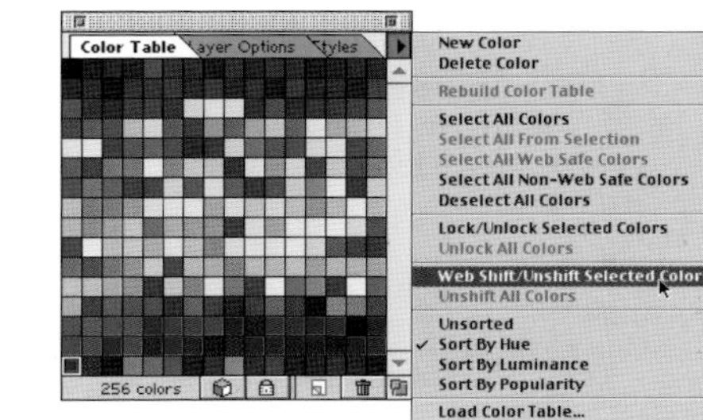

4 View your change in the image window.

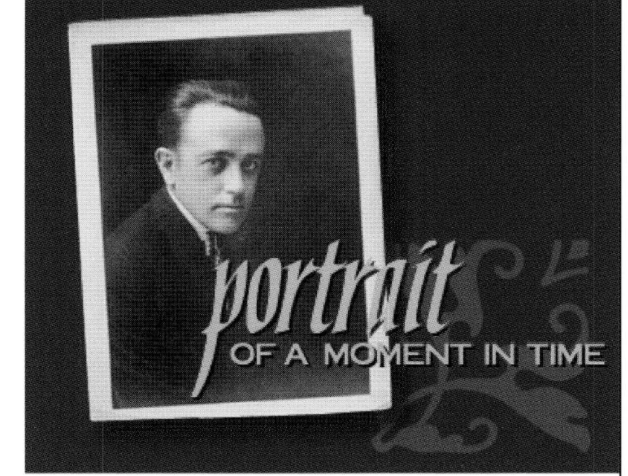

5 You can also select an area of the image with the Marquee or Magic Wand, for example, and then choose Select All From Selection in the Color Table palette's pop-up menu.

6 The colors in the selected area are selected in the Color Table palette, too, and you can now choose Web Shift/Unshift Selected Colors from the pop-up menu to make them Web safe.

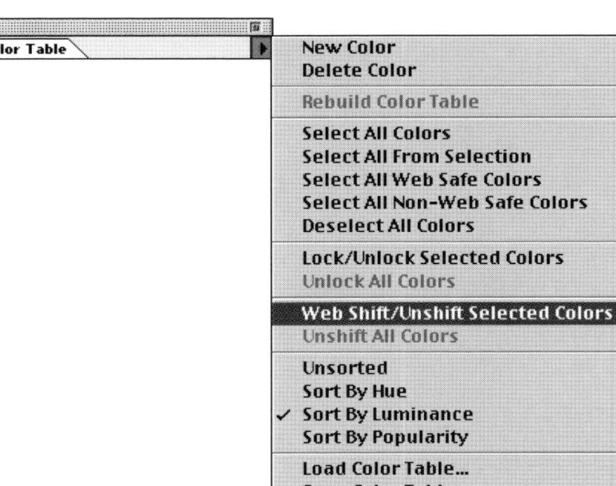

7 You can make similar changes in Photoshop by choosing Save for Web from the File menu and using the Eyedropper tool to select all the pixels of a certain color.

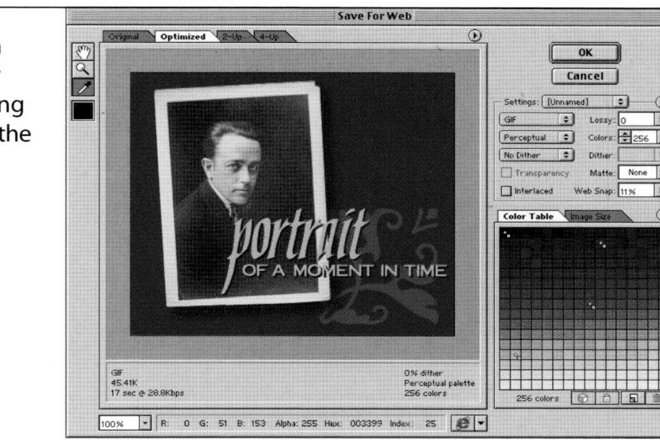

8 Here is what your final GIF image will look like on a 256-monitor (left) and on a monitor that supports millions of colors (right).

Understanding Palettes and Dithering

Before saving graphics as GIF, you must choose a palette for your file. The adaptive palette uses colors based on what's in the image, and the Web palette uses colors that are supported by 256-color monitors on both Macintosh and Windows. When you choose to apply dithering to the file, colors present in the palette are placed in adjacent pixels of the image to approximate the missing color. Dithering will also occur on the visitor's computer if it has a 256-color monitor and the browser has to display a photographic image with millions of colors, or if you create a GIF that uses a color outside of the 216 colors in the Web-safe palette. If you want to be sure that your colors aren't dithered by visitors' browsers regardless of their platform or the number of colors their monitor can display, choose 216 or fewer colors from the Web-safe palette for your GIF. *—Irv Kanode*

Casey Caston
CNET
www.cnet.com

Dithering Only Part of an Image

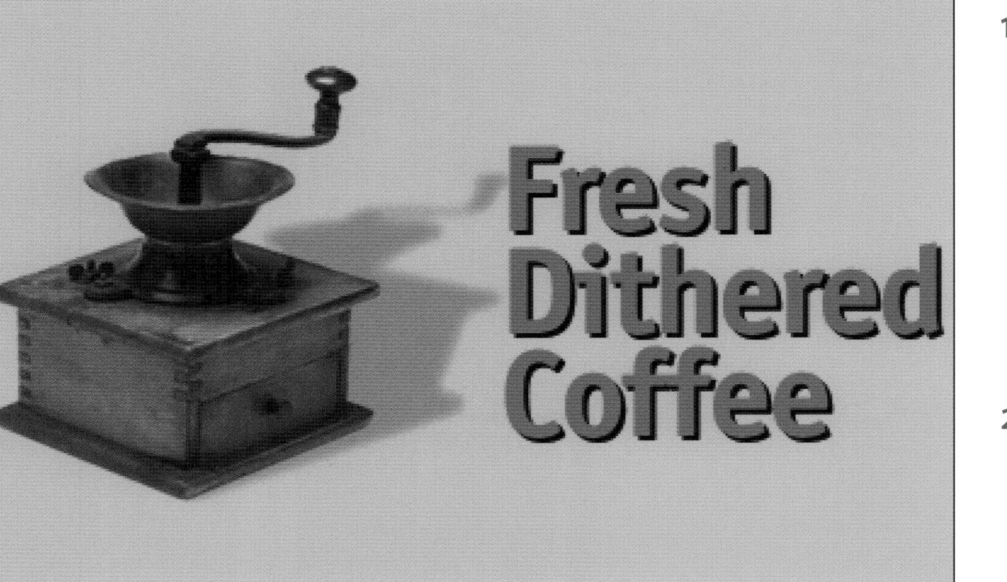

Dithering can make anti-aliased type appear fuzzy and unclear, but sometimes you might want to purposely dither an image for effect, such as with a drop shadow, even when you use the Web-safe palette. Instead of jeopardizing the legibility of any type in the image, a better solution is to dither just the portion of the image that will benefit from it. CNET senior designer and production specialist Casey Caston explains how.

1 Open the original RGB file in Photoshop.

2 Select the area that you want to dither by Command-clicking (Control-clicking) the layer name in the Layers palette. (To execute this tip with a flattened image, select the area that you want to dither with the Lasso or Marquee tool, or make a quick mask, and skip ahead to Step 5.)

3 If the graphic has a blurry edge or is mostly transparent (like this shadow), you may need to add to your selection. Choose Similar from the Select menu to catch any trapped transparent areas. You should now have the entire area selected (note that it goes well outside of the "solid" edge of the shadow).

4 Add any additional areas that you want to dither. Press Command-Shift (Control-Shift) while you click on the layer name to add that layer's contents to the selection area. To remove a layer, press Command-Option (Control-Alt) while you click.

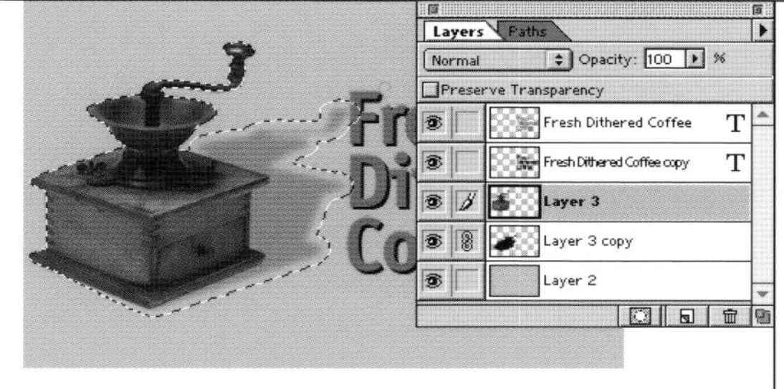

5 Choose Copy Merged from the Edit menu to copy from all the layers to the Clipboard. (If you're working with a flat file, just Copy.) Keep your selection active.

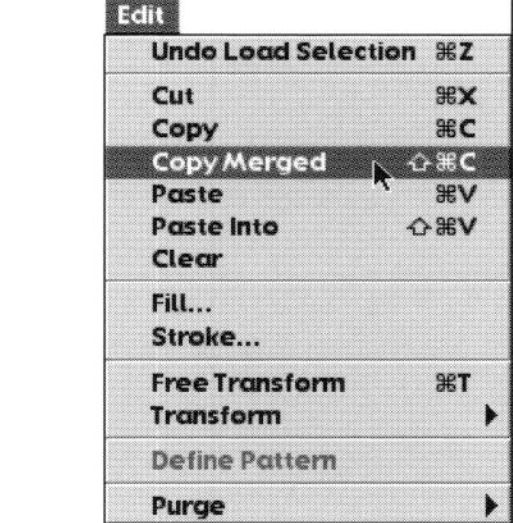

6 Convert the RGB image to indexed color by choosing Mode from the Image menu. (Flatten the layers as prompted.) Use an ordered palette, such as the Web palette; do not use the adaptive palette or an exact palette. Do not use dithering.

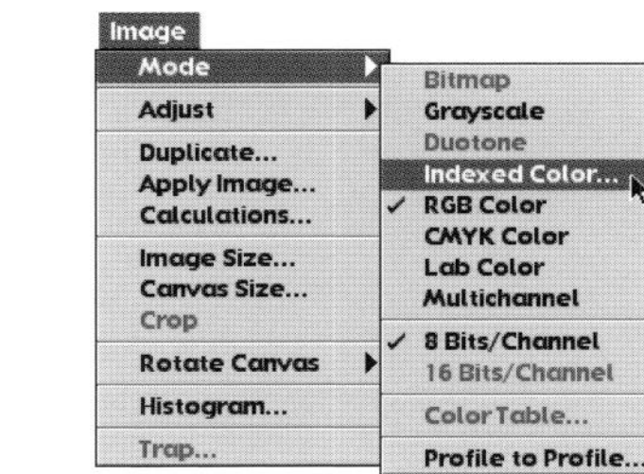

7 Paste the RGB contents of the Clipboard into the selected area in the indexed color file.

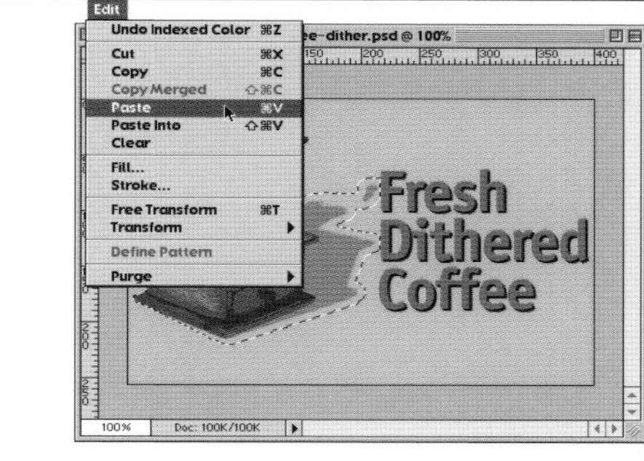

8 Photoshop automatically applies a diffusion dither to the pasted area using the indexed palette you've specified, but the rest of the file remains nondithered, and you can choose Save For the Web from the File menu to save it as a GIF.

Melissa Crowley
Fluid Design & Development
www.fluid.com
www.redbean.com

Expanding on the Web-Safe Palette

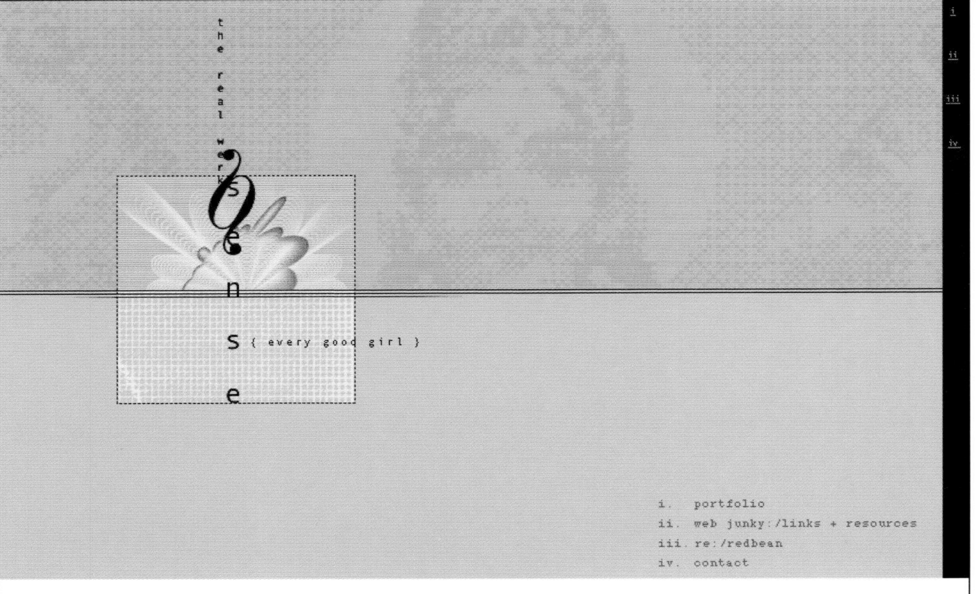

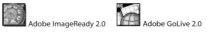

The palette of Web-safe colors is harsh and restrictive, with saturated hues that are too garish to use in many backgrounds and graphics, particularly for corporate sites. One way to soften a background is to alternate 1-pixel lines of two Web-safe colors of similar hue. This creates the appearance of unique yet browser-safe colors, similar to the way halftones help printed pieces achieve the appearance of more colors than the press can actually produce. ImageReady makes it super easy to create these "dithered" patterns with its DitherBox filter.

1 Start by creating a new file in ImageReady of an appropriate size, such as 200-x-200 pixels. In the New Document dialog box, you can make the contents of the first layer white, transparent, or the background color.

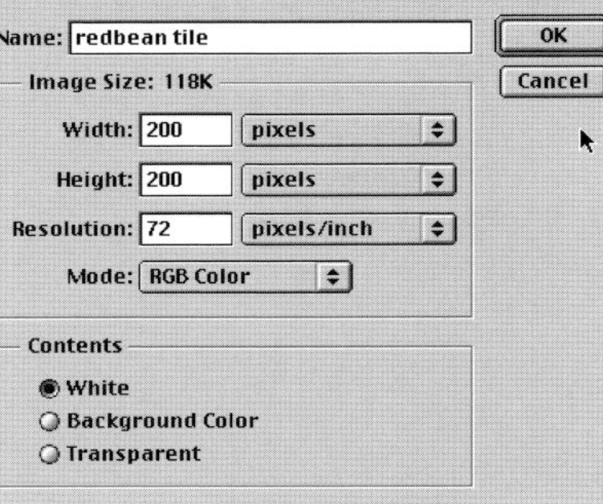

2 Fill the tile with a Web-safe color. Choose Make Ramp Web Safe from the Color palette's pop-up menu, or check the Only Web Colors box in the Color Picker to select your color, and then choose Fill from the Edit menu. Use the foreground color—255/153/000 in our example—as your Contents.

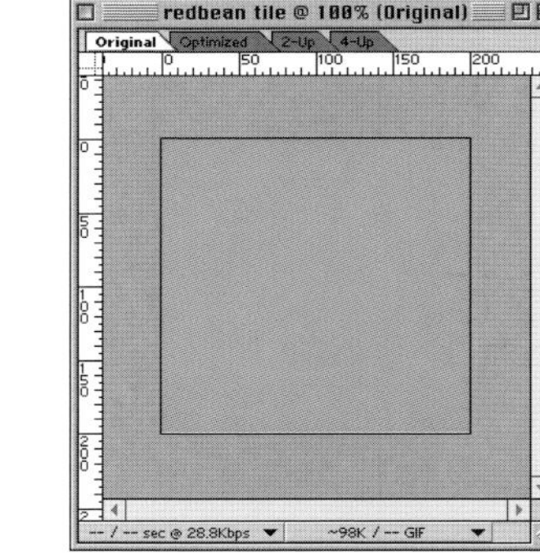

3 Choose Other from the Filter menu, and then choose DitherBox. The filter applies a 2-x-2 default dither pattern with a second color.

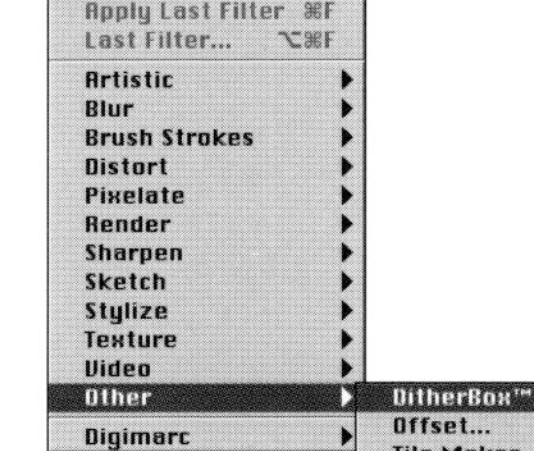

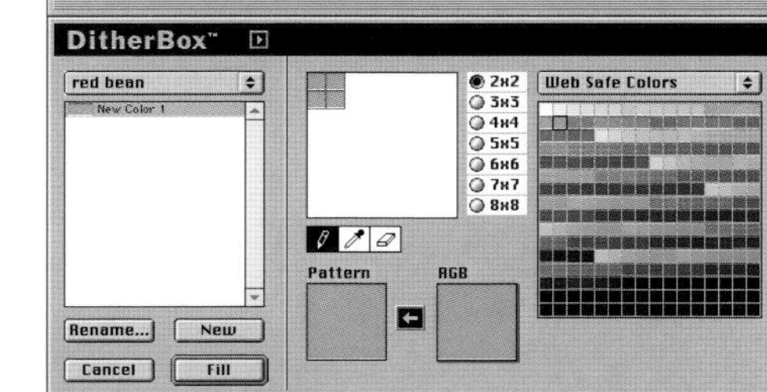

Adobe ImageReady 2.0 Adobe GoLive 2.0

4 To change a pixel in the dither pattern grid, select a new color in the Web Safe Colors palette, and with the Pencil tool click the appropriate pixel in the dither pattern grid. To delete a color, use the Eraser tool and click in the grid.

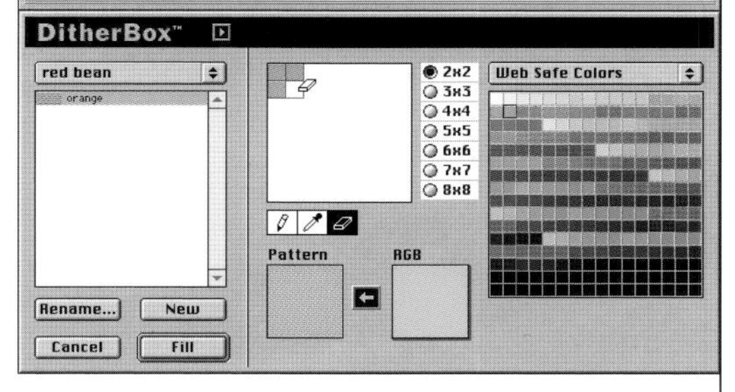

5 You can make the pattern grid as large as 8-x-8 pixels, with several colors and any creative pattern. As you experiment, keep in mind that similar hues work best, especially if you want the pattern to be subtle. To make a color seem less saturated, use white as one of your colors. We created a pin-stripe pattern using a simple 2-x-2 grid, adding a second orange hue.

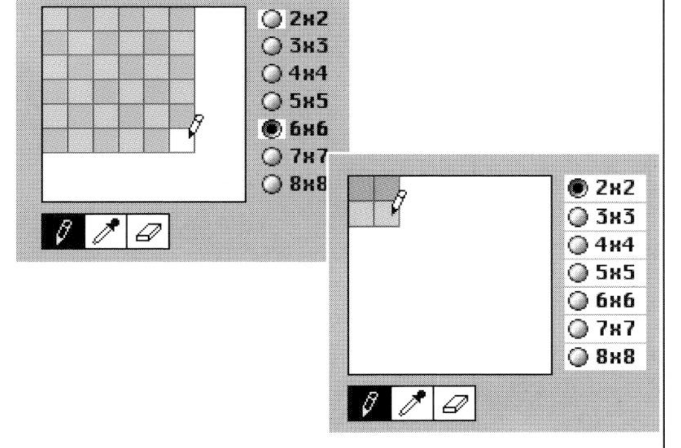

6 The Pattern box shows a preview of each edit that you make. When you're satisfied, click Fill.

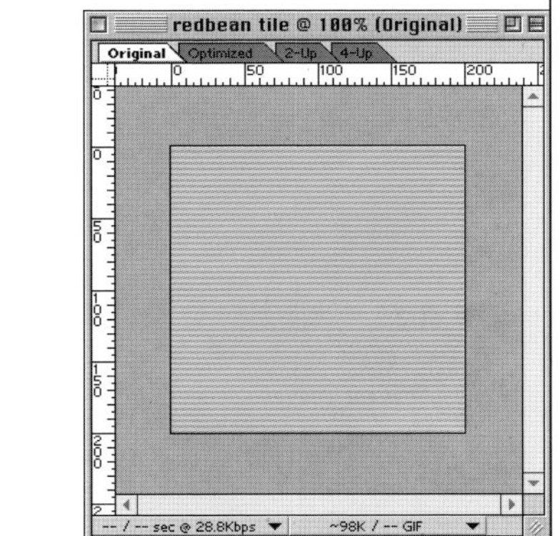

7 You can also apply the dither to a selected area of an image: Use any of the Marquee tools, or make a specific layer of the image visible in the Layers palette, to apply the dither to that area or layer.

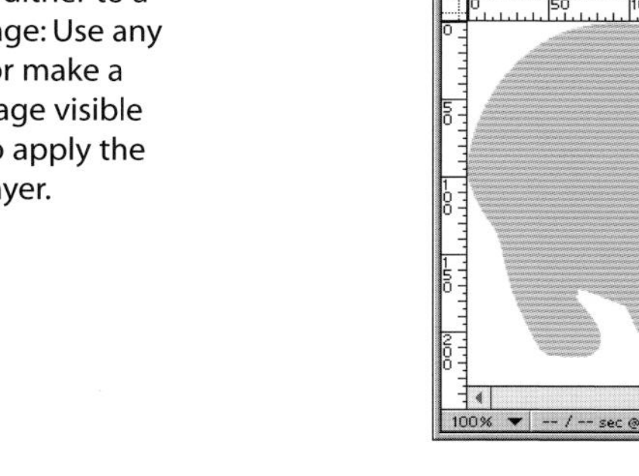

8 Since you know the exact number of colors used in the file, 2 in this case, you can optimize your GIF nice and small.

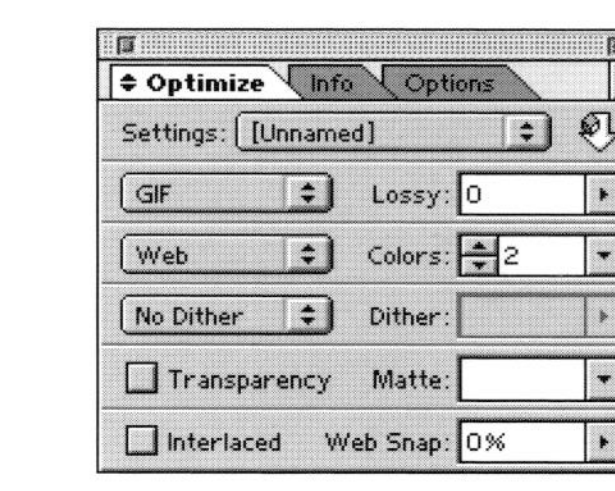

9 To apply the tile to an HTML page background, click the Page icon in a document window in GoLive to access the Page Inspector. Check the Image box in the Background section, and browse to select your tile file.

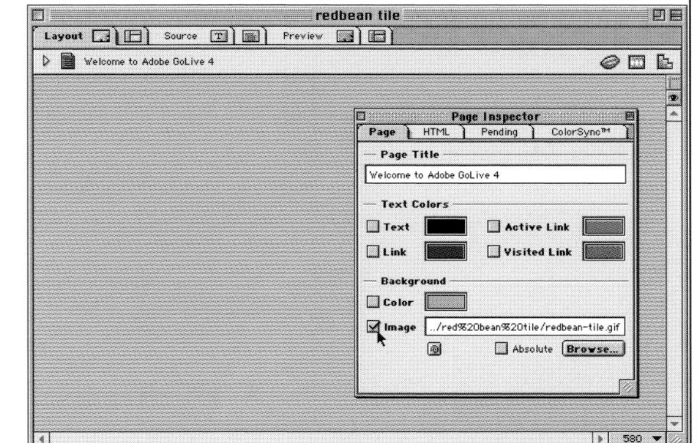

Amy Franceschini
Futurefarmers
www.futurefarmers.com

Creating Drop Shadows

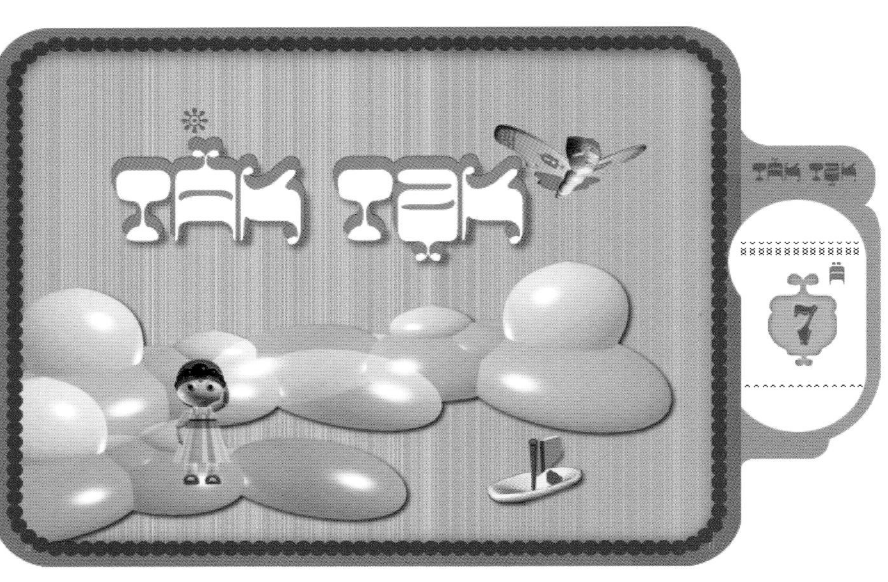

A drop shadow is a fundamental design element that enhances the appearance of graphics and images in print and on the Web. Photoshop makes drop shadows easy to create with a Layer Effects command, but you don't have to be limited to that approach. Here's a way to create a drop shadow for a graphic on the Web—a 3D object in our example—that gives you more flexibility. You can, for example, fill the shadow with a gradient to give it depth, or distort the shadow to give the illusion that the object is sitting on a flat surface. In any case, the object should reside on its own layer when you create a drop shadow.

1 Duplicate the layer that contains the image or graphic that you want to shadow. Choose the Duplicate Layer command from the Layer menu or from the Layers palette pop-up menu.

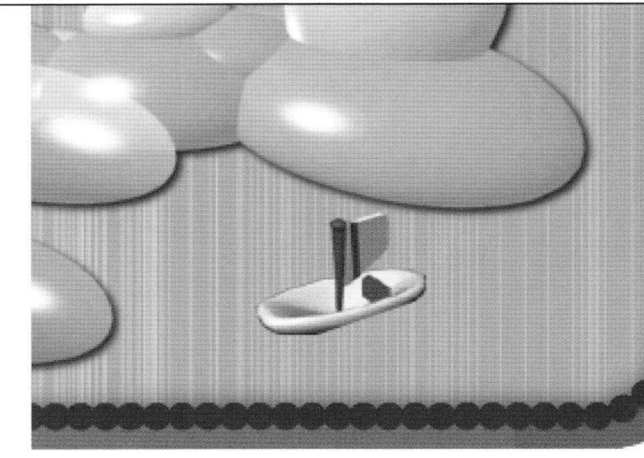

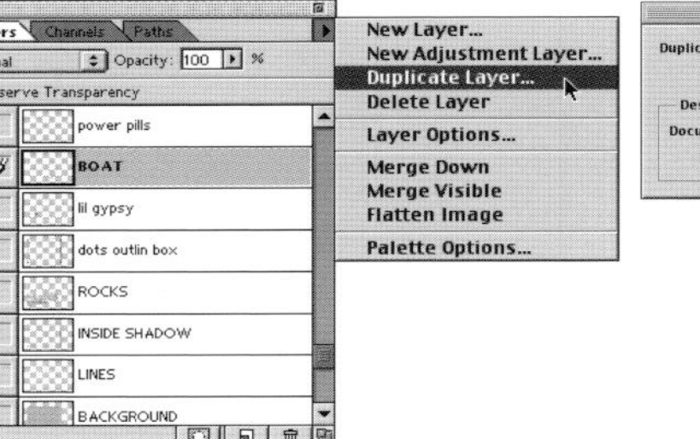

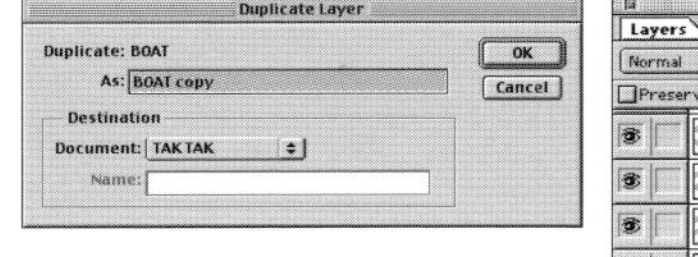

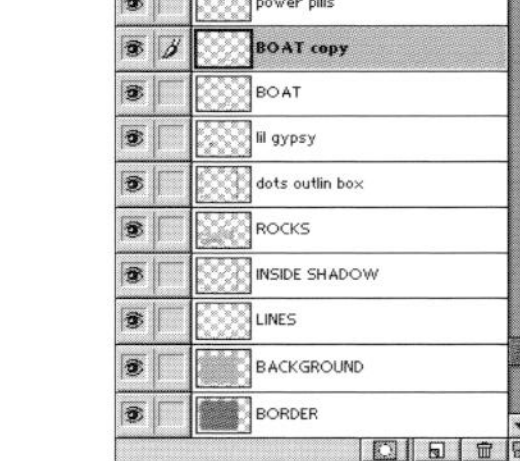

2 Command-Click (Control-Click) the duplicate layer's name in the Layers palette to select its contents.

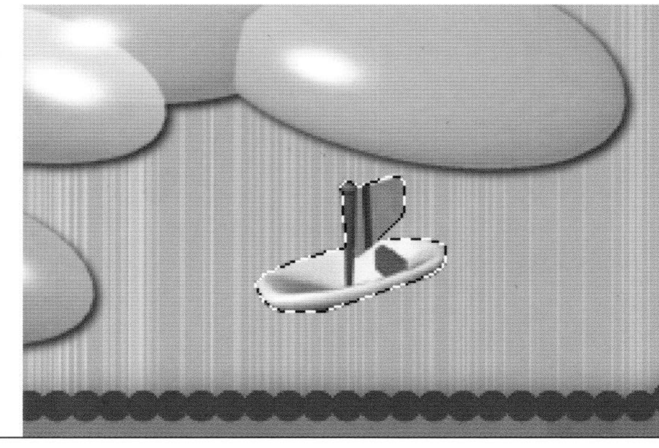

3 Use the Fill command in the Edit menu to fill the area with black (or whatever color you want for your shadow).

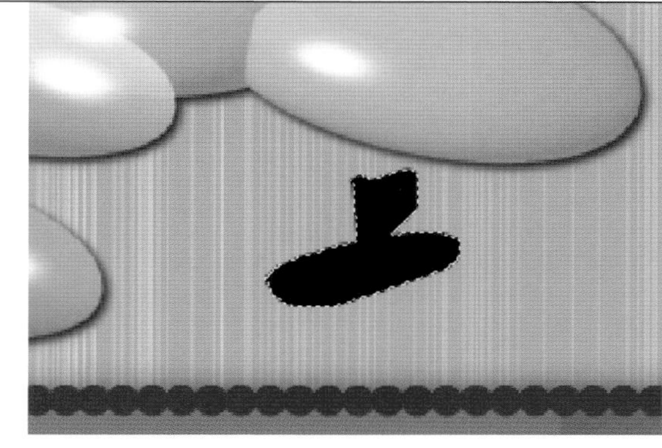

4 Choose Deselect from the Select menu and apply the Gaussian Blur filter. Choose a radius of 1.4 to 1.7 pixels. Anything greater begins to look sloppy on the Web.

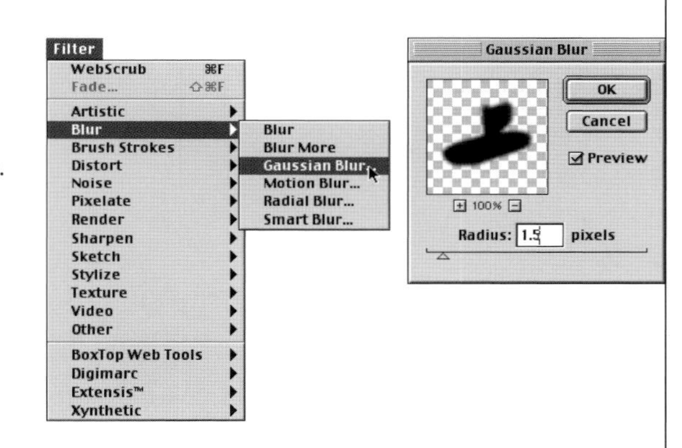

5 Use the Move tool and the arrow keys to shift the shadow 1 to 4 pixels to the right or left and 1 to 4 pixels up or down. The amount that you offset the shadow depends on how big your object is, how exaggerated you want the shadow to appear, and the direction of the light source.

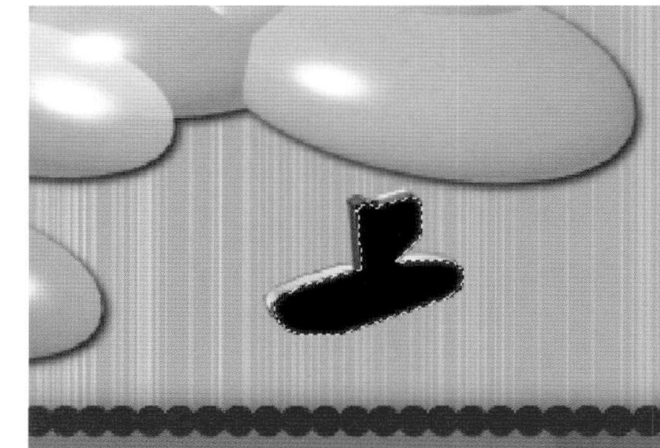

6 Decrease the opacity of the shadow layer to 75 percent or so, according to what looks best for your design, and move the shadow layer below the object layer.

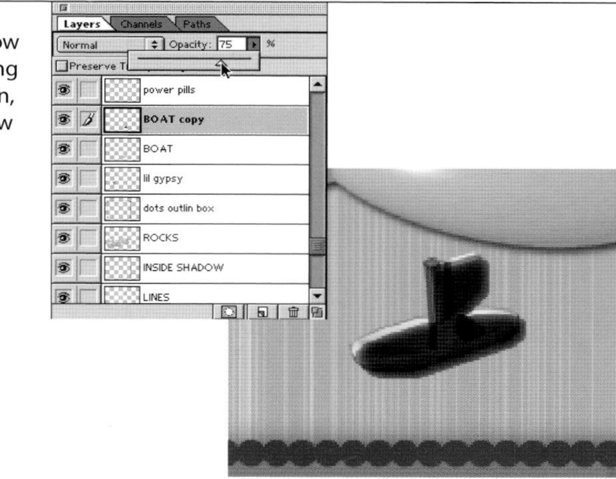

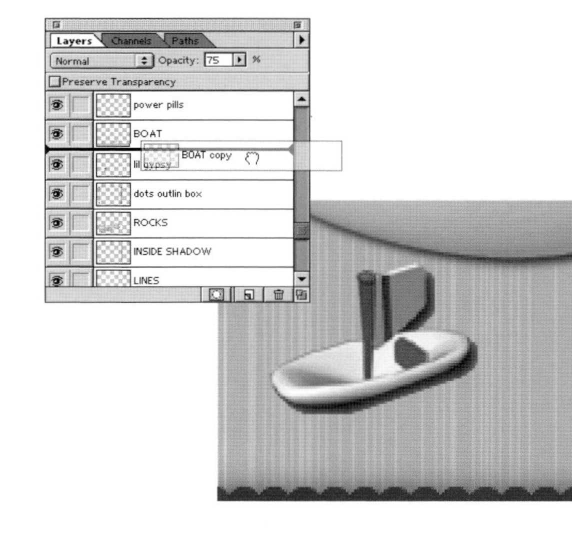

Florian Fangohr
HOT
www.hotstudio.com

Tiling a Background Pattern

Although HTML tables and sliced images allow designers to produce highly graphical pages with small file sizes, there are still other ways to prepare background images. Muted patterns behind text create a pleasing effect, for example. Since browsers can automatically tile a graphic file, repeating it across the Web page, you don't need to construct HTML tables or worry about matching colors across image slices. ImageReady makes it particularly easy to create tiles for backgrounds with its Tile Maker filter. Here's how.

1 In Illustrator or Photoshop, create an image from which you'll marquee a tile. Experiment with Illustrator's Scatter brushes or pattern swatches, and apply either program's filters. The bubbles in this tile, for example, were created in Illustrator using gradient fills and then edited in Photoshop with blending modes. As you're designing, keep in mind that small patterns work best for tiled backgrounds, and try to work with a Web-safe palette.

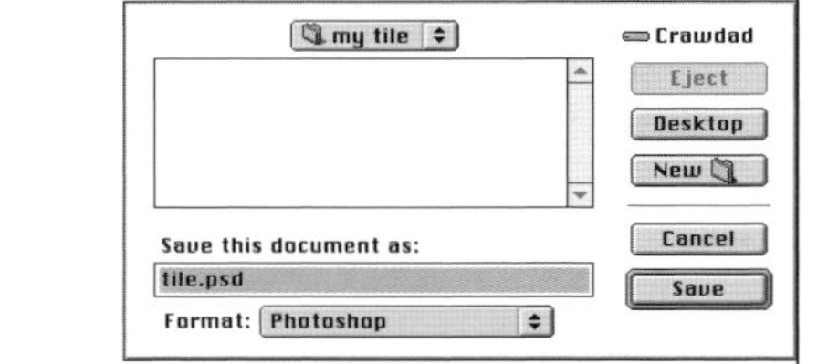

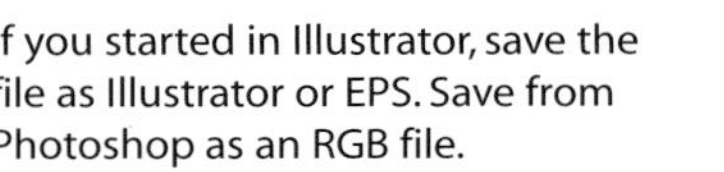

2 If you started in Illustrator, save the file as Illustrator or EPS. Save from Photoshop as an RGB file.

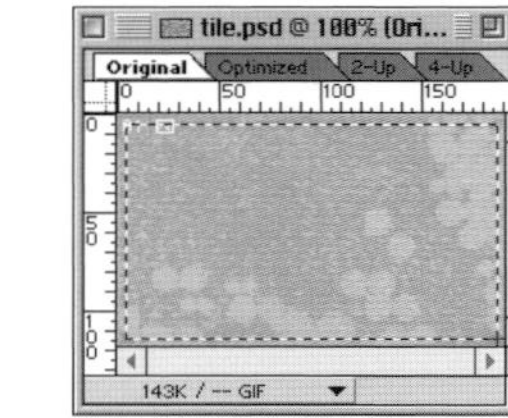

3 Open the image in ImageReady, and select an area that you want to use for your tile with the rectangular Marquee tool. You might have to experiment with size and position to select an area that creates a good pattern and yet is small enough.

 Adobe Illustrator 8.0  Adobe Photoshop 5.5  Adobe ImageReady 2.0  Adobe GoLive 4.0

4 Choose Tile Maker from the Filter menu (under Other). Select the Blend Edges option and specify a width. A percentage between 5 and 15 works best. Check Resize Tile to Fill Image so that the tile isn't reduced by the amount specified in Width. The Kaleidoscope Tile option flips and duplicates the selection horizontally and vertically to create an abstract design. Click OK.

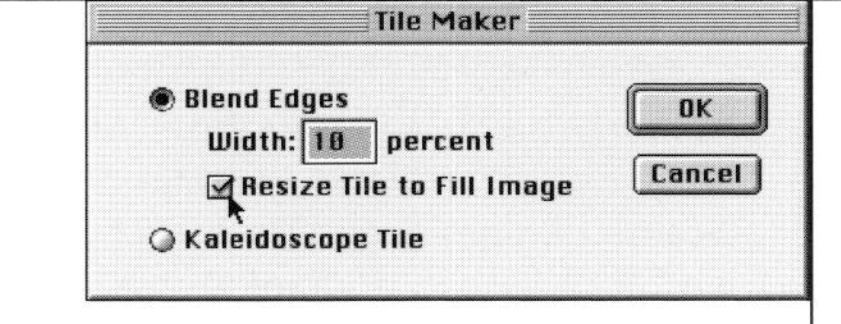

5 Choose Crop from the Image menu to reduce the file to the size of the tile. Opt to delete cropped areas. Click OK.

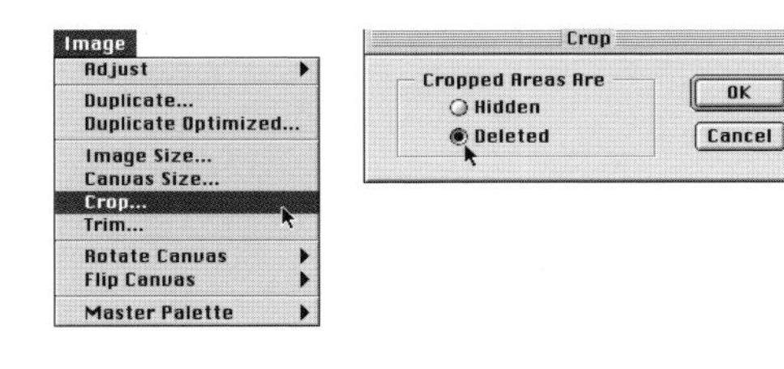

6 To preview your tile as a background in a browser, choose HTML Background from the File menu. Click the View As Background button.

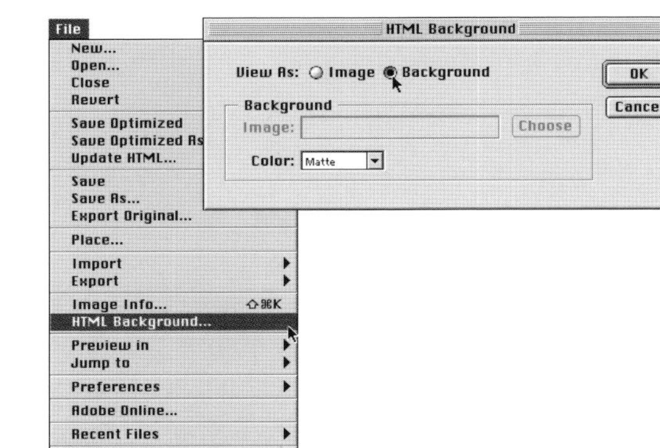

7 Choose Preview In from the File menu and choose your preferred browser.

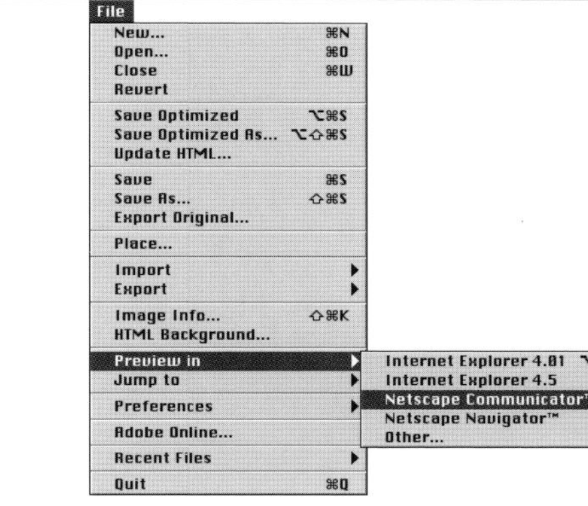

8 Optimize your tile as a GIF. If it contains transparency you might want to deselect the Transparency check box and apply a matte color such as white. Choose Save Optimized As from the File menu.

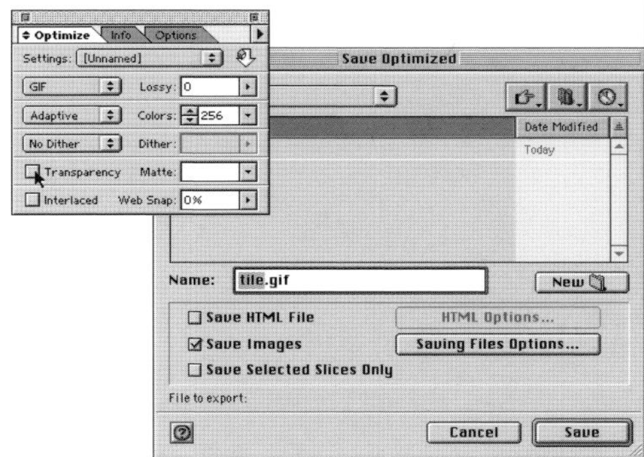

9 To place your tile on a page in GoLive, click the Page icon in the document window to access the Page Inspector. In the Background section, check the Image box and browse to select your tile.

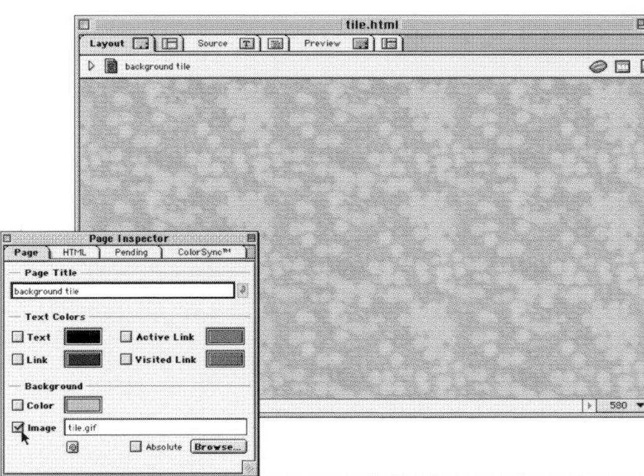

Jason Kottke
www.kottke.org

Creating Static Motion

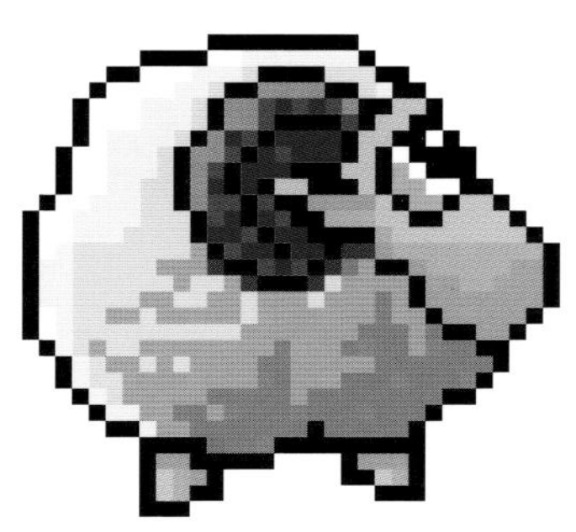

If you want to create the illusion of motion in your graphics without actually animating them—for example, in a banner ad for a site that won't accept animation—you can use stroked outlines in Photoshop to simulate the effect. Minneapolis-based designer Jason Kottke explains how.

1 Place the graphic that you want to "animate" in its own layer by copying the selected area and pasting it into a new layer (layer1).

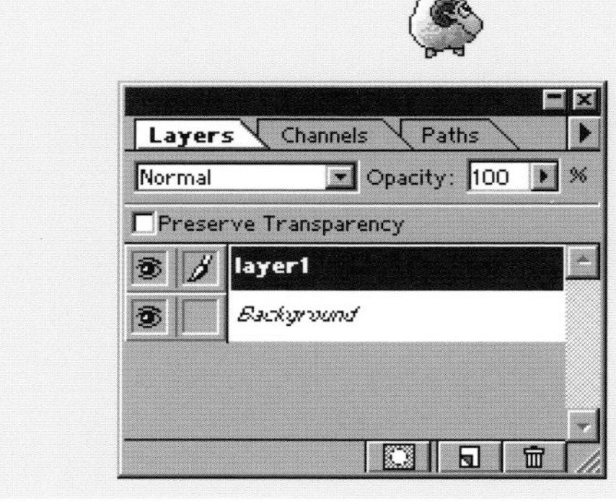

2 Command-click (Control-click) layer1 in the Layers palette to select its contents.

3 Make a new layer (layer2), click it in the Layers palette, and drag to place it under layer1.

4 While layer2 is active, make a 1-pixel stroke inside the selection by choosing Stroke from the Edit menu. Black usually works best for this, but choose the color based on what goes with the background of your graphic.

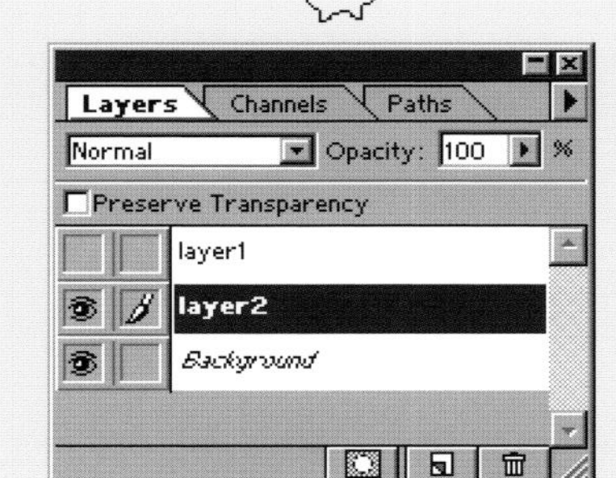

5 Deselect all, and then duplicate layer2 using the Layers palette pop-up menu and paste it into several new layers—we did it four times in this example, layers 3 through 6—for as many "frames" as you want for your implied animation.

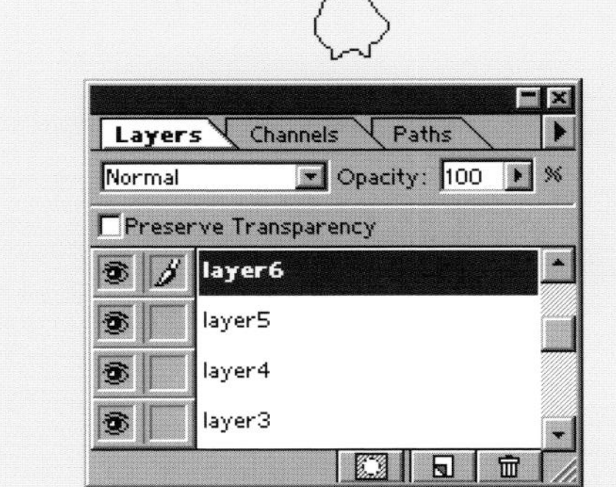
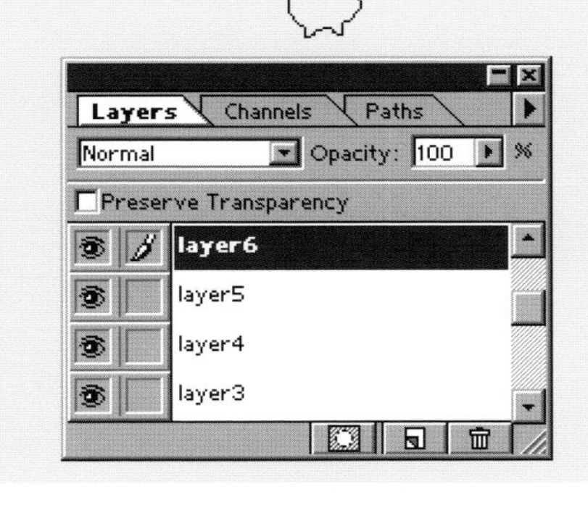

6 Use the Move tool and arrow keys to nudge the outlines in each layer so that they appear to trail the graphic in layer1. If the outlines are only 5 pixels apart, then the image might appear to be moving slowly, but if the outlines are 15 pixels apart, the motion appears to be faster. Vary the distance between the outlines to give the illusion of acceleration or deceleration.

7 Modify the opacity of the outline layers so that the farthest one out is dimmest and the closest one to the graphic is darkest. Again, this may take some tweaking, but this step completes the sense of motion for the object.

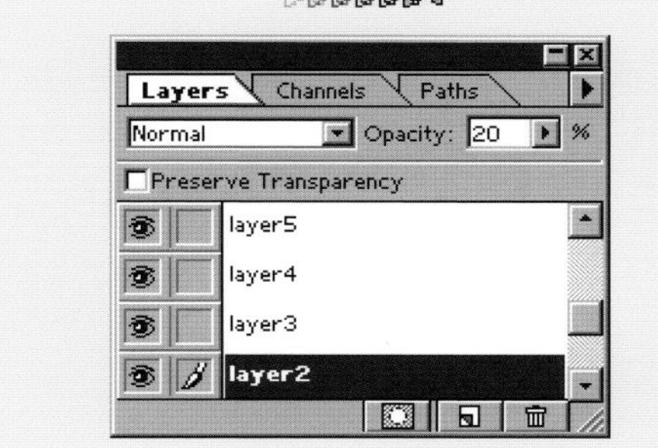

8 Finally, you can add other elements to your graphic. Just make sure that when you save this as a GIF, you use enough colors to keep the outlines of the "animation" visible.

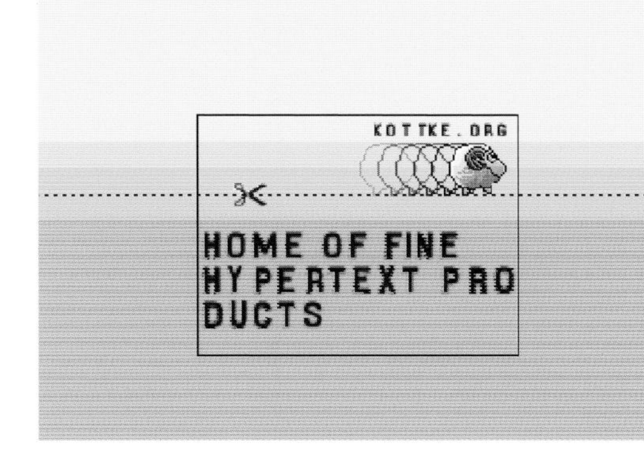

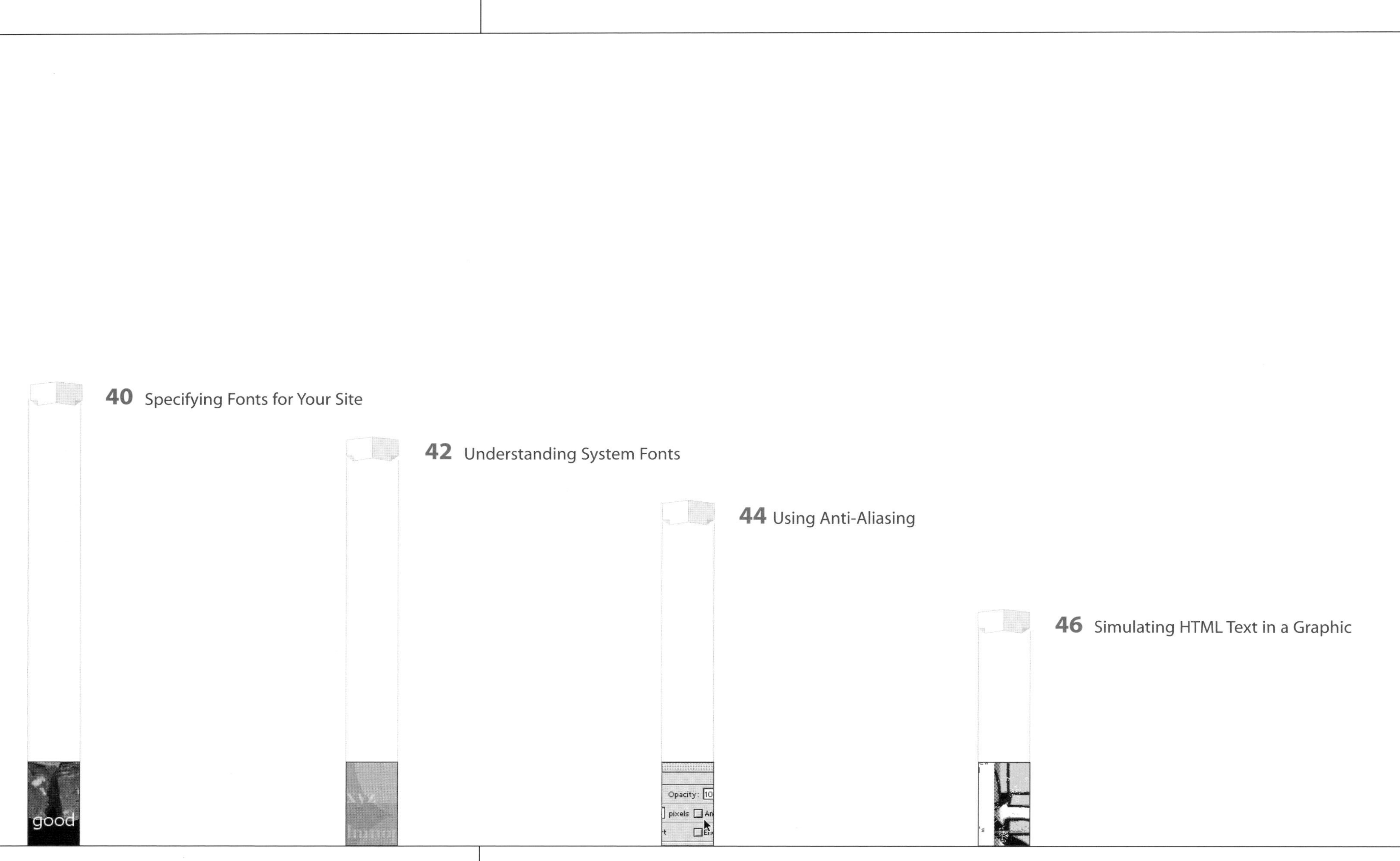
good
xyz
lmno
Opacity:
pixels

Chapter 3

Managing Type

Renee Anderson
HOT
www.hotstudio.com

Specifying Fonts for Your Site

Presenting text as a graphic is one of the few ways a designer can have control over the way type appears in a browser, but it's not always a viable option. It adds bulk in the form of a graphic file to your site and it isn't as flexible as real text. Another option is GoLive's font sets, which instruct a browser to use specific fonts to display a page. If the first typeface you specify isn't on the visitor's system, the browser looks for the second typeface, and so on. So if you want text to appear in Verdana but your visitor doesn't have it, you can specify the next best thing, such as Arial, as a backup. At the least, you may ensure that what you want to appear in a sans serif face doesn't become serif in the browser.

1 Specify font sets before opening a document. Choose Font from the Style menu to access the Font Set Editor dialog box. Click the New button under the Font Sets scrolling list to make a new set.

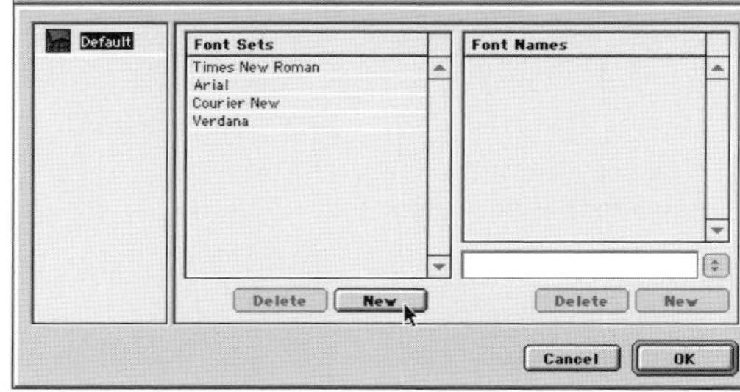

2 An empty font set appears in the Font Sets scrolling list. To add a font to the set, choose one from the pop-up menu under the Font Names list. The set assumes the name of this font. To add other fonts, click the New button under the Font Names list and select another font from the menu. To specify a font that's not on your system, type the name into the box.

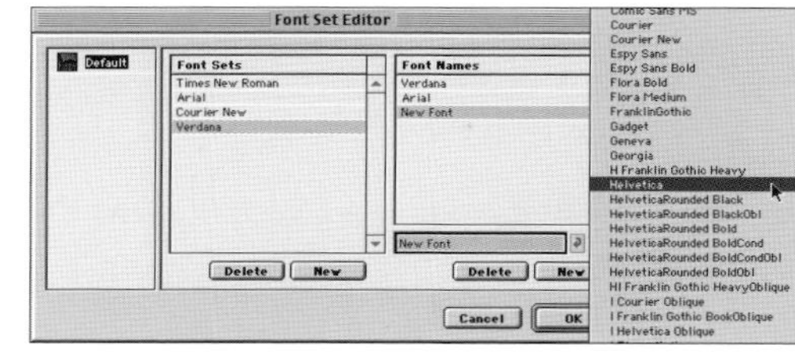

3 You've just added a global font set that will be available to all future documents you create. To see a list of your global font sets, relaunch GoLive, open a document, and choose Font from the Style menu. The sets are listed under the Edit Font Sets command.

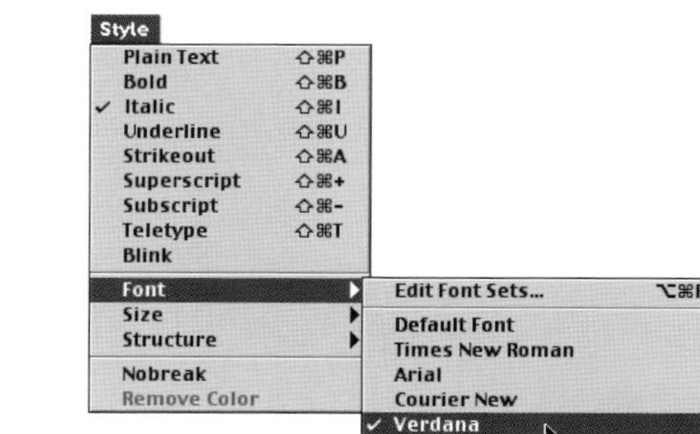

4 You can also create font sets for specific pages. Open a new document and in the Font Set Editor, click the Page icon, and then create your set. The set will be available only to that document and will appear with global sets under the Font command in the Style menu.

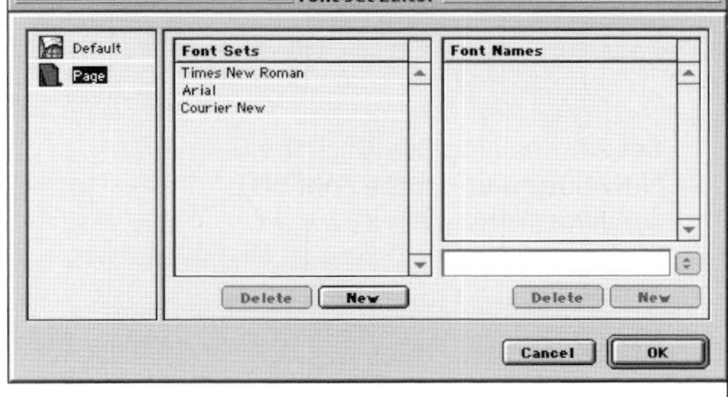

5 To create a font set that is available to every page you create for an entire site, choose New Site from the File menu to create a new site, and then click the Fontsets tab in the site window.

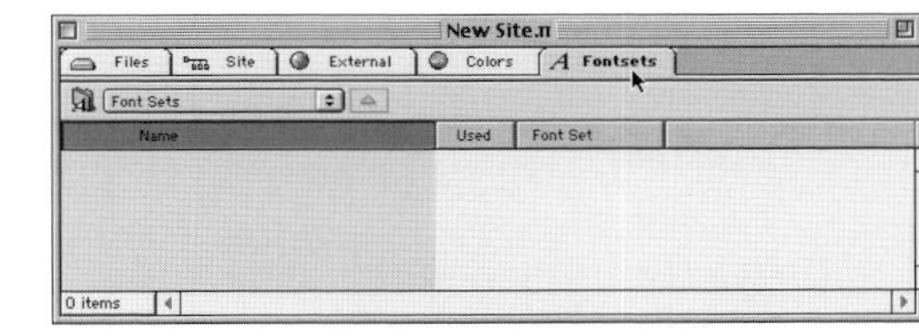

6 From the Site menu, choose the New command and select Font Set, or drag a Font Set icon from the Site tab of the Palette onto the site window.

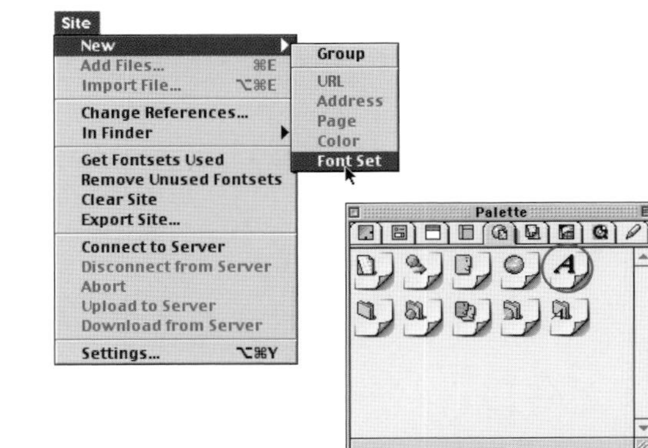

7 In the Font Set Inspector, name your set (and press Return) and select the fonts you want to include from the pop-up menu.

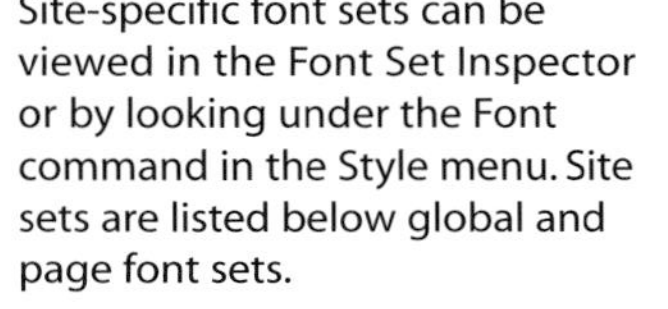

8 Site-specific font sets can be viewed in the Font Set Inspector or by looking under the Font command in the Style menu. Site sets are listed below global and page font sets.

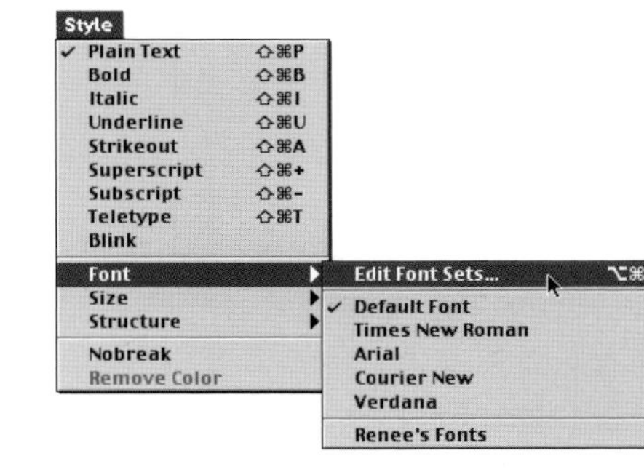

9 Open a new page from the Site menu and type in some text. It uses the first font in your default global set. Select the text and change the font to your site-specific set from the Font command in the Style menu.

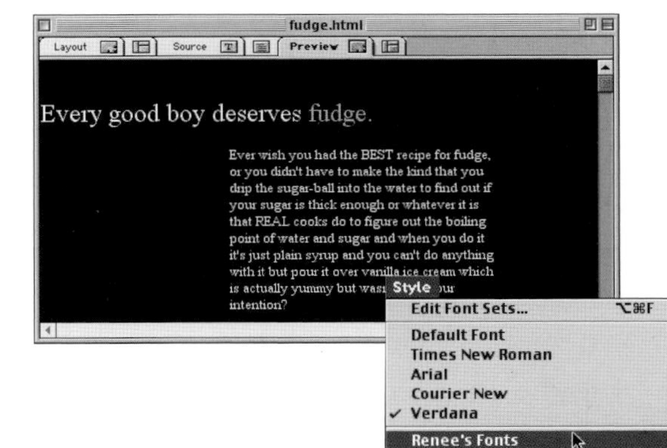

Gregory Ramsperger
HOT
www.hotstudio.com

Understanding System Fonts

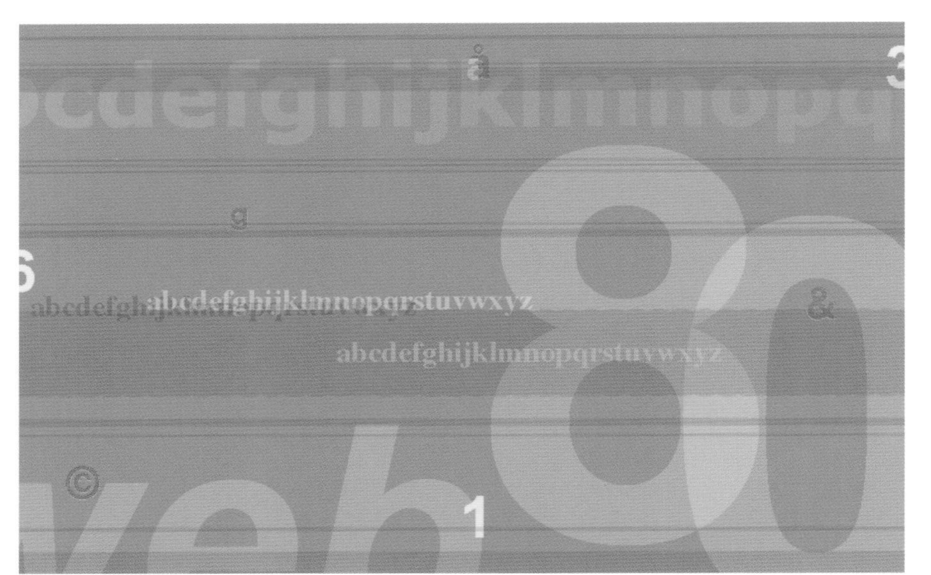

Typography is the cornerstone of good design: The judicious use of type ensures continuity and flow within your pages. But when you're designing for the Web, it's best to make two assumptions: One, site visitors will not have the typeface you specify for your pages on their system; and two, if the visitors do happen to have the typeface you specify, the way the type is displayed in their browsers will be significantly different from what you intended. Although you can specify preferred fonts in HTML and GoLive, sometimes it's safer and simpler to rely on system fonts so that you can be assured of what your visitors will see in their browser. And it helps to know and understand the differences between the fonts that come with the Mac OS; Microsoft Windows (all versions); and some flavors of UNIX, such as Red Hat Linux and SGI IRIX.

System Fonts

Consistent type on Web pages is severely hampered by platform incompatibilities. Geneva, for example, has been standard on the Macintosh since before the rise of the Web, but it is not available for other operating systems. Below are the typefaces that ship with the Mac OS and Microsoft Windows; notice that only versions of Courier, Times, and Symbol are common to both platforms.

Mac OS	Microsoft Windows
Charcoal	Arial
Chicago	Courier New
Courier	Symbol
Geneva	Times New Roman
Helvetica	Wingdings
Monaco	
New York	
Palatino	
Symbol	
Times	

Popular Fonts

A variety of popular typefaces can be downloaded for free or are shipped with various software packages. Arial, Verdana, and Impact, for example, are often considered part of the "canon" of typefaces largely because they are included with the standard installation of Internet Explorer and Microsoft Office on both Macintosh and Windows. Nevertheless, choose and use them with care—they are not ubiquitous.

8pt	Arial	Verdana	Impact
12pt	Arial	Verdana	Impact
16pt	Arial	Verdana	Impact
24pt	Arial	Verdana	Impact

Cross-Platform Font Appearance

Compounding the problem of not knowing what fonts are on your visitors' systems is the fact that it's hard to control the size of type on the Web. It's a good idea to always specify point size in your HTML code, since you can never be sure if visitors' browsers support Cascading Style Sheets. Unfortunately, point size is relative, not absolute, and the same font appears larger or smaller depending on the platform on which it's viewed. Using Cascading Style Sheets in conjunction with system fonts gives you the best shot at controlling how type will appear to site visitors, regardless of platform. Although style sheets don't give absolute control over character width, they do let you specify both line height and point size in pixels, giving you the same degree of accuracy of placement as you can achieve with images, so type displays nearly identically on all platforms. Here is how identically sized Times, Arial, Helvetica, and Verdana appear on various platforms.

Times

Mac OS

All you need is ignorance and confidence;
then success is sure. - Mark Twain
Originality is the art of concealing your source. -Franklin Jones

Microsoft Windows

All you need is ignorance and confidence;
then success is sure. - Mark Twain
Originality is the art of concealing your source. -Franklin Jones

Red Hat Linux

All you need is ignorance and confidence;
then success is sure. – Mark Twain
Originality is the art of concealing your source. –Franklin Jones

SGI IRIX

All you need is ignorance and confidence;
then success is sure. – Mark Twain
Originality is the art of concealing your source. –Franklin Jones

Arial

Mac OS

All you need is ignorance and confidence;
then success is sure. - Mark Twain
Originality is the art of concealing your source. -Franklin Jones

Microsoft Windows

All you need is ignorance and confidence;
then success is sure. - Mark Twain
Originality is the art of concealing your source. -Franklin Jones

Red Hat Linux*

All you need is ignorance and confidence;
then success is sure. – Mark Twain
Originality is the art of concealing your source. -Franklin Jones

SGI IRIX*

All you need is ignorance and confidence;
then success is sure. – Mark Twain
Originality is the art of concealing your source. –Franklin Jones

* Arial is not available for Red Hat Linux or SGI IRIX, so browsers on those platforms usually default to Times.

Helvetica

Mac OS

All you need is ignorance and confidence;
then success is sure. - Mark Twain
Originality is the art of concealing your source. -Franklin Jones

Microsoft Windows

All you need is ignorance and confidence;
then success is sure. - Mark Twain
Originality is the art of concealing your source. -Franklin Jones

Red Hat Linux

All you need is ignorance and confidence;
then success is sure. – Mark Twain
Originality is the art of concealing your source. –Franklin Jones

SGI IRIX

All you need is ignorance and confidence;
then success is sure. – Mark Twain
Originality is the art of concealing your source. –Franklin Jones

Verdana

Mac OS

All you need is ignorance and confidence;
then success is sure. - Mark Twain
Originality is the art of concealing your source. -Franklin Jones

Microsoft Windows

All you need is ignorance and confidence;
then success is sure. - Mark Twain
Originality is the art of concealing your source. -Franklin Jones

Red Hat Linux*

All you need is ignorance and confidence;
then success is sure. - Mark Twain
Originality is the art of concealing your source. -Franklin Jones

SGI IRIX*

All you need is ignorance and confidence;
then success is sure. – Mark Twain
Originality is the art of concealing your source. -Franklin Jones

* Verdana is not available for Red Hat Linux or SGI IRIX, so browsers on those platforms usually default to Courier.

Julia Hummelt
HOT
www.hotstudio.com

Using Anti-Aliasing

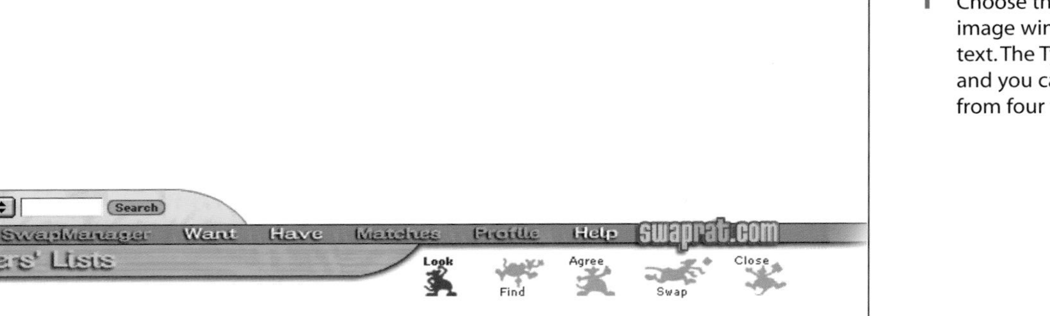

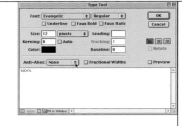

When adding type or line art to an image or graphic, you have the option of applying anti-aliasing. This technique reduces jaggy edges of letterforms and lines and smoothes the appearance of the type or line art against its background. Anti-aliasing is generally recommended for making type much more readable on 72-ppi computer screens, but it's not always appropriate. You should always consider the point size of your type and the background behind the letterforms or objects in your image. Also, keep in mind that anti-aliasing increases file size (because it adds color pixels to the edges of the type), which is always a consideration when publishing to the Web.

1 Choose the Type tool and click in the image window where you want to add text. The Type Tool dialog box appears, and you can enter text and choose from four types of anti-aliasing.

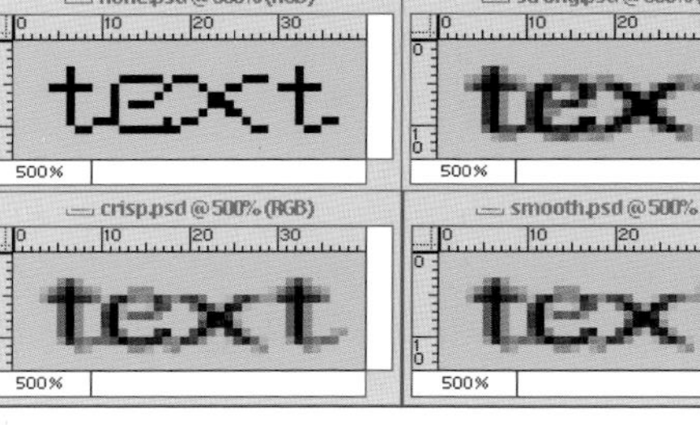

2 Clockwise from the top left, the four types of anti-aliasing are None; Crisp, which makes type appear sharper; Smooth, which makes type appear smoother; and Strong, which makes type appear bolder. The effect is difficult to replicate in print, which is a higher resolution medium, so we're showing the examples here at 500 percent.

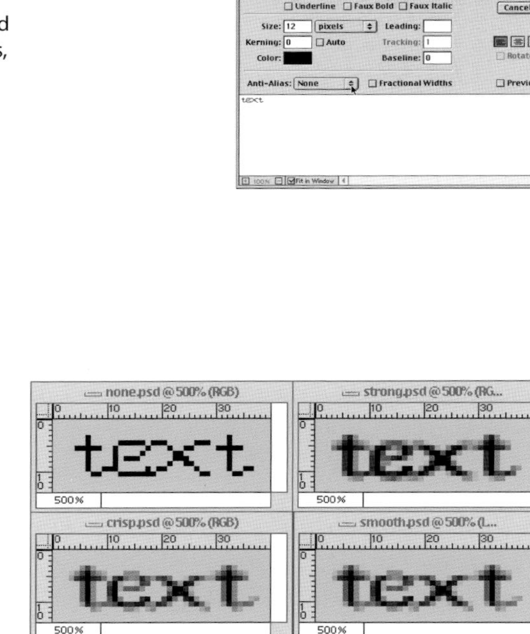

3 On some occasions you'll want to leave your type aliased: When working with small point sizes—9 points or less—anti-aliasing may make type appear blurry. The names of these buttons are aliased; the mice drawings are anti-aliased. The effect also depends on the typeface, so you may want to experiment with the anti-aliasing settings.

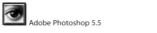

4 Also, be careful when using anti-aliasing with type over transparent graphics, patterned backgrounds, or backgrounds of a similar color to the type. In these cases, anti-aliasing might make the type difficult to read. The small type in the Update List button at right is aliased, for example; the Members' Lists text is anti-aliased.

5 You can also apply anti-aliasing to lines as you draw. Here you see the difference between a shape drawn with anti-aliasing (left) and one without (right). The 500 percent close-up of the aliased shape (below) highlights the sharp edges of the line's pixels against the background.

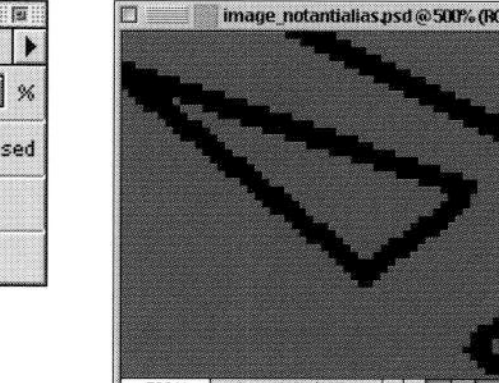

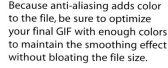

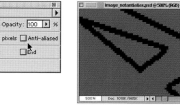

6 When you import a vector file from Illustrator into Photoshop, you're prompted with a dialog box that asks how you want to rasterize the file. The rule of thumb is to leave the Anti-aliased box unchecked if your drawing is mainly straight lines; applying anti-aliasing would diminish the lines' sharpness. Do apply anti-aliasing if your drawing includes rounded or curved shapes and lines.

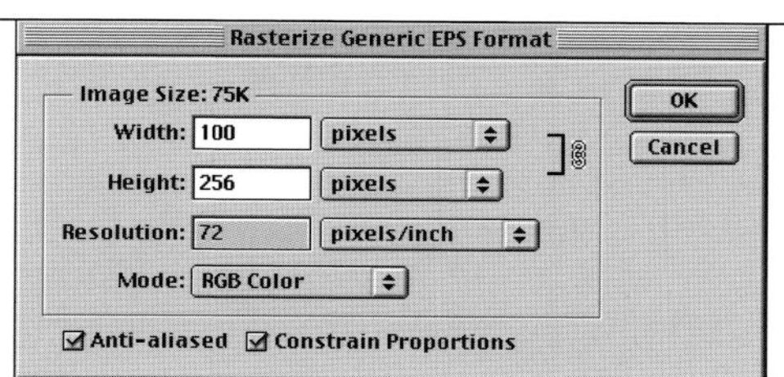

7 Because anti-aliasing adds color to the file, be sure to optimize your final GIF with enough colors to maintain the smoothing effect without bloating the file size.

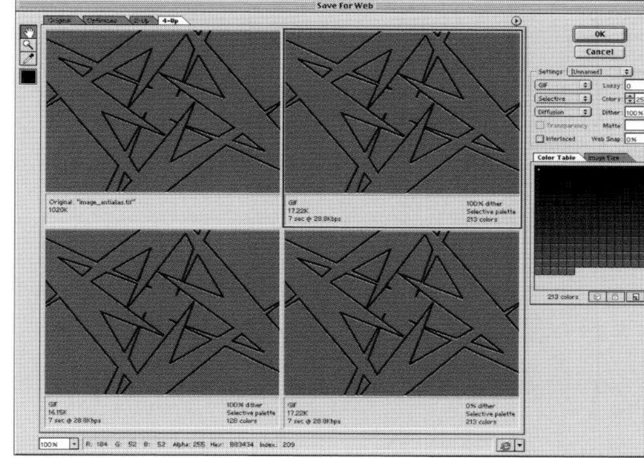

Sharpening Tiny Type

To make tiny aliased type in an image appear clearer and smoother, add or replace crucial pixels of solid color (where the letter naturally curves) with semi-transparent pixels. This is particularly useful for the internal spaces in lowercase a, c, e, and s as well as uppercase B, R, and P, which often close up. And keep in mind that sans serif typefaces such as Geneva or Arial work best at small point sizes, because serifs can obscure the letterform.

—Casey Caston

Jason Kottke
www.kottke.org

Simulating HTML Text in a Graphic

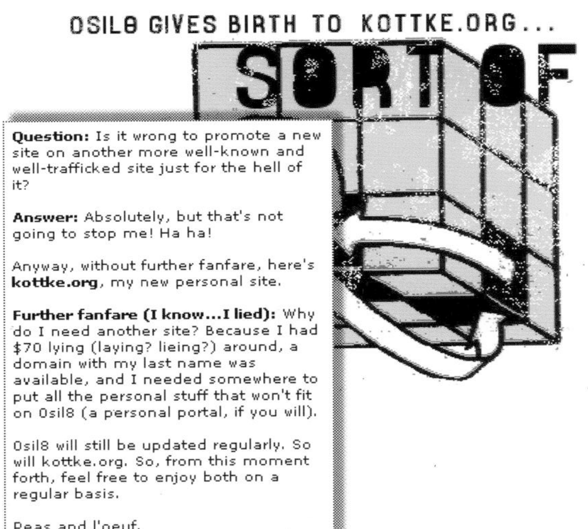

Sometimes you need a bit of aliased text for a design, and although you want it to look like HTML, you don't want to leave it to the browser to render. You may, for example, want navigational items or paragraph line breaks to display identically across browsers and platforms. Whatever the reason, you can code the text in HTML, take a screen capture as it appears in a browser, and then use the graphic in your design. Jason Kottke says he uses this technique frequently because it saves him time and gives him greater control over the appearance of text.

1 Using GoLive, lay out the desired HTML text with tables, Cascading Style Sheets, or whatever techniques you wish. In this example, we're laying out some text at an extremely small point size in a narrow table cell.

```
<table cellpadding=0 cellspacing=0 border=0 width=220>

<tr>
<td align=left valign=top><font size="-2" face="verdana,arial,geneva">

<b>Question:</b> Is it wrong to promote a new site on another more well-known and well-trafficked
site just for the hell of it?<br> <br>

<b>Answer:</b> Absolutely, but that's not going to stop me! Ha ha!<br> <br>

Anyway, without further fanfare, here's <b>kottke.org</b>, my new personal site.<br> <br>

<b>Further fanfare (I know...I lied):</b> Why do I need another site? Because I had $70 lying
(laying? lieing?) around, a domain with my last name was available, and I needed somewhere to put
all the personal stuff that won't fit on Osil8 (a personal portal, if you will).<br> <br>

Osil8 will still be updated regularly. So will kottke.org. So, from this moment forth, feel free to
enjoy both on a regular basis.<br> <br>

Peas and l'oeuf.

</font></td>
</tr>

</table>
```

2 Click the Show in Browser button to preview the text in your preferred Web browser, and take a screenshot by pressing Command-Shift-3 (Print Screen).

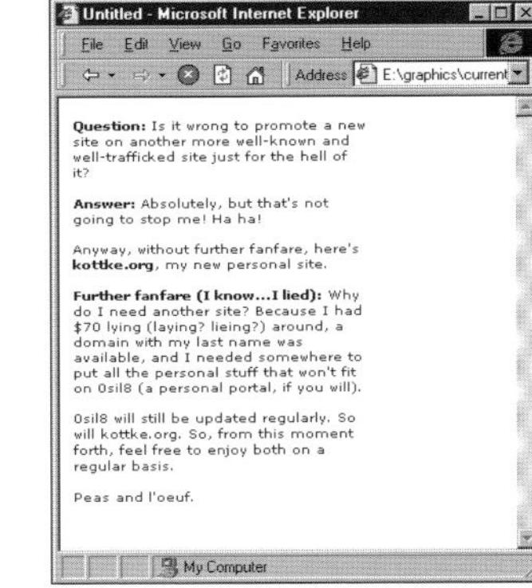

3 Open the screenshot of your type in Photoshop and double-click the background layer name in the Layers palette to change it to a regular layer. Use the Marquee tool to select the area that contains the text, and then copy and paste the type into the file that contains the image background. This automatically creates a new layer.

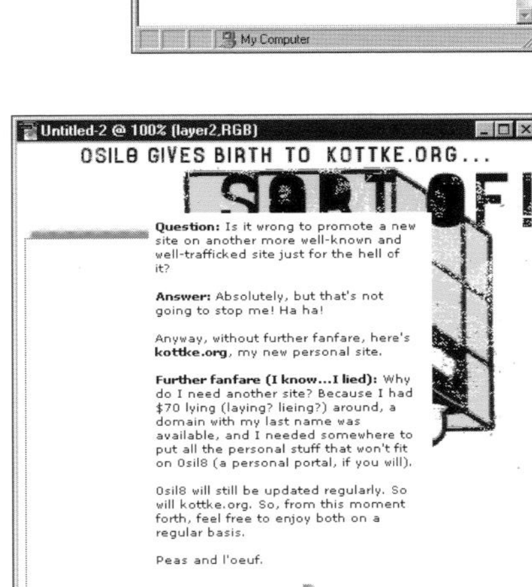

Adobe Photoshop 5.5  Adobe GoLive 4.0

4 Select the Magic Eraser tool in the Tool palette. Specify a Tolerance of 0 and deselect the Anti-aliased and Contiguous check boxes in the Magic Eraser Options palette.

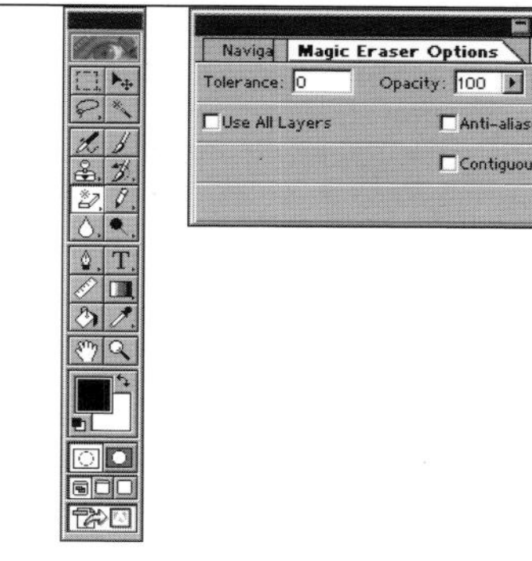

5 Click in the white area of the screen capture to remove all of the white pixels.

6 Use the Move tool to drag the text into position in your design. Tweak the text if necessary—change the color, for example—and save the file.

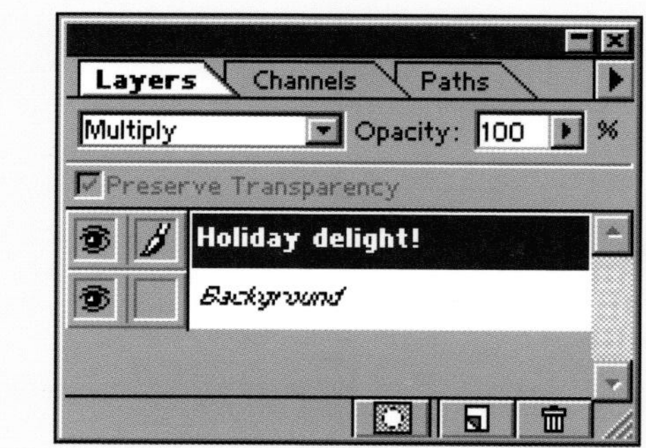

Options for Selecting Text

If you want to do this technique and your text is black, try the following instead of Steps 4 and 5: Select the layer with the text you pasted in Step 3. In the Layers palette, choose Multiply as your mode and specify your Opacity as 100 percent. This leaves just your black text pixels in the layer, and you can use the Move tool to position them. *—HOT*

Jason Kottke
www.kottke.org

Creating a Quick 3D Text Effect

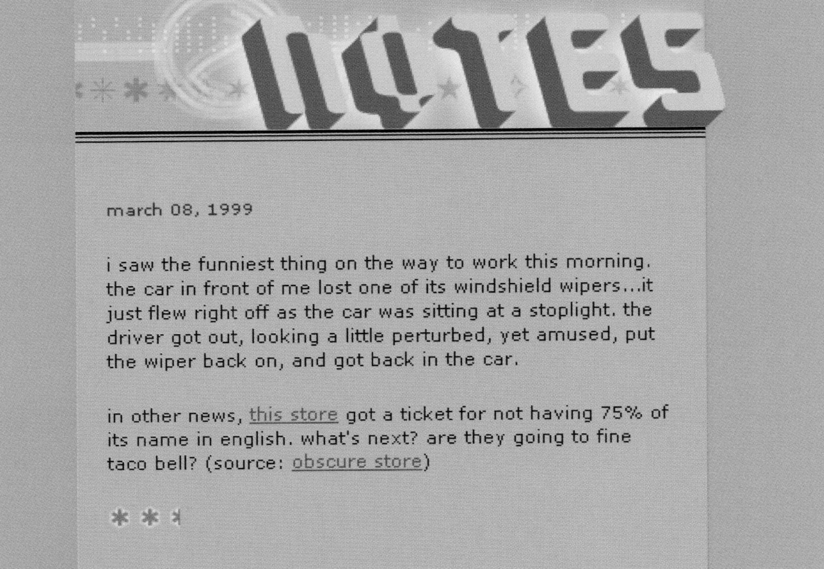

This tip is for those of you who don't have one of those nifty 3D text plug-ins for Photoshop. For best results, use a heavy sans serif typeface, a large point size, and a relatively large tracking value.

1 Type your text into a Photoshop document. Turn the type layer into a regular layer by choosing Type, Render Layer from the Layer menu.

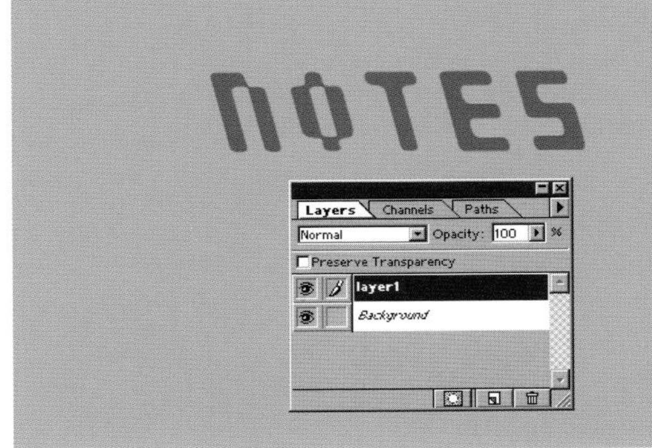

2 Copy the layer with your text by choosing Duplicate Layer from the Layers palette pop-up menu, or click it and drag it onto the Create New Layer icon at the bottom of the palette.

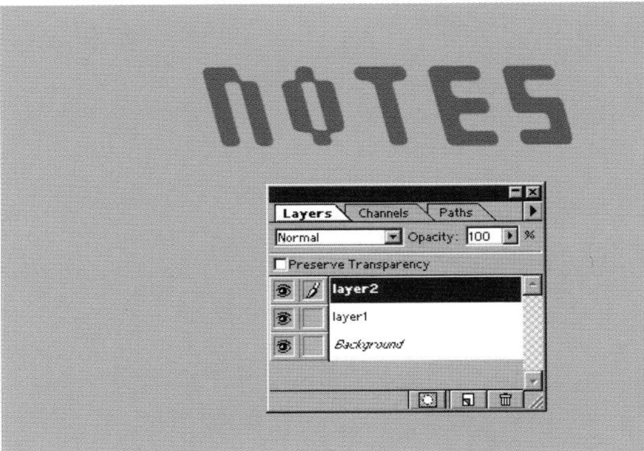

3 With your copied layer active, use the Move tool and the arrow keys to shift the contents 1 pixel horizontally and 1 pixel vertically. In our example, it's been moved up and to the right.

4 Continue to duplicate and nudge the contents of layers until you achieve the desired depth for your 3D effect.

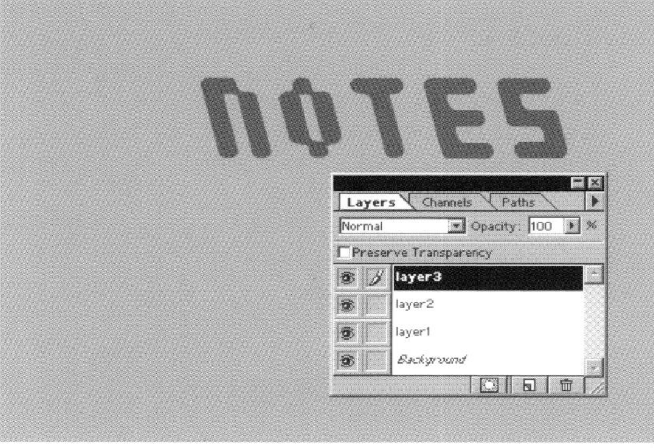

5 Make sure the layers are offset progressively. Now select the top layer (which may be the original text or the furthest offset layer, depending on how you duplicated the layers), choose Fill from the Edit menu, and fill the contents with a different color. Check the Preserve Transparency box. Then click OK.

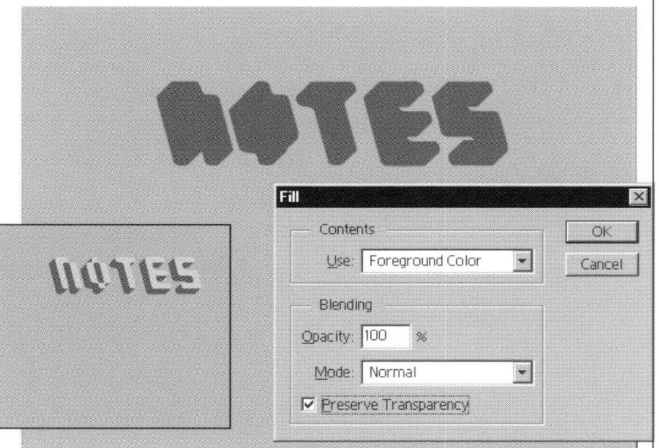

6 Add some background graphics to help make the text pop up.

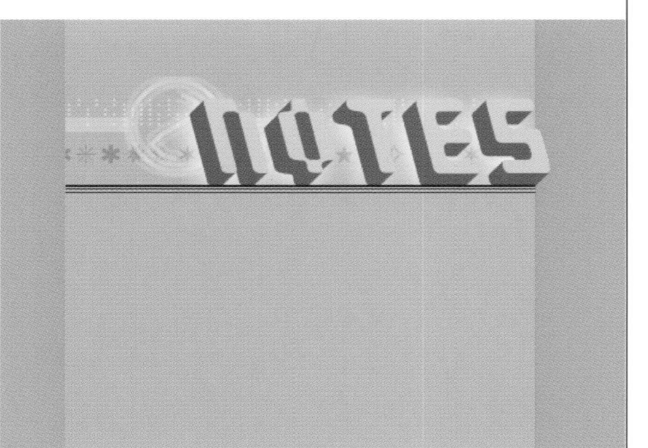

7 For a softer look, graduate the color of the top three or four layers so it looks like a beveled edge; or make the text in the top layer the same color as the background, and apply a 1-pixel stroke inside the type using the color of the 3D shadow.

8 When you're satisfied, choose Save for Web from the File menu. Optimize the graphic as a GIF. Because you're using solid colors, you can reduce the number of colors in your adaptive palette to just a few without sacrificing image quality.

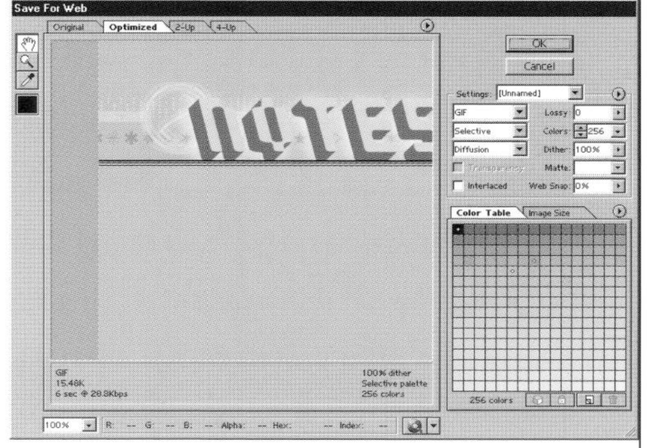

Steve Piasecki
www.sirius.com/~stevepi

Applying Style Sheets to HTML Pages

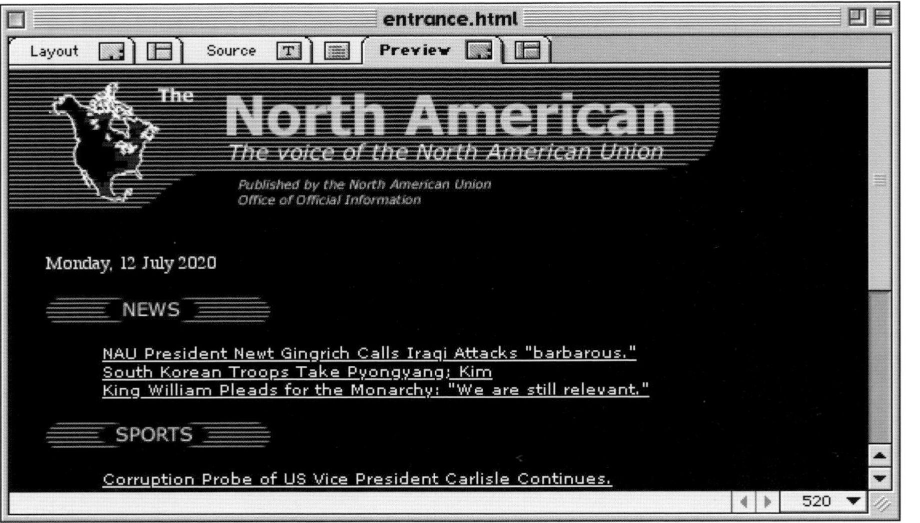

Cascading Style Sheets, like style sheets used in page layout programs for print, let designers control the appearance and positioning of type and graphics on the Web. You can, for example, create headline, paragraph, and banner styles that specify how text and graphics should be displayed relative to the browser window or to other elements. You can specify attributes such as the size, spacing, and color of text as well as the spacing and margins for images and graphics. (For a guide to GoLive's CSS capabilities, see "Understanding Style Sheet Attributes," page 54.) Style sheets make it easy to keep designs consistent across pages, but you have to apply them cautiously: Different browsers support different CSS attributes, so you have to test pages extensively to be sure that what you design is what visitors see.

1 With a new HTML document open, click the Page icon in the document window and set the basic properties in the Page Inspector. In case there's a problem with a viewer's browser applying the style sheet, set the default text color as white so that it appears over the black background.

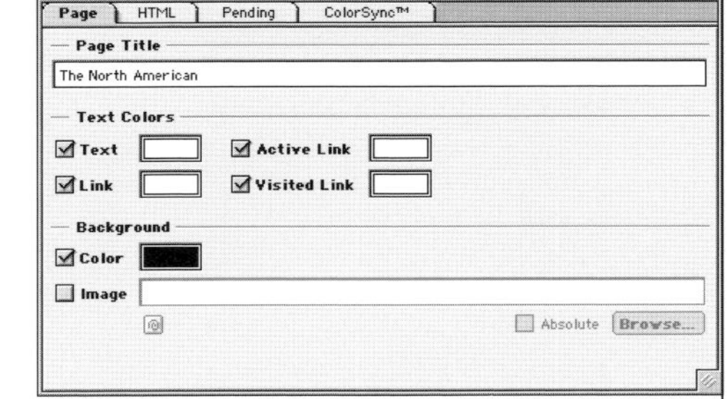

2 Place images and type text on the page, not worrying about exact placement for the moment. Avoid using tables and frames when you know you'll be applying a style sheet—they complicate positioning. Create URL links by selecting text or graphics, clicking the New Link button in the toolbar, and specifying the URL in the Link tab of the Text or Image Inspector. Save the document.

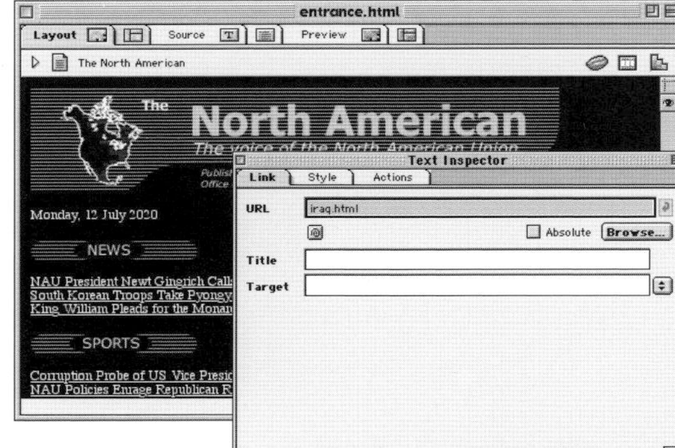

3 Choose New Special from the File menu, and open a New Stylesheet Document. You will use this style sheet document to apply formatting to the page you just prepared.

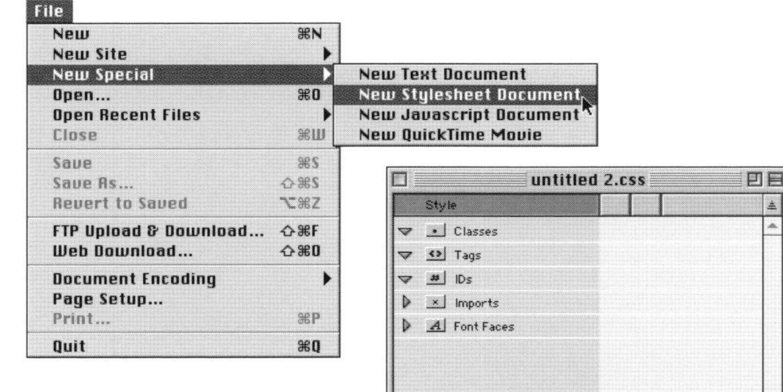

4 Click the New Class button in the toolbar (the far-left button, with a dot in the middle) to create a new style class. In the CSS Selector Inspector, name the class in the Basics tab; the name should describe the properties of the class or what it is modifying. We called ours "mastheadgraphic" because it will be used to position the masthead graphic.

5 Click the Position tab in the CSS Selector Inspector. To ensure that the masthead graphic appears in the upper-left corner of the browser window, we set the positioning Kind to Absolute, specifying the Left and Top values as 0 pixels. Because style classes with absolute positioning are separate from the main document, the masthead will reside on a "layer" above the other page elements.

6 Create a second style class to position the date. Name it "date" in the Basics tab of the CSS Selector Inspector, and then switch to the Block tab and set the top margin to 100 pixels so that it falls 6 pixels below the masthead graphic, which is 94 pixels high. Set the left margin to 15 pixels to allow for some space on the left.

7 Now it's time to position the section header graphics. Create a new style class named "sectionheadergraphic," with a top margin of 10 pixels and a left margin of 15 pixels. This will position each section header graphic 10 pixels below the previous block and will maintain the 15 pixel offset from the left side of the browser window.

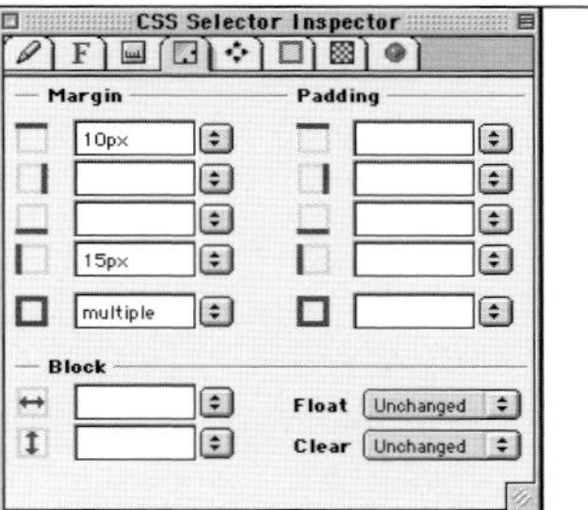

8 Create a fourth style class for the news headlines. Ours is named "smlheadlinewhtver10," with a top margin of 5 pixels (so that the first headline will fall 5 pixels below the graphic above it) and a left margin of 50 pixels (so that the text will be indented from the left a bit more than the other elements).

9 Since this style class will format text, switch to the Font tab of the Inspector. Select white in the Color field and set the Size to 10 points. Specify a font family by clicking the New button and choosing a primary font from the pop-up menu. Specify alternate faces also, and end the list with a generic family name, such as sans serif.

Steve Piasecki
www.sirius.com/~stevep/nau

CONTINUED...

Applying Style Sheets to HTML Pages

10 To specify a color for URL text links, set a link tag style. Click the New Tag button in the toolbar (the one with the carets, next to the New Class button) and set some properties in the Inspector. Name the style "l" in the Basics tab and set the color to white in the Font tab.

11 Create a second style tag and name it "l:hover." This style, which will be applied to a text link, changes the color of the text when the mouse cursor is positioned over it. Set the color to silver. (See "Naming CSS Elements" on page 53 for more information about using colons in CSS style names.)

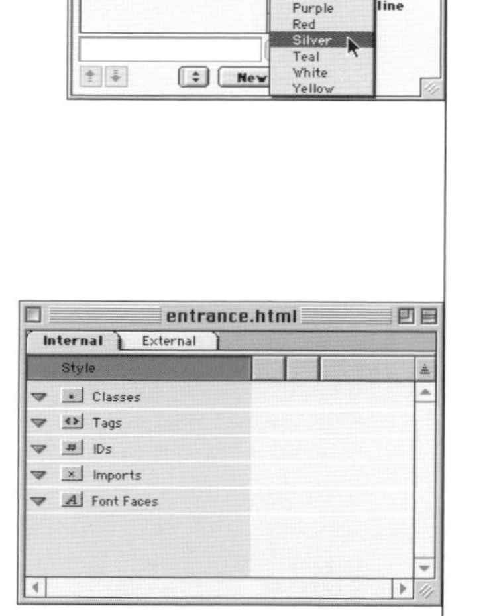

12 Save the style sheet with a .css extension. To apply the style sheet to your HTML document, you must link the two. Click the Style Sheet button at the top right of your HTML document window (the button with the stair-step icon) to access the style sheet window.

13 Click the External tab in the style sheet window; it will be empty. Click the New Item button in the style sheet toolbar (another button with a stair-step icon) and set the URL of your style sheet in the External Style Sheet Inspector to complete the link.

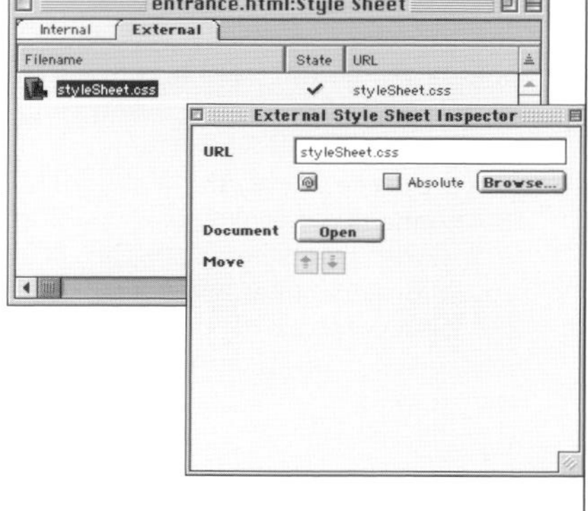

14 The link tag style will be applied to links automatically, but you have to manually apply the style classes. Start from the bottom of your HTML document and work upward. Select the last set of news headlines. In the Style tab of the Text Inspector, check the style "smlheadlinewhtver10" as a Div, which is short for division and refers to a selected section of text.

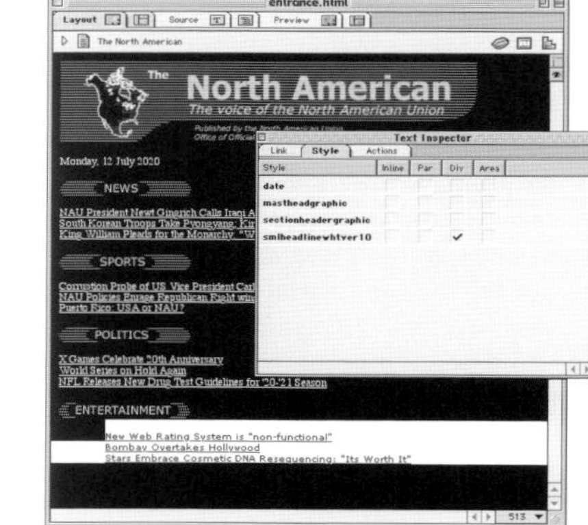

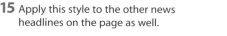

15 Apply this style to the other news headlines on the page as well.

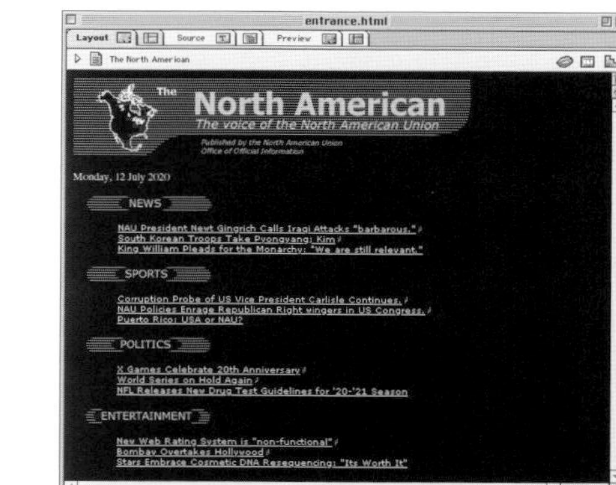

16 Now select the last section header graphic by dragging the I-beam cursor from left to right across it, which lets you edit the graphic's text properties. Apply the style "sectionheadergraphic" as a division in the Style tab of the Text Inspector. Repeat for the other section header graphics.

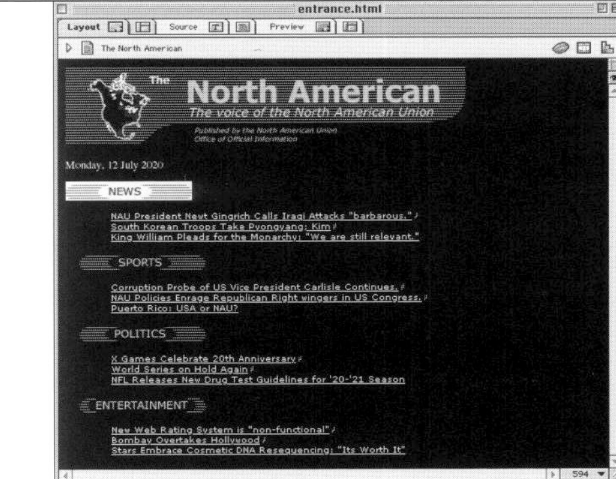

17 Select the date and apply its style in the Text Inspector. A large space will appear above the date that allows for the masthead graphic and the 6-pixel offset that you specified in the style.

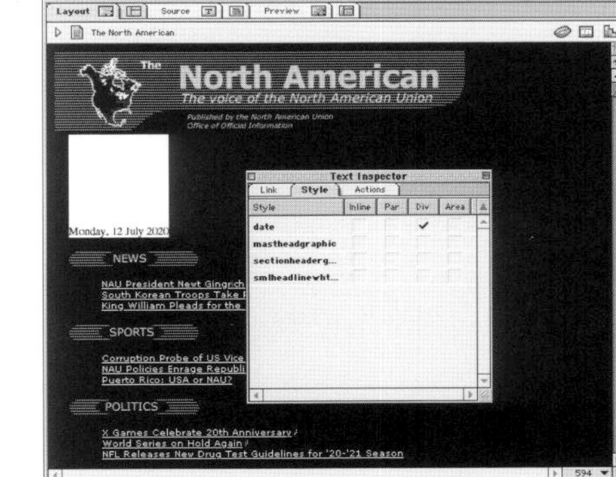

18 Finally, apply the style for the masthead graphic. To see the graphic's absolute positioning, switch to the Preview tab of the document window.

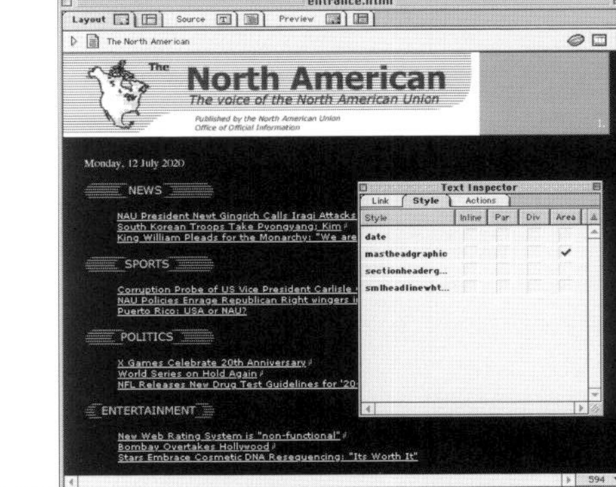

19 Preview the styled HTML page in multiple browsers (choose Show in Browser from the Special menu to access all the browsers on your system) before saving it. The l:hover tag we created in Step 11, for example, works in Internet Explorer but not Netscape Navigator.

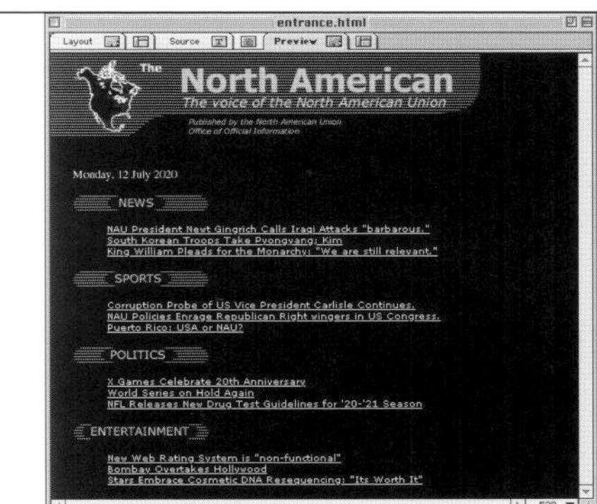

Naming CSS Elements

When creating and applying CSS styles, choose a naming convention carefully. Web browsers are often unable to decipher style names that include spaces or nonalphanumeric characters such as underscores and hyphens. Style names are case independent and should always begin with a letter.

One exception to the rule is the use of colons. Colons cans be used to delineate several behaviors of a single class. For instance, the anchor tag has four pseudo-classes. The default behavior of a hypertext link is determined by naming the style "a:link", and "a:visited" defines the properties of a visited link; the "a:active" and "a:hover" are considered dynamic pseudoclasses that change the characteristics of links as they are clicked or as the mouse cursor hovers above them. *—Gregory Ramsperger*

Gregory Ramsperger
HOT
www.hotstudio.com

Understanding Style Sheet Attributes

	GoLive Attribute	CSS Equivalent	Description
FONT	Color	Color	Sets the font color.
	Size	Font-size	Sets the font size in absolute or relative terms.
	Line Height	Line-height	Sets the vertical space given to the type, overriding browser settings.
	Font	Font-family	Defines which fonts should be used in your order of preference.
	Style	Font-style	Sets type as normal (roman), oblique, or italic
	Decoration	Text-decoration	Adds underlining, strikethrough, and other formatting options.
TEXT	Text Indent	Text-indent	Indents the first line of text in a block.
	Word Spacing	Word-spacing	Sets the space between words.
	Letter Spacing	Letter-spacing	Sets the space between characters within a word.
	Vertical Align	Vertical-align	Positions the text vertically on the line.
	Font Variant	Font-variant	Selects small caps.
	Transformation	Text-transform	Controls capitalization and case of text in a block.
	Alignment	Text-align	Applies horizontal alignment to a block of text.
BLOCK	Margin	Margin-top	Sets the margin around a block of text; may be a negative value.
		Margin-right	
		Margin-bottom	
		Margin-left	
	Padding	Padding	Sets the padding around a block of text; must be a positive value.
		Padding-top	
		Padding-right	
		Padding-bottom	
		Padding-left	
	Width	Width	Sets the width of an object or text block.
	Height	Height	Sets the height of an object or text block.
	Float	Float	Allows a defined block (a floating box) to wrap around another element.
	Clear	Clear	Clears or allows floating boxes around an element.
POSITION	Positioning Kind	Position	Defines the absolute or relative positioning of a floating element.
	Positioning Left	Left	Defines the horizontal distance from the origin.
	Positioning Top	Top	Defines the vertical distance from the origin.
	Z-Index	Z-Index	Controls the stacking order of floating elements.
	Overflow	Overflow	Controls what happens when an element's content exceeds its size.
	Visibility	Visibility	Controls the visibility of an element.
	Clipping	Clip	Allows you to crop portions of an image.

GoLive lets you define three kinds of styles: classes, which can be applied to individual blocks of text in an HTML document; tags, which apply to entire groups of HTML elements; and IDs, which can be applied to unique paragraphs or ranges of text. Here's a guide to the CSS attributes (sometimes called *properties*) that GoLive supports.

	GoLive Attribute	CSS Equivalent	Description
BORDER	Border	Border Border-top-width Border-right-width Border-bottom-width Border-left-width Border-width Border-color Border-style Border-top Border-right Border-bottom Border-left	Sets width, color, and style of the border.
BACKGROUND	Image	Background Background-image	Specifies a background image.
	Color	Background Background-color	Specifies a background color.
	Repeat	Background Background-repeat	Controls the tiling of a background image.
	Attach	Background Background-attachment	Allows for a fixed background or one that scrolls with the page.
	Top, Left	Background Background-position	Defines the position of the top-left corner of the background image.
LIST & OTHERS	Image	List-style List-style-image	Sets an image as the list marker.
	Style	List-style List-style-type	Sets a style for the list marker.
	Position	List-style List-style-position	Defines where the list marker is placed relative to the content.
	Other Property	—	Allows for the inclusion of CSS attributes not listed in GoLive, primarily for use with future additions to style sheets.

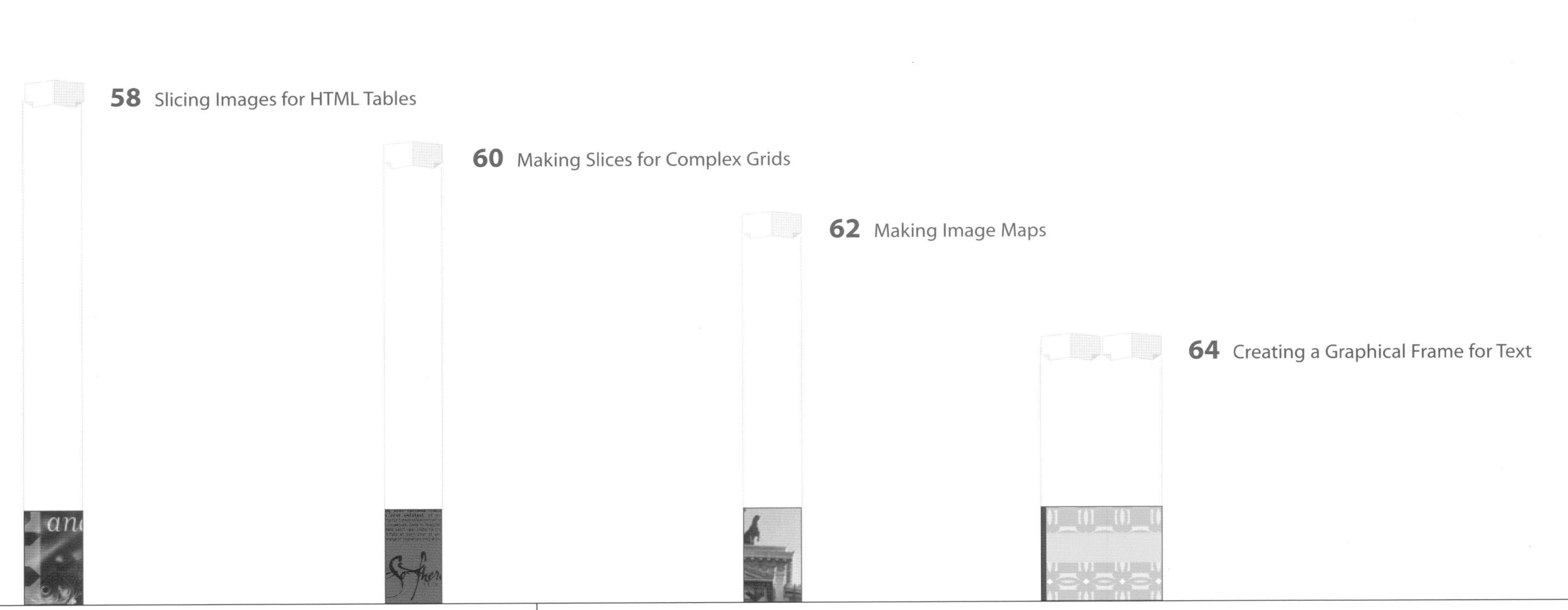

Chapter 4

HTML, Tables, and Frames

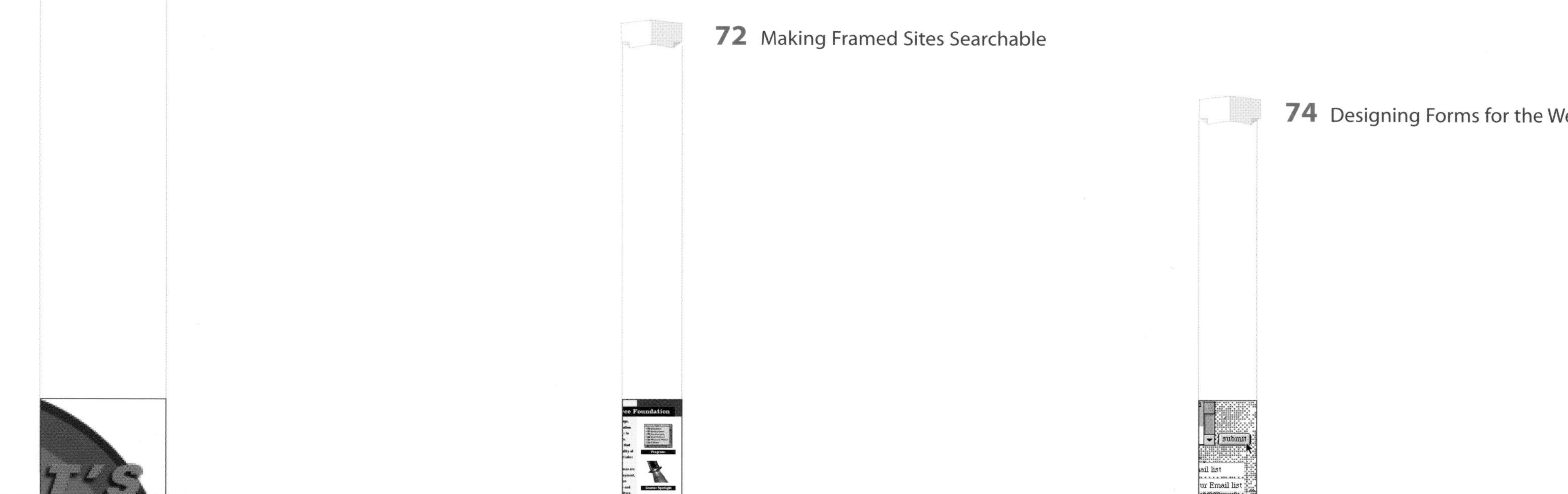

Casey Caston
CNET
www.cnet.com

Slicing Images for HTML Tables

When you prepare Web pages using HTML tables and large images or backgrounds, you need to cut up the image into areas that fit into your HTML table grid. These smaller, "sliced" images load individually and can have navigational links and rollover effects applied to them. Keep in mind, however, that a sliced image takes longer to download than an unsliced image. You can slice up an image in Photoshop, defining your slices on a separate layer and cutting and pasting them into new files, but it's much easier in ImageReady, where you can use the program's slice feature.

1 Open your image in ImageReady and drag guides out from the rulers to represent how you want the image to be sliced.

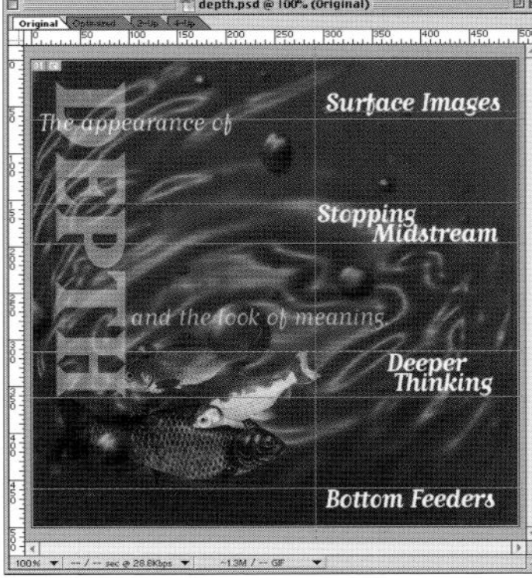

2 From the Slices menu, choose Create Slices from Guides.

3 Alternatively, use the Slice Select tool to click and drag to define an area you want to slice. ImageReady automatically divides the remaining area into the smallest number of additional slices required to complete an HTML table for the file.

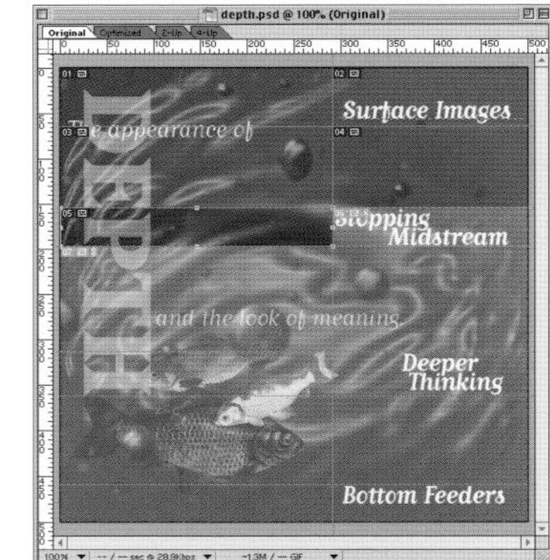

4 Edit your slices by clicking and dragging their handles, or change their dimensions in the Slice palette. If you create overlapping slices, ImageReady automatically divides underlying slices into subslices for the final HTML. To edit these "auto slices," select them and choose Promote to User-slice from the Slices menu. You can also create slices from selections by choosing Create Slice from Selection from the Slices menu.

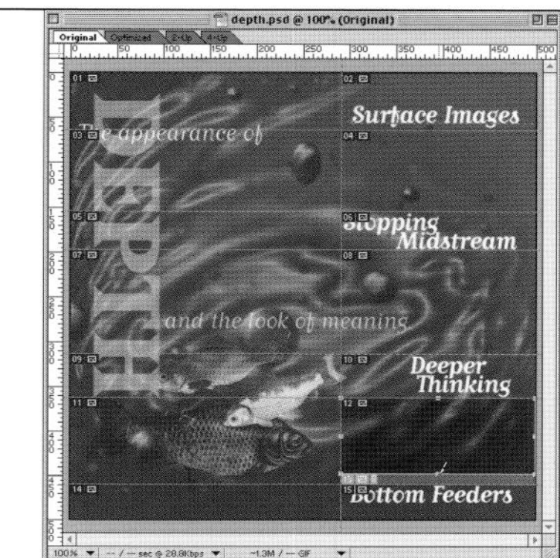

5 When you're satisfied, choose Save Optimized As from the File menu. If you started with a JPEG, you might want to specify each slice as a GIF in the Optimize palette before you save. (See "Creating Slices from a GIF," below.)

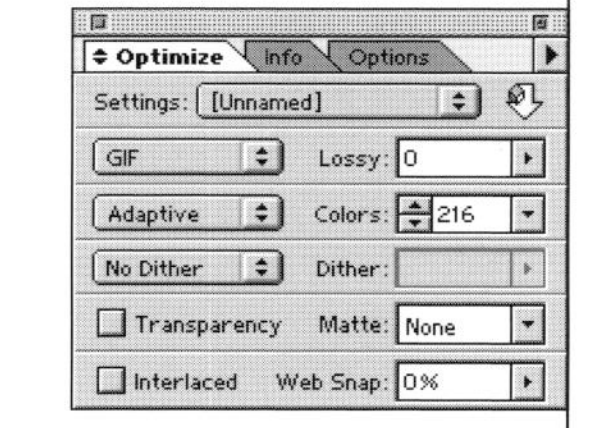

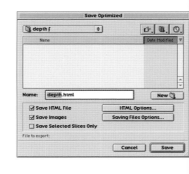

6 In the Save Optimized dialog box, choose Save HTML File and Save Images to render all of the slices as well as the HTML code for the image's table. ImageReady automatically creates a folder called "images" for your slices.

7 Here is the assembled graphic in a browser, along with the HTML code for its table.

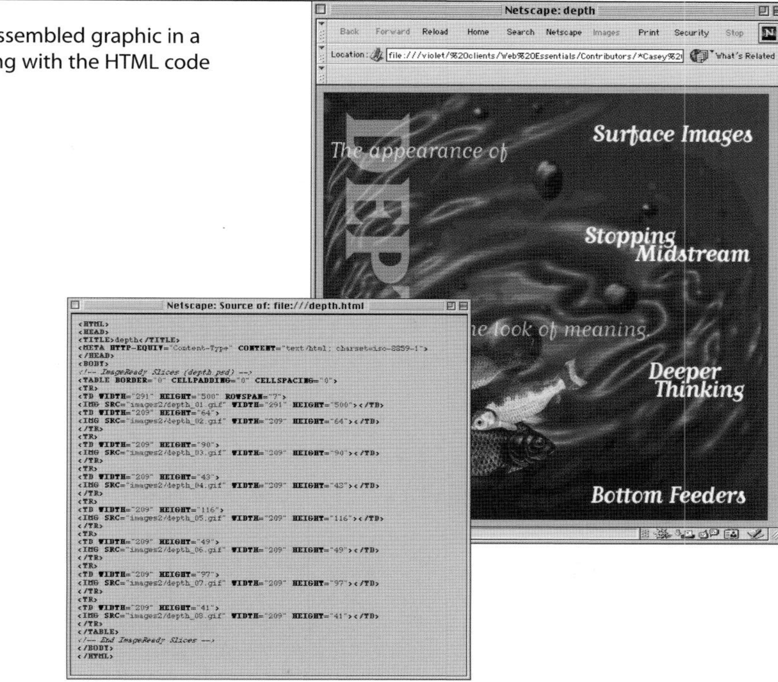

Creating Slices from a GIF

Before slicing up an image for an HTML table, convert it to GIF. That way, you don't have to convert all of the slices individually before you save them as separate files. Also, GIF is preferred over JPEG for slices—as well as for rollover button effects—because you don't have to worry about colors not matching when the slices or buttons are viewed side by side in a browser. *—Casey Caston*

Frank Kolodziej
www.cacophony.com

Making Slices for Complex Grids

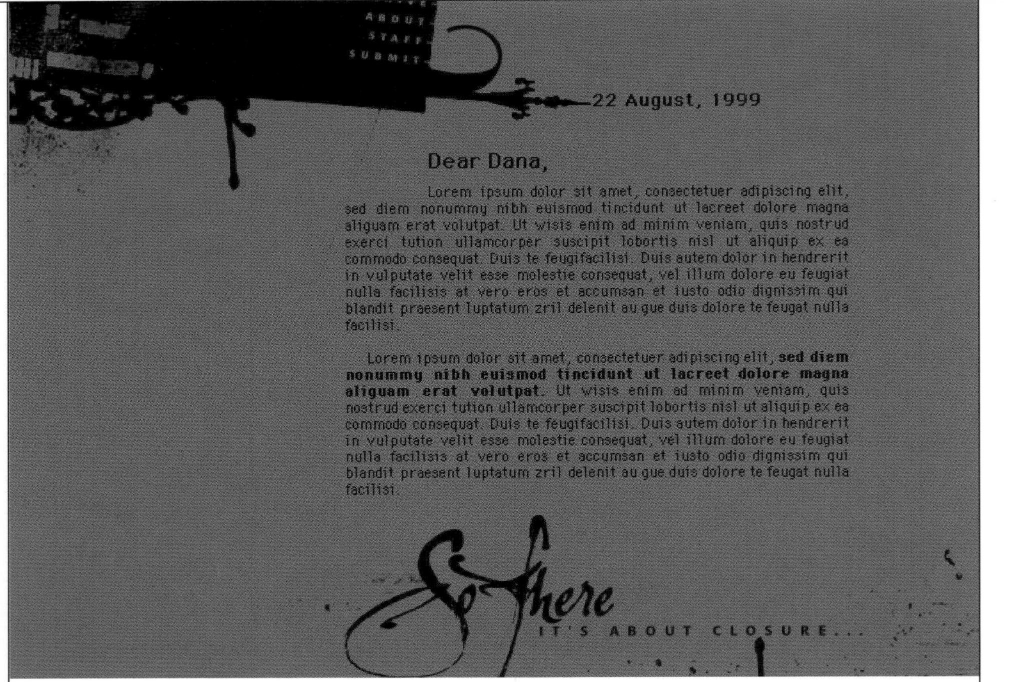

Since slices slow download times, it's important to really think about how you're going to slice images for HTML tables: Slicing by simply cropping along Photoshop's guides or by using ImageReady's Create Slices from Guides command is easy, but it doesn't tailor the slices to your particular needs. Sometimes only part of the image needs to be in a table, or, depending on the content of your image, you may need to create multiple table grids. Or you may want to put more than one slice in a table cell. Frank Kolodziej shows how to slice up an image in ImageReady with all of these complex elements.

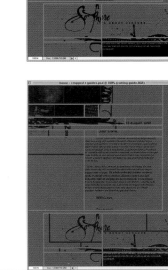

1 Create a new layer over your flattened image and draw the grid of your table using the Line tool. Our example actually has two tables: one in the upper-left portion of the image, another in the lower right. Set the Line tool at 2 pixels, no anti-aliasing, so you know that the cell borders lie exactly between the two pixels.

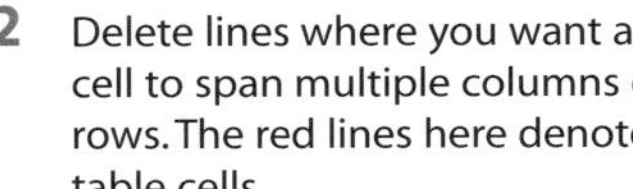

2 Delete lines where you want a cell to span multiple columns or rows. The red lines here denote table cells.

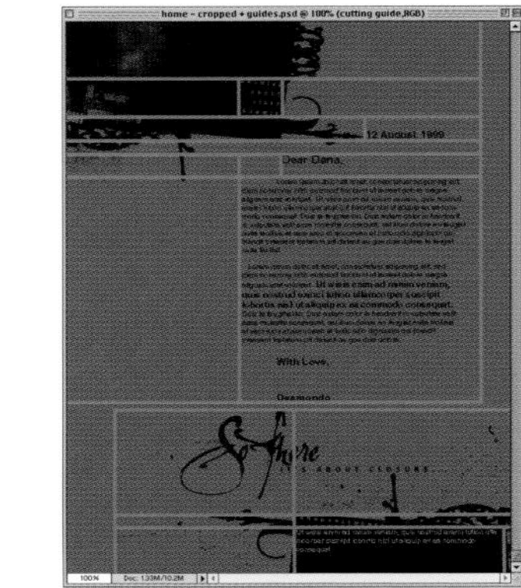

3 Define your image slices where they deviate from cell parameters by drawing with 2-pixel lines in a different color, such as blue. The navigation cell, for example, has four slices, each of which will be a rollover.

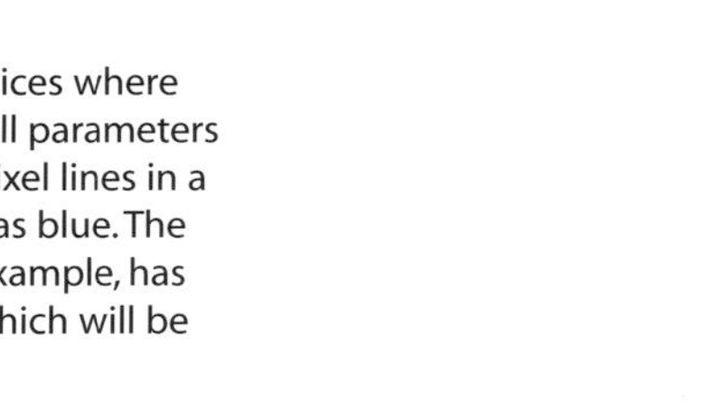

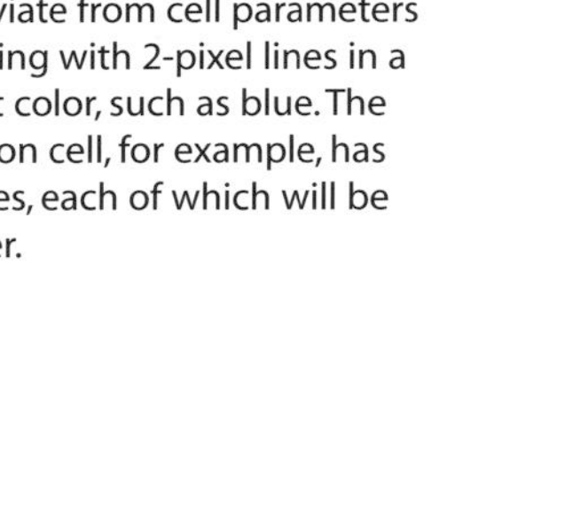

4 Use the Slice Select tool to cut up the image, using the red and blue lines as guides. To edit any slices created automatically by ImageReady, first select them and choose Promote to User-slice from the Slices menu.

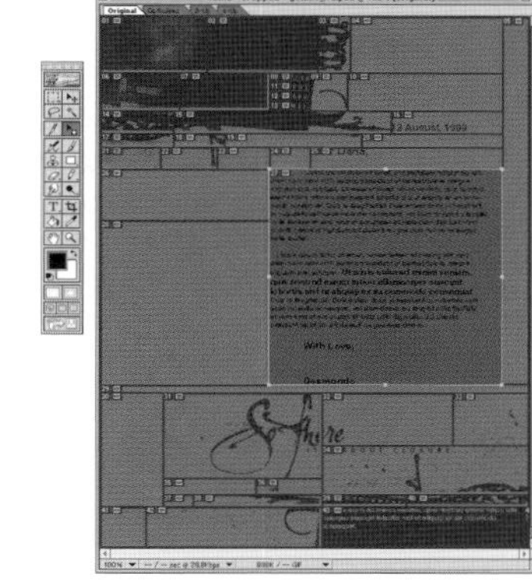

5 In the Slice palette, indicate URL links and name your slices, if you prefer to customize the names instead of letting ImageReady do it automatically when it saves.

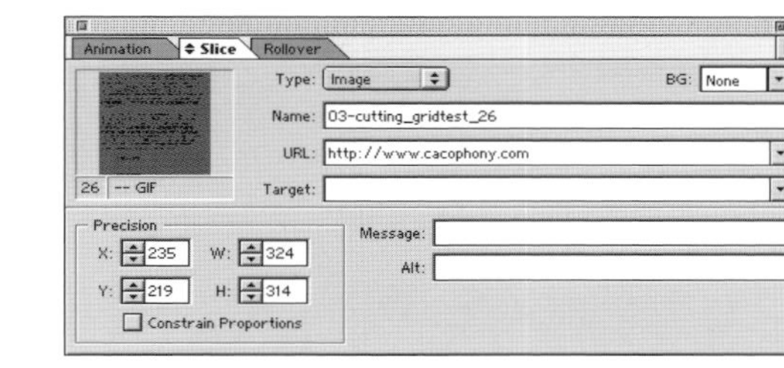

6 To add a rollover effect to a slice, such as one of the four navigational slices, click to select it, and then click the "Create new rollover state" icon in the Rollover palette. Rollover states are based on visible layers, so in the Layers palette, toggle off visibility for the layers that you don't want to appear in when a mouse cursor rolls over the slice, and toggle on the layers that you do want.

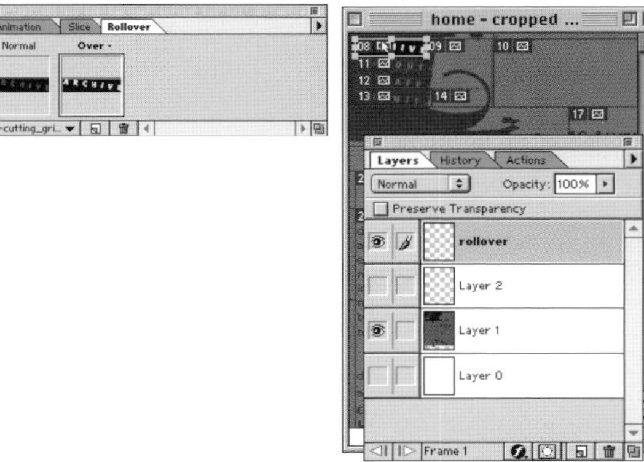

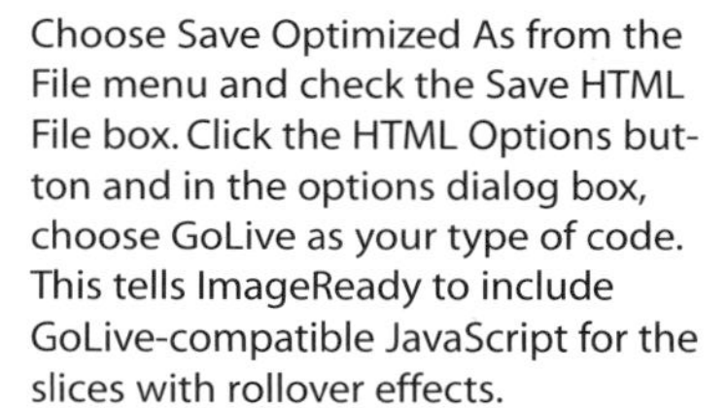

7 Delete the lines layer, and then optimize the slices in the image as GIF, using an appropriate palette and settings. These were saved with 16 colors using the perceptual palette, with transparency, so that the black text and graphics appear over a background color as specified in an HTML editor.

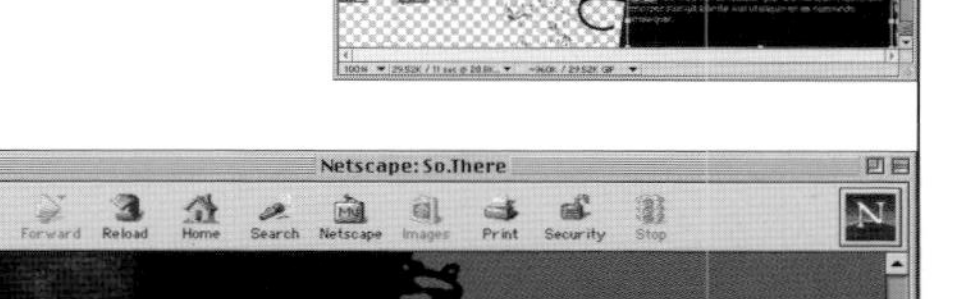

8 Choose Save Optimized As from the File menu and check the Save HTML File box. Click the HTML Options button and in the options dialog box, choose GoLive as your type of code. This tells ImageReady to include GoLive-compatible JavaScript for the slices with rollover effects.

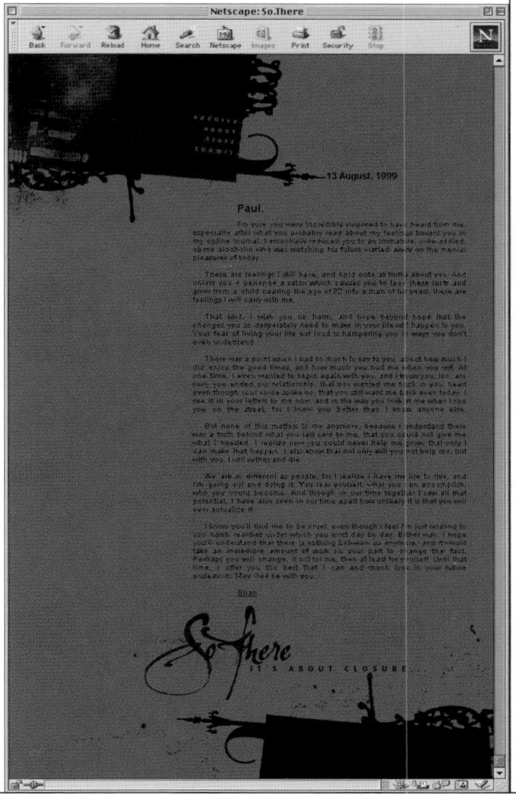

Casey Caston
CNET
www.cnet.com

Making Image Maps

Image maps are a great design tool for the Web. They communicate with a visually interesting message that offers subtle functionality via "hotspot" links, sparing the designer from having to use boring and garish plain text links. It's easy to create image maps in ImageReady: Simply define each hotspot on a different layer and save the file with HTML code that defines the hotspot coordinates. Watch out for a couple of pitfalls, however: Don't overlap hotspots and avoid stray non-transparent pixels in a layer or you will complicate the HTML code.

1 Open the file and start by creating hotspots for areas of the flattened image, such as the statues shown here. Create a new layer using the Layers palette pop-up menu and define your first hotspot. Either paint roughly over the element in the image that you want to be "hot," or marquee the area and fill it with a color.

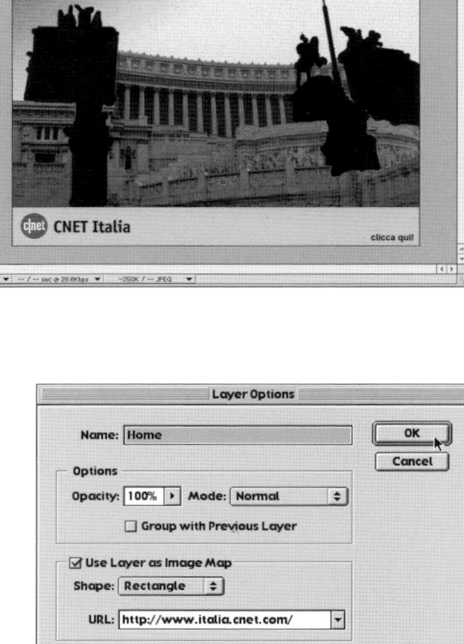

2 Repeat the process of creating new layers and defining each hotspot that you want in the image. It can be helpful to fill or create the areas with a solid color such as black or white, but you don't have to. Just keep in mind that ImageReady will create a hotspot from any pixel in the layer that is not transparent.

3 Double-click a hotspot layer and check Use Layer as Image Map in the Layer Options dialog box. Specify the URL link and the hotspot's shape. A rectangle works well because it generates a small amount of code (only four coordinates) but the area it defines is blocky and, well, rectangular.

4 A polygonal hotspot creates a more dynamic shape, albeit with more HTML code: You can outline an object and ImageReady will omit any transparent or near-transparent pixels, such as the sky behind the statue, from the hotspot. Use the Tolerance slider here: The higher the value, the more semitransparent pixels are included in the hotspot shape.

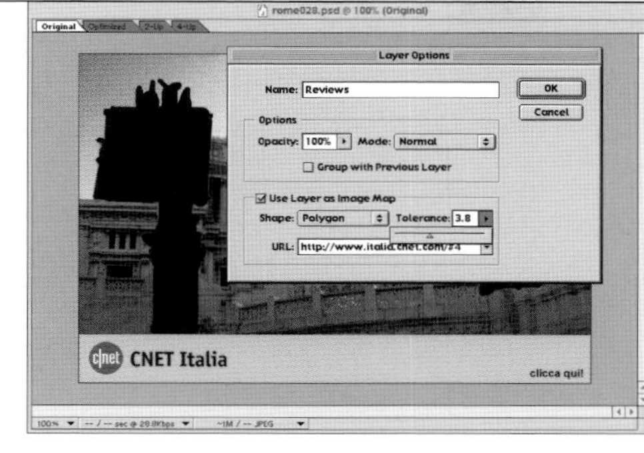

5 If you want an element of your image to be a hotspot and it is already on a separate layer—such as the yellow bar across the bottom of this page—you can specify the layer itself as an image map.

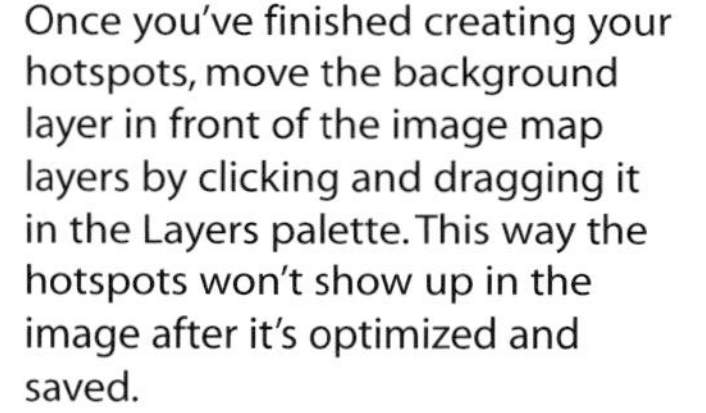

6 If you have overlapping hotspots, such as these two statue areas, browsers will automatically resolve the discrepancy. But instead of letting the browser use its own default hierarchy, clearly define the hotspots yourself. Command-click (Control-click) in the Layers palette to select one of the overlapping hotspots, switch to the overlapping layer, and press Delete.

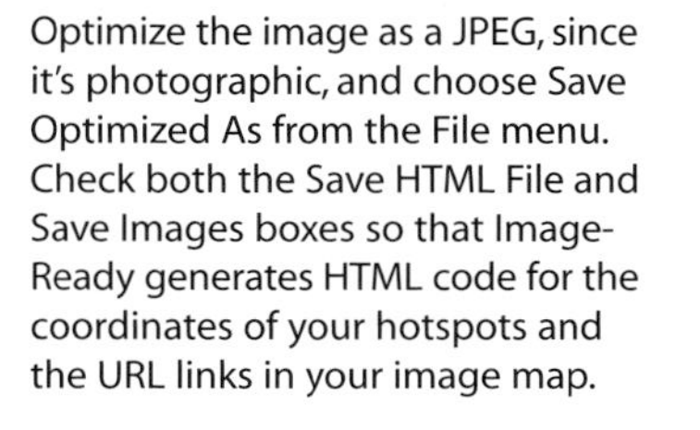

7 Preview your hotspots anytime by clicking the Optimized tab in the image window and choosing Preview In from the File menu. Choose the browser you want to use.

8 Once you've finished creating your hotspots, move the background layer in front of the image map layers by clicking and dragging it in the Layers palette. This way the hotspots won't show up in the image after it's optimized and saved.

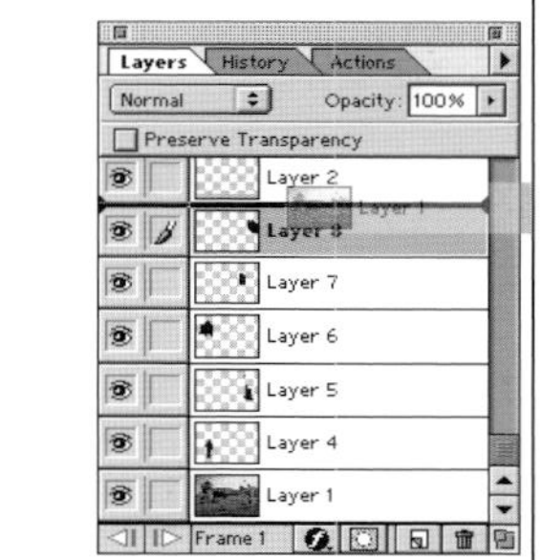

9 Optimize the image as a JPEG, since it's photographic, and choose Save Optimized As from the File menu. Check both the Save HTML File and Save Images boxes so that ImageReady generates HTML code for the coordinates of your hotspots and the URL links in your image map.

Geoffrey Brown
ZeroZine
www.zerozine.com

Creating a Graphical Frame for Text

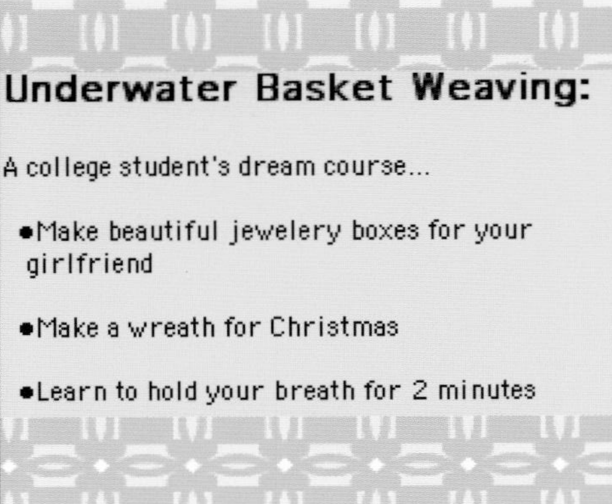

Underwater Basket Weaving:
A college student's dream course...
•Make beautiful jewelery boxes for your girlfriend
•Make a wreath for Christmas
•Learn to hold your breath for 2 minutes

Sometimes you want to spiff up the display of HTML text, but you don't want to go as far as turning it into a graphic, and applying a border in an HTML table is too dull. Here's a way to create a graphical frame that resides in an HTML table and can expand vertically to fit as much text as you require. The trick is to not specify a height for the table cells and to apply background colors that match the placeholder graphics so that as you add text and the cell expands, the design is seamless. This technique adds some flair in the form of color, rounded corners, and patterns, which you can't do with simple HTML table borders and cells.

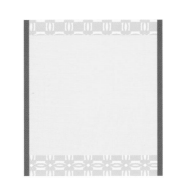

1 Draw a box in Illustrator using the Rectangle tool. Our example is 250 points wide by 300 points high. Give the box a heavy stroke, say, 10 points. Since the stroke is centered over the path of the box, it adds 5 points to all four sides of the perimeter, making the box a total of 260 points wide by 310 points high. When the art is opened in ImageReady, 1 point will equal 1 pixel.

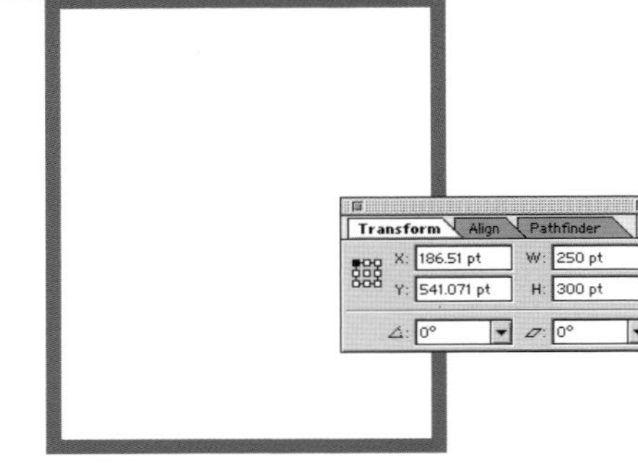

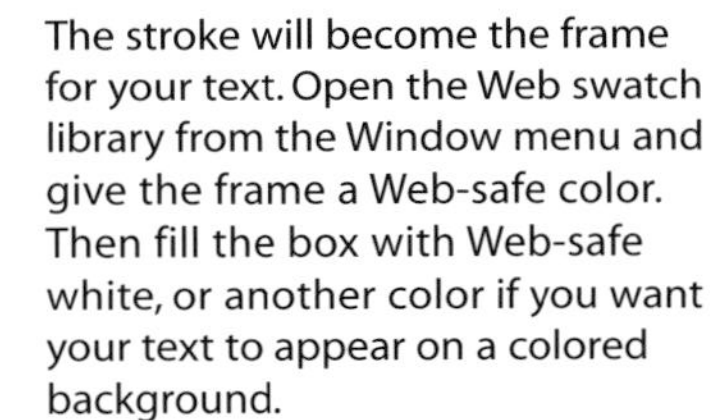

2 The stroke will become the frame for your text. Open the Web swatch library from the Window menu and give the frame a Web-safe color. Then fill the box with Web-safe white, or another color if you want your text to appear on a colored background.

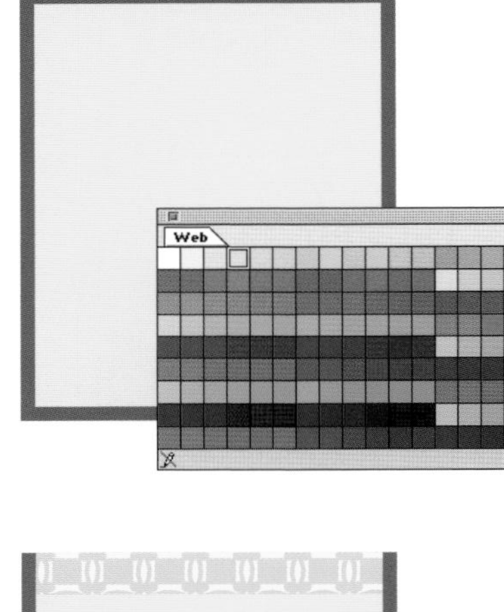

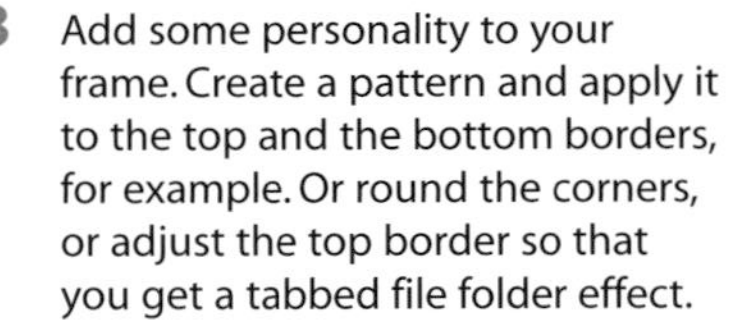

3 Add some personality to your frame. Create a pattern and apply it to the top and the bottom borders, for example. Or round the corners, or adjust the top border so that you get a tabbed file folder effect.

 Adobe Illustrator 8.0  Adobe ImageReady 2.0  Adobe GoLive 4.0

4 Save the file as an Illustrator EPS file. You can also export as a Photoshop 5 file, specifying the RGB color model and 72-dpi resolution.

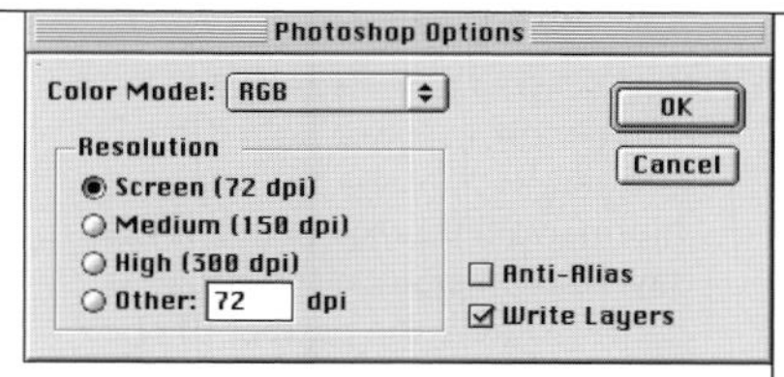

5 Open it in ImageReady. Click OK in the Rasterize Options dialog box. The software will size the image appropriately.

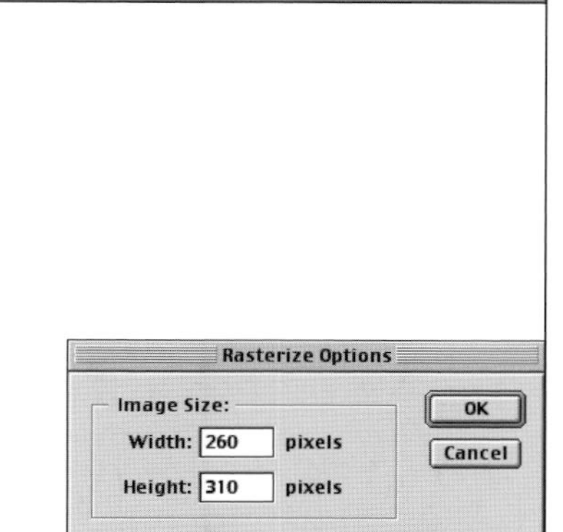

6 Drag four guides out from the rulers and snap them to the inner edges of the frame as shown.

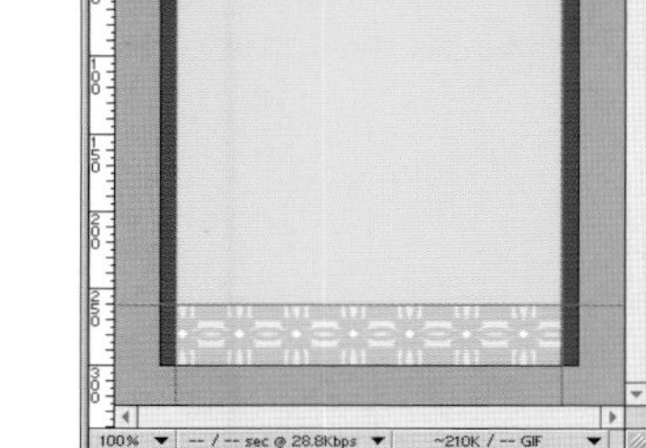

7 Choose Create Slices from Guides from the Slices menu to cut up your framed box for an HTML table. ImageReady creates nine slices.

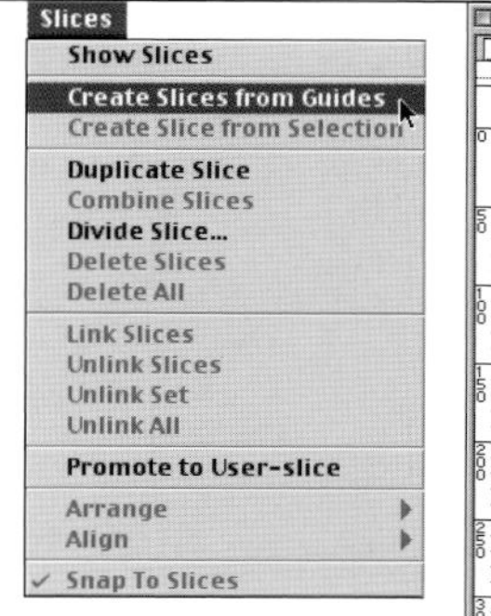

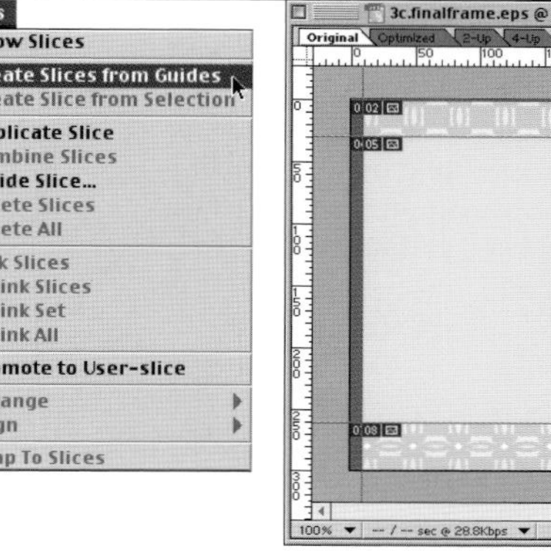

8 Select the three top slices with the Slice Select tool and choose Combine Slices from the Slices menu. Repeat this step for the bottom three slices.

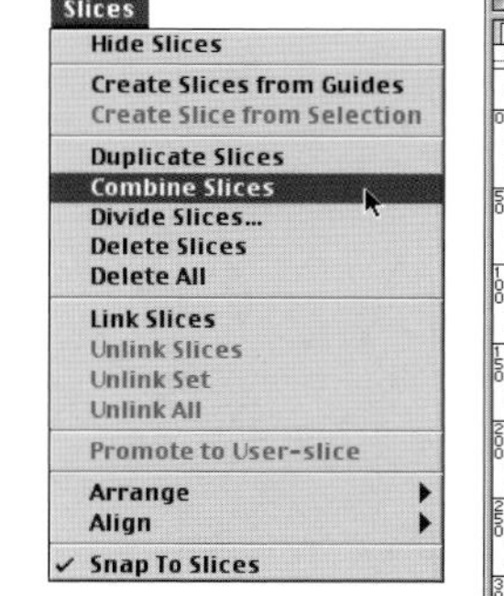

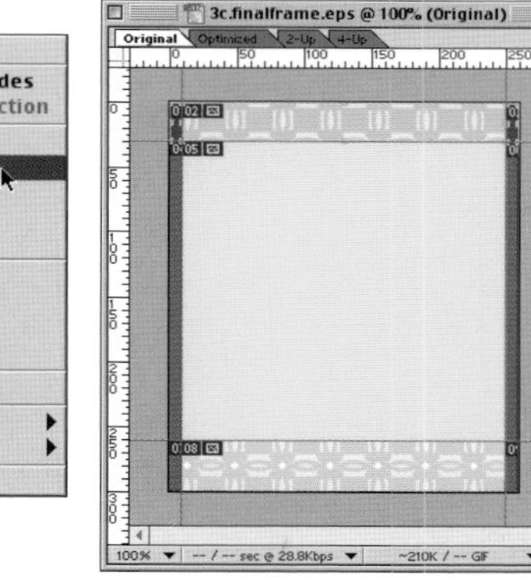

9 This leaves you with five slices. In our example, the slices for the top and bottom borders are 260 pixels wide, the center is 240 pixels wide, and the remaining two blue vertical slices are each 10 pixels wide.

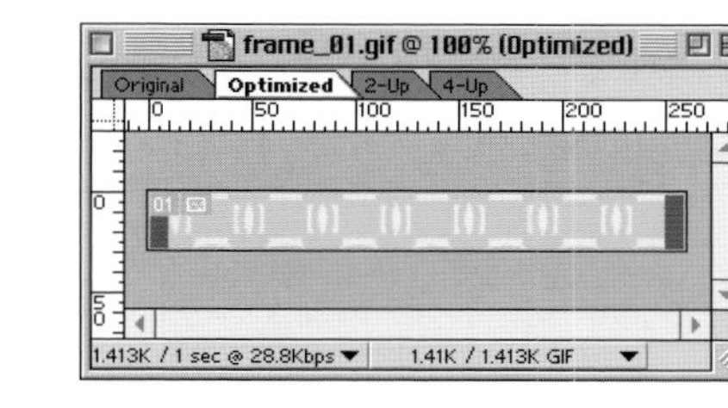

Geoffrey Brown
ZeroZine
www.zerozine.com

Creating a Graphical Frame for Text

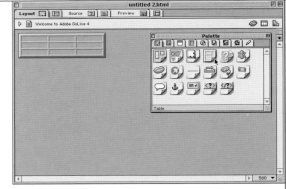

10 Optimize your slices as GIF. For the slices in the middle row, which are each a solid Web-safe color, you can use two colors and the Web palette. For the top and bottom slices, which have a colored pattern, you'll need more colors.

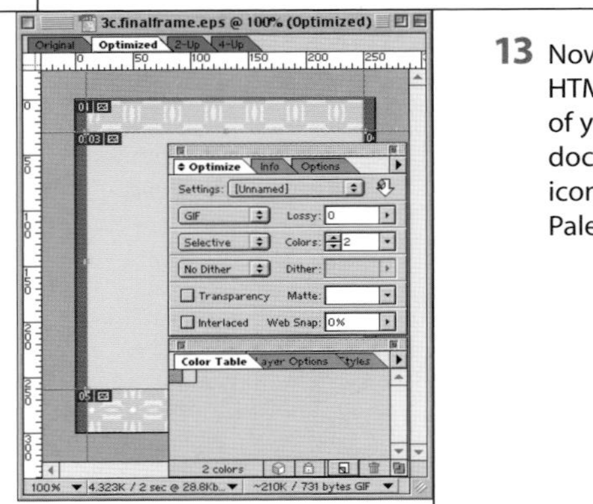
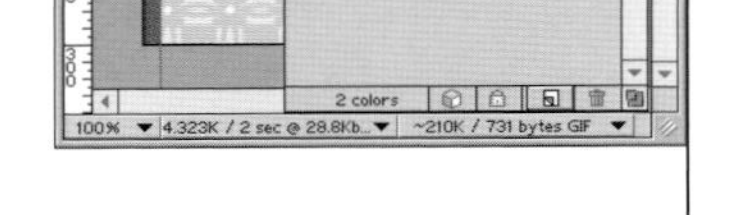

11 Choose Save Optimized As from the File menu and save the images.

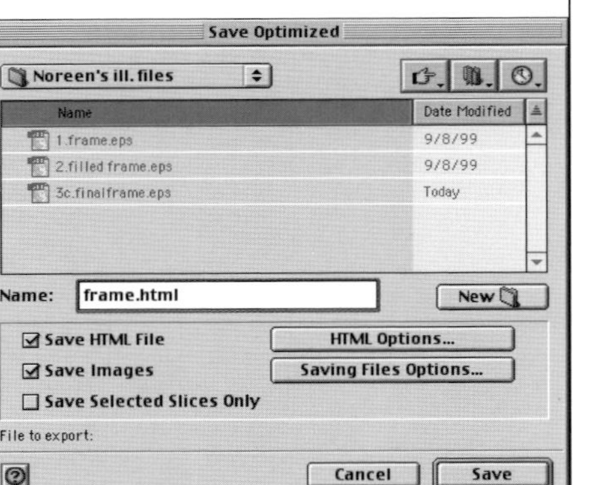

12 Open each slice you created from the middle row and resize each one so that it's just 1 or 2 pixels tall: Choose Image Size from the Image menu and change the Height value, unchecking the Constrain Proportions box.

13 Now you're ready to create an HTML table that will hold the slices of your graphical frame. In a new document in GoLive, drag a Table icon from the Basic tab of the Palette onto your page.

14 In the Table Inspector, specify 3 columns, 3 rows, and set the width of the table to that of the whole frame—260 pixels, in our example. Set the cell spacing, cell padding, and border properties to 0. Leave Height blank.

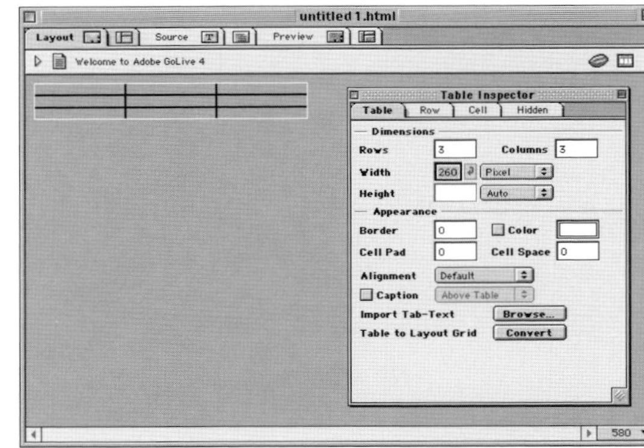

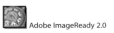

15 Merge the three cells in the top row into one: Click the right or bottom edge of the upper-left cell, and in the Cell tab of the Table Inspector, change the Column Span to 3. Repeat for the bottom row.

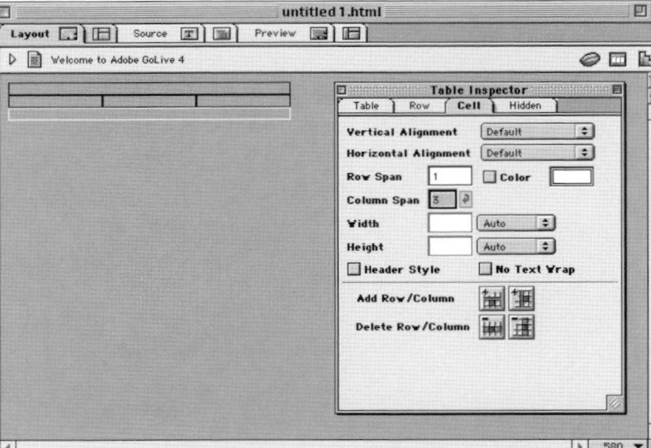

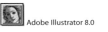

 Adobe Illustrator 8.0  Adobe ImageReady 2.0  Adobe GoLive 4.0

16 Set the width of each cell in the middle row to correspond to the width of the slices you've created: from left to right, 10, 240, 10 pixels. Again, leave Height blank. Set the Alignment of the middle cell, where the text goes, to Top. Click to select each cell and specify the measurements in the Cell tab of the Table Inspector.

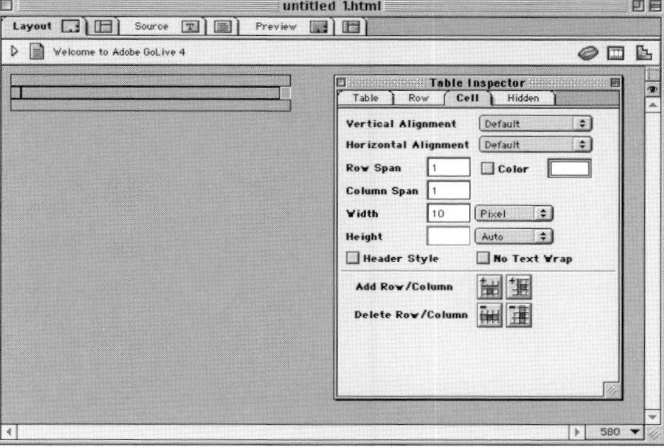

17 Back in ImageReady, find the hexadecimal value of your center area and of the frame by holding the Eyedropper tool over the colors and reading the Info palette. Then in the Cell tab of the Table Inspector in GoLive, check the Color box, and then click the well and specify those values as the background colors for the three cells in the middle row. (For a Hex/RGB conversion chart, see pages 108–109.)

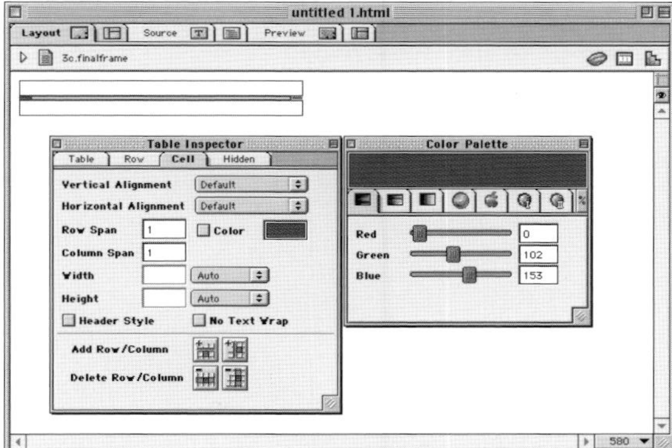

18 Place your slices in their cells. Drag an Image icon from the Basic tab of the Palette onto a cell, click the Browse button in the Image Inspector, and specify the appropriate slice. The graphics serve as placeholders for the middle cells; without them, the cells (and their background colors) won't appear in browsers. You don't need to place a slice in the text cell, however: The text itself serves as a placeholder.

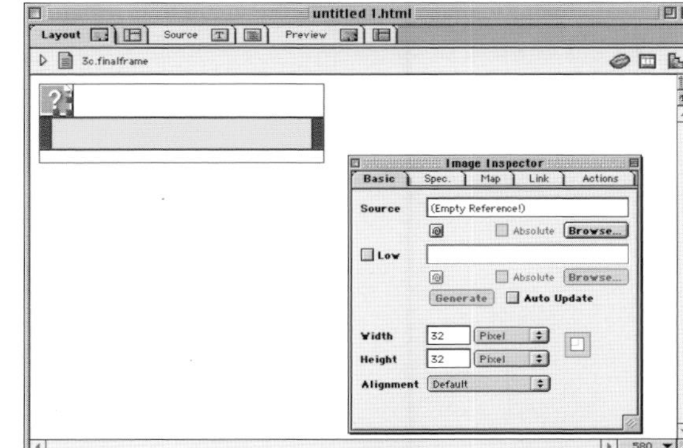

19 The height of each cell accommodates the graphic placed inside. When you add text to the middle cell, the height of the cell expands accordingly, and the color of the frame is seamless.

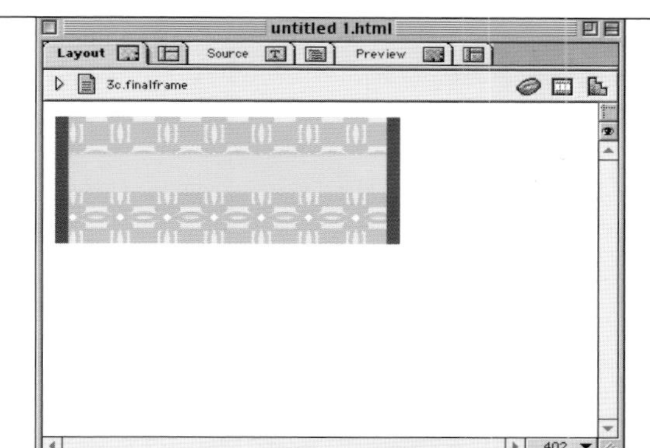

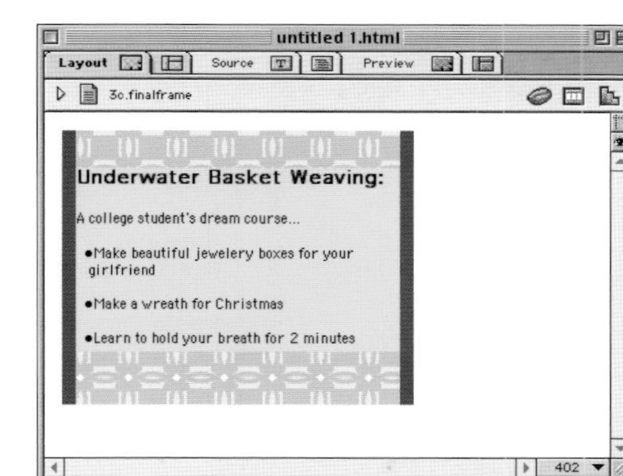

Ben Seibel
Ben Seibel Graphic Design
www.mindspring.com/~bseibel

Setting Up Tables with Drop Shadows

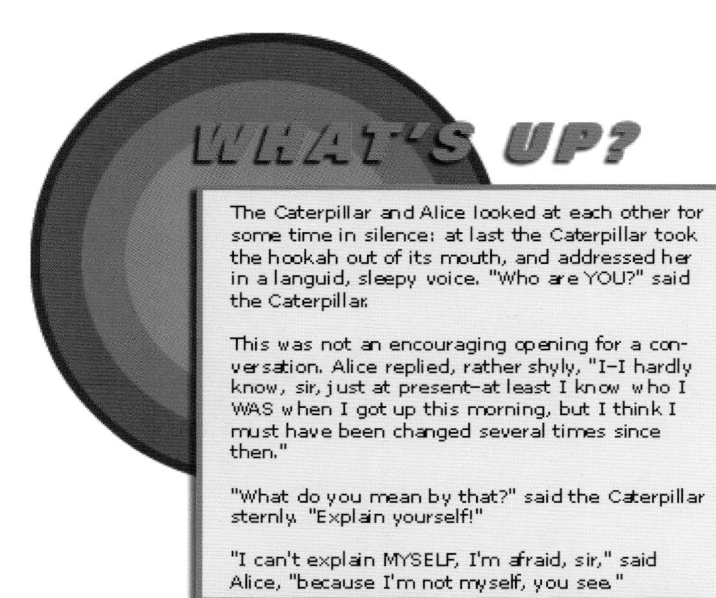

WHAT'S UP?
The Caterpillar and Alice looked at each other for some time in silence: at last the Caterpillar took the hookah out of its mouth, and addressed her in a languid, sleepy voice. "Who are YOU?" said the Caterpillar.
This was not an encouraging opening for a conversation. Alice replied, rather shyly, "I–I hardly know, sir, just at present–at least I know who I WAS when I got up this morning, but I think I must have been changed several times since then."
"What do you mean by that?" said the Caterpillar sternly. "Explain yourself!"
"I can't explain MYSELF, I'm afraid, sir," said Alice, "because I'm not myself, you see."

Once you get the hang of surrounding HTML text with expandable graphical frames, you can start using more sophisticated techniques. You can include other elements of design—background graphics behind the frame, for example, or drop shadows in the graphical frame. Designer Ben Seibel shows how to prepare the frame in Photoshop and ImageReady and import and place the slices in nested tables in GoLive.

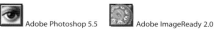

1 Before you start creating effects in Photoshop and Web pages in GoLive, sketch out your table.

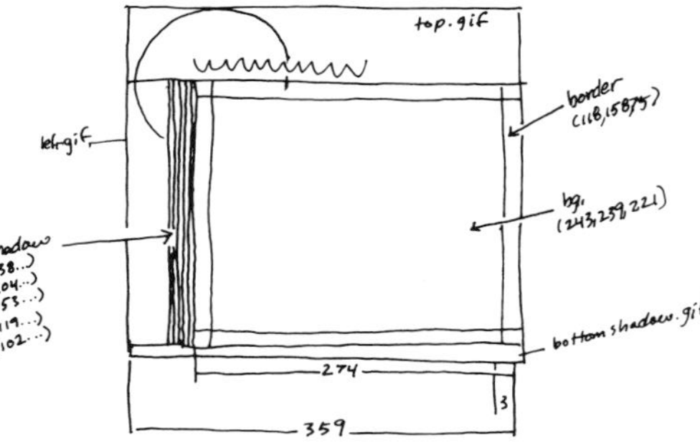

2 Open Photoshop's Preferences dialog box and set the grid to one pixel with one subdivision.

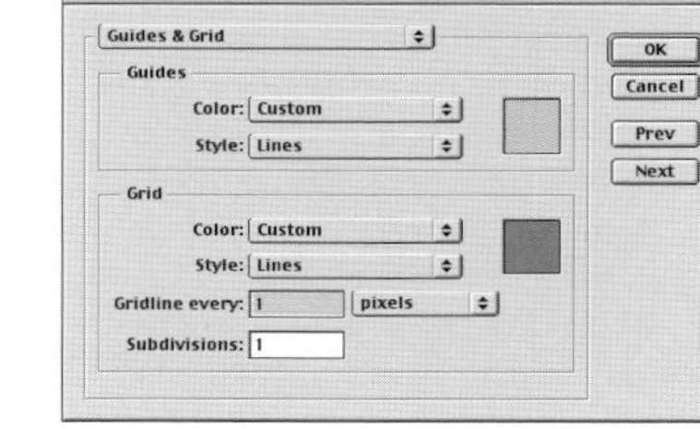

3 Turn on the rulers and the grid in your Photoshop document. Then draw the main elements of your table (in our example, the table consists of a rectangle that overlaps a multicolored circle) and zoom in to about 300 percent.

 Adobe Photoshop 5.5  Adobe ImageReady 2.0  Adobe GoLive 4.0

4 Position guides around elements of your image to correspond with your HTML table.

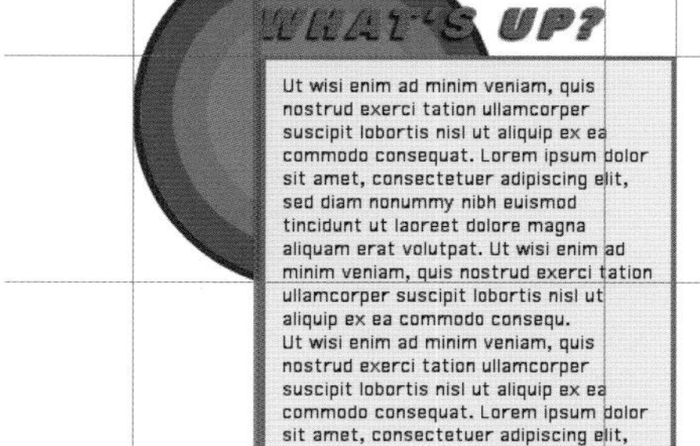

5 Add the drop shadow using Layer Effects. In our example, we added a shadow on the left and bottom sides of the text rectangle. Zoom up to about 1,600 percent and position a vertical guide between each column of pixels that makes up the shadow's vertical gradient.

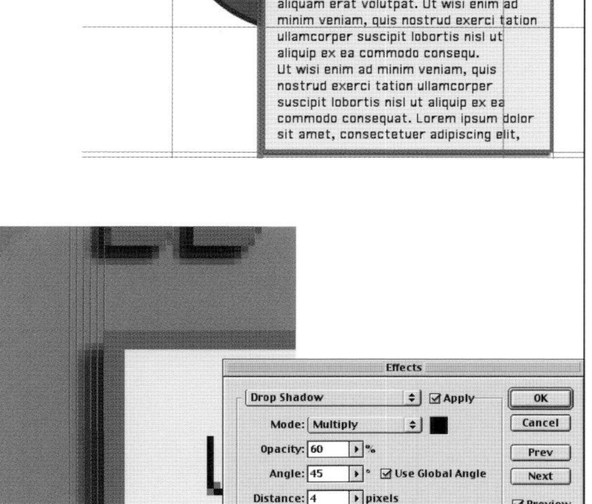

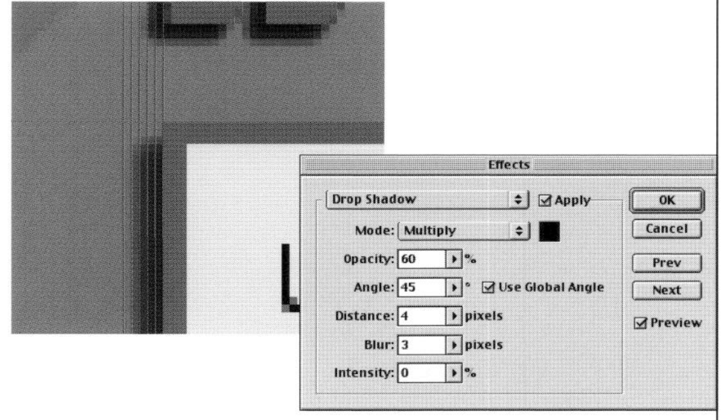

6 Click the Jump To button to open the document in ImageReady.

7 Using the Slice tool, cut the image into blocks following the guides.

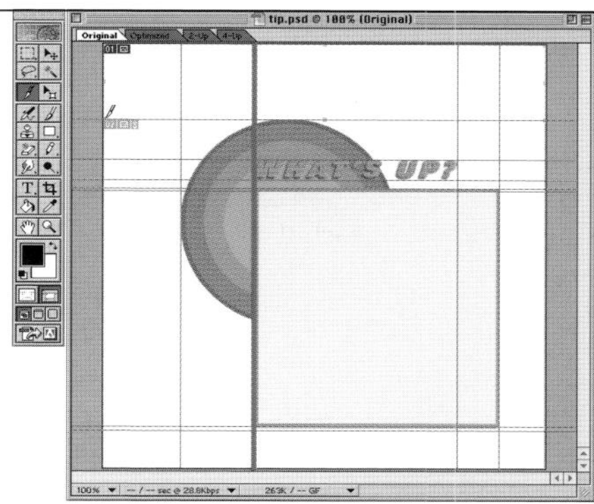

8 Next we'll give a name to each slice and specify that certain slices act as spacers in our table. From the Window menu, choose Show Slice. Using the Slice Select tool, select each slice in turn, and give it a logical name that reflects its position and/or function in the overall graphic. For any slice that you want to serve as a spacer (a placeholder), choose No Image from the Type pop-up menu.

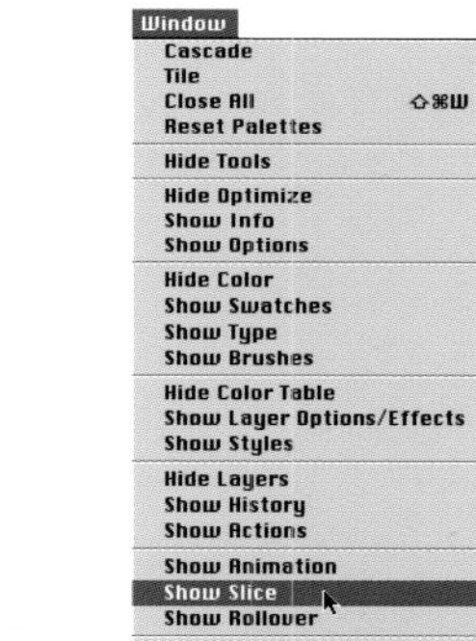

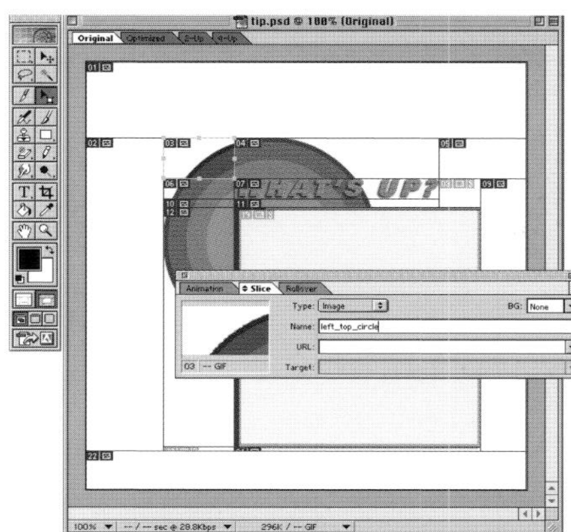

Ben Seibel
Ben Seibel Graphic Design
www.mindspring.com/~bseibel

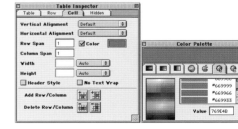

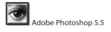

Setting Up Tables with Drop Shadows

9 Now prepare the slices for Web use. Click the 4-Up tab and select the first slice. Choose Show Optimize from the Window menu and adjust the optimization settings to taste. Repeat for each slice.

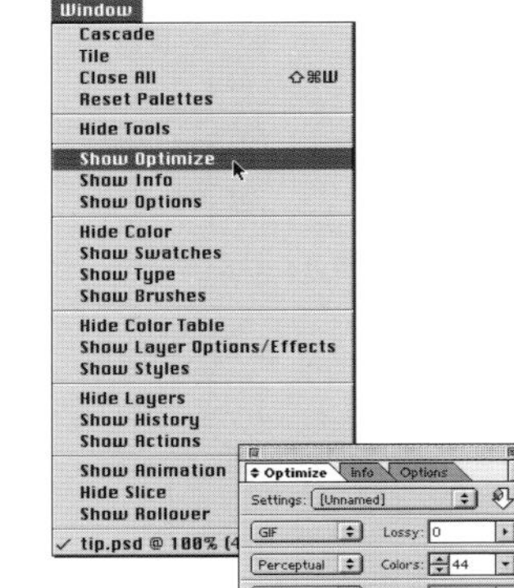

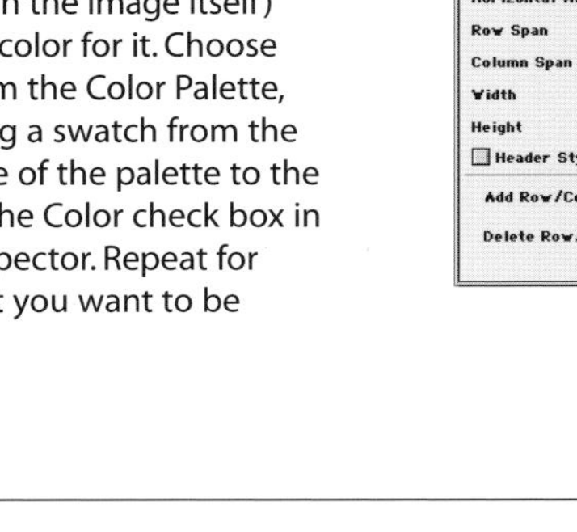

10 We're ready to transfer the slices to GoLive and start building our table. Select only the slices you need for the table (Shift-click to select multiple slices, or click outside the image area or in an auto-slice and drag out a marquee to select many slices quickly). Choose Jump to Adobe GoLive from the File menu, and make sure the Save Selected Slices Only box is checked. If you don't select specific slices, ImageReady will add placeholder GIFs where you might not want them, which might cause problems down the line.

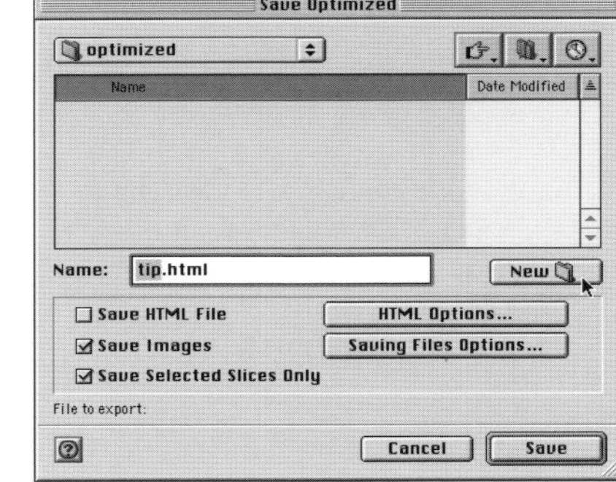

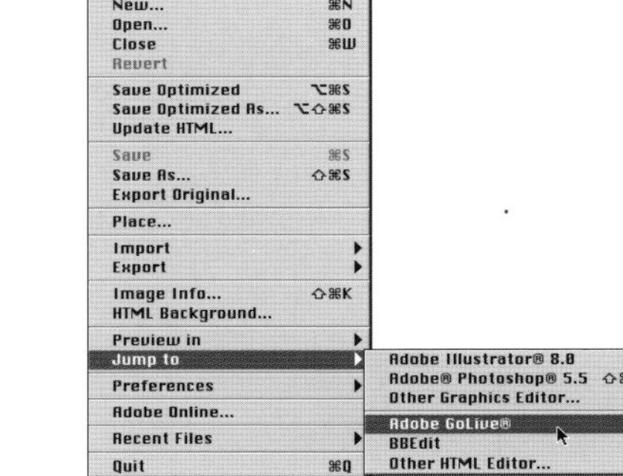

11 In GoLive, select a cell that will be expandable (click the edge of the cell, not within the image itself) and define a color for it. Choose the color from the Color Palette, and then drag a swatch from the preview pane of the palette to the box next to the Color check box in the Table Inspector. Repeat for each cell that you want to be expandable.

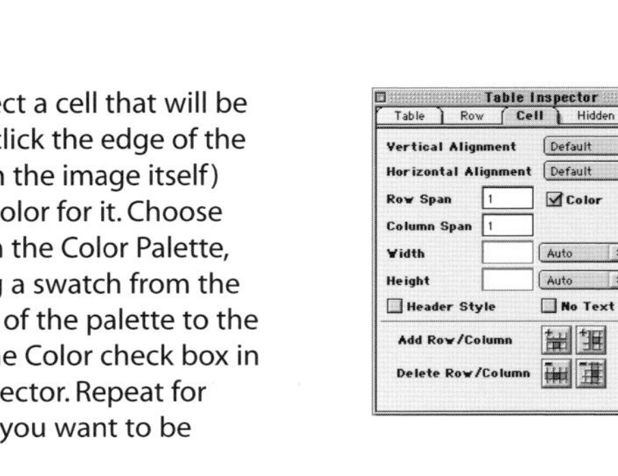

Adobe Photoshop 5.5 Adobe ImageReady 2.0 Adobe GoLive 4.0

12 Select the image of the shadow beneath the expandable cell (this time don't select the cell, but the image within). The Basic tab on the Image Inspector should appear. We'll change the image so it expands to fit the cell as the table stretches to the right to accommodate the flow of text. Choose Percent from the pop-up menu next to the Width box and type 100 into the box.

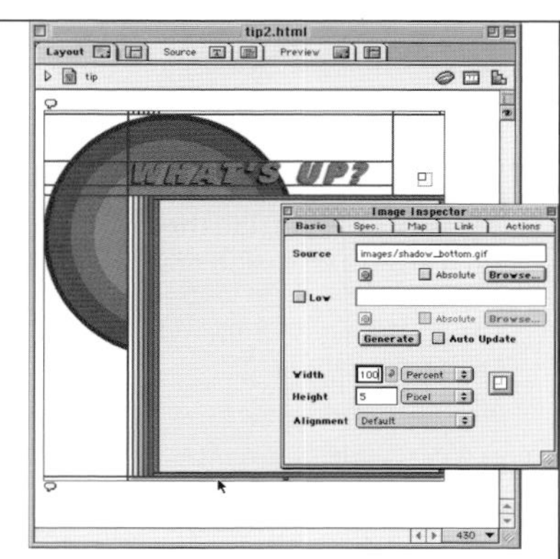

tip2.html
Image Inspector

13 Next select the cell containing the image to the left of the expanding cell. In the Cell tab of the Table Inspector, change the Vertical Alignment to Top. This causes the image to stay put even when the text cell expands downward.

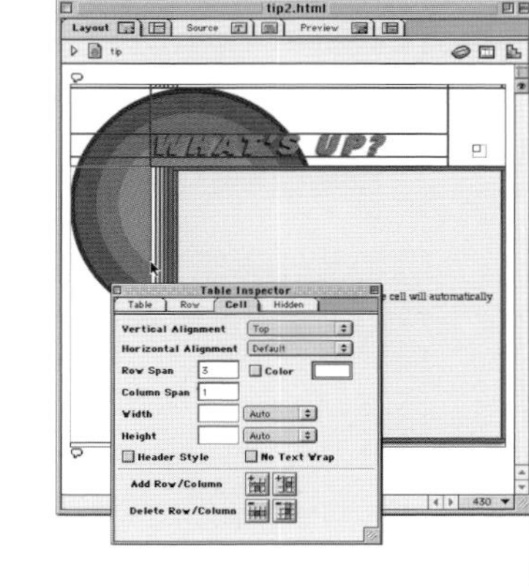

tip2.html
Table Inspector

14 Select the image within the expanding cell and delete it. Move the cursor over the cell and when the cursor changes to the I-beam shape, click and begin typing. The cell will expand to the right and down to accommodate your text. Since you can't give a single cell any padding, drag a 1-cell table into the text cell and give it some padding to indent the text.

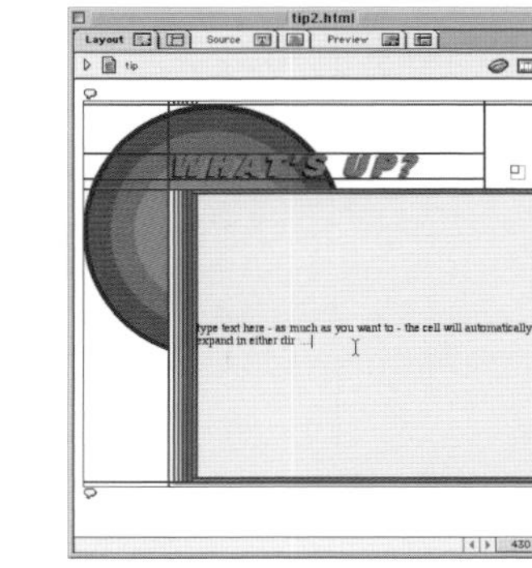

tip2.html

15 Click the Preview tab to check the GoLive document and then save it. You should also preview it in a Web browser. Try pasting more text into the table or changing the point size. The table and its shadow will stretch to accommodate it.

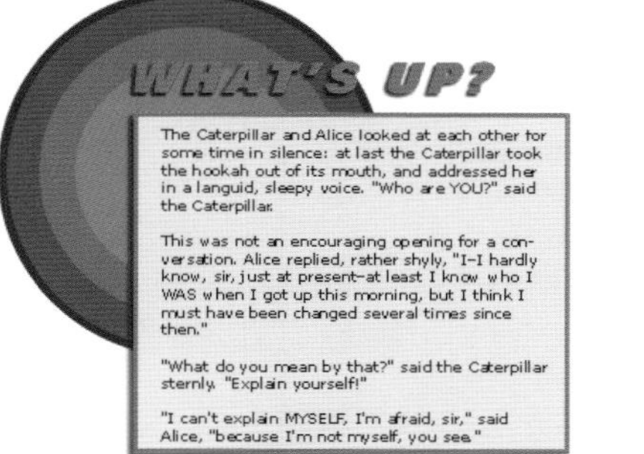

WHAT'S UP?
The Caterpillar and Alice looked at each other for some time in silence: at last the Caterpillar took the hookah out of its mouth, and addressed her in a languid, sleepy voice. "Who are YOU?" said the Caterpillar.
This was not an encouraging opening for a conversation. Alice replied, rather shyly, "I–I hardly know, sir, just at present–at least I know who I WAS when I got up this morning, but I think I must have been changed several times since then."
"What do you mean by that?" said the Caterpillar sternly. "Explain yourself!"
"I can't explain MYSELF, I'm afraid, sir," said Alice, "because I'm not myself, you see."

Anne-Marie Concepción
Seneca Design & Consulting
www.senecadesign.com

Making Framed Sites Searchable

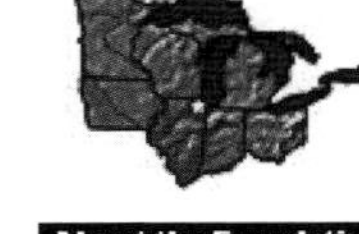

The Joyce Foundation
Search
Site Map
Feedback
Based in Chicago, the Joyce Foundation supports efforts to strengthen public policies in ways that improve the quality of life in the Great Lakes region.
Its program areas are Education, Employment, Environment, Gun Violence, Money and Politics, and Culture.
Programs
Publications
Application Guidelines
Grantee Spotlight
Media Packet
About the Foundation
What's New!

When you design a Web site using frames, you may unintentionally limit the searchability of your content. That's because search engine robots (called "bots" for short), which troll the Web in search of new and updated HTML documents to add to their indexes, stop at the frameset definition document and never find their way to the content of the HTML documents inside the frames. You can overcome this problem, however, by using metatag keywords and comment tags, and by editing the <NOFRAMES> section of the frameset definition document to improve your framed site's ranking in search engine matches lists.

1 To add keywords to every framed page of your site that you'd like to come up as a link in a search engine matches list, open the frameset document in GoLive. In Layout view, click the triangle to the left of the Page icon to open its head section. Then open the Head tab of the Palette.

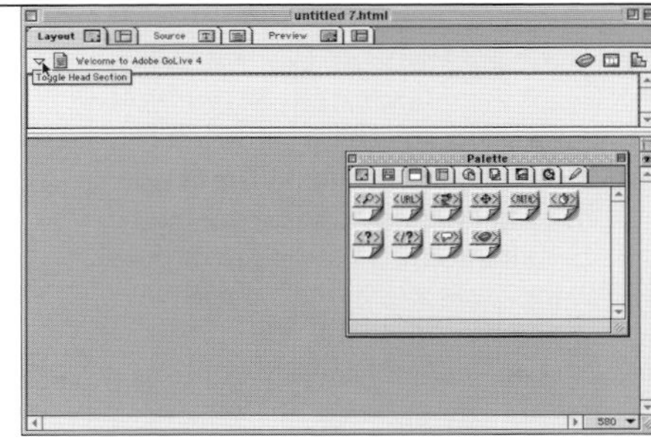

2 Drag the Keywords placeholder icon and drop it onto the frameset page's head section.

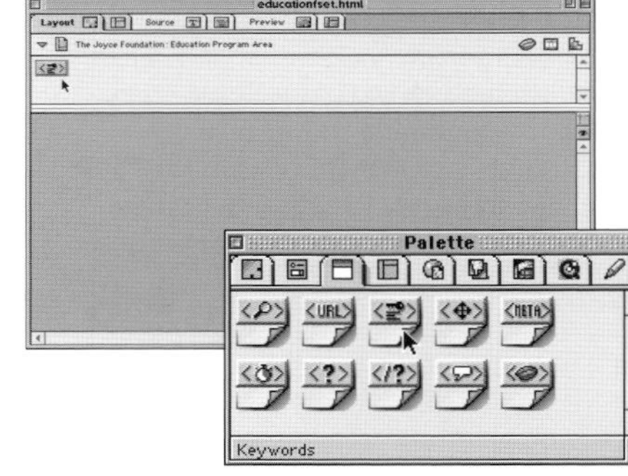

3 Double-click the icon to open the Keywords Inspector. Add as many keywords and phrases as you wish, including the typical search terms that you think your prospective visitors might use. Don't go overboard, as bots might think you're trying to spam the search engine and, as a result, bypass you altogether.

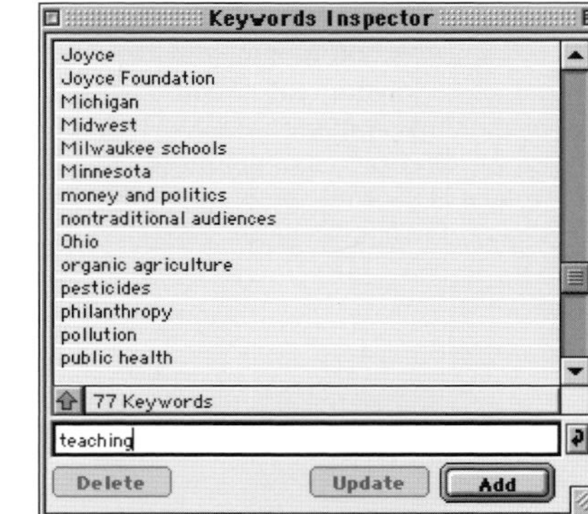

4 To reuse keywords for multiple frameset pages or modify them to reflect a particular section's content, drag the Keywords icon from the frameset page's head section and drop it into the Custom tab of the Palette. Then, instead of starting with an empty Keywords Inspector in subsequent pages, you can drag the icon from the Custom tab of the Palette.

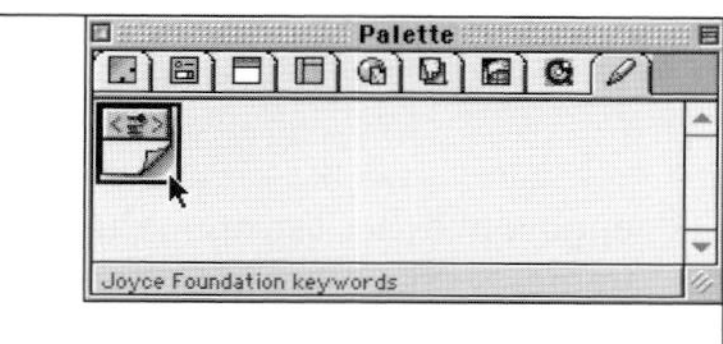

5 Some search engines index comments tags, so drag the Comment icon from the Head tab of the Palette to the frameset page's head section, as you did with the Keywords icon.

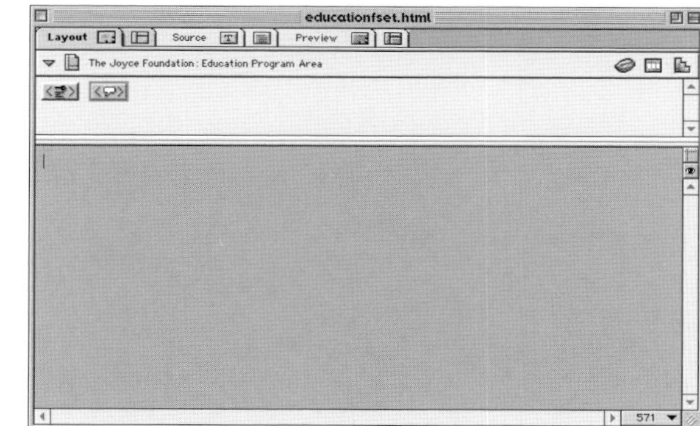

6 Double-click the Comment icon to open the Comments Inspector, and type in your text. You can reuse the comments on other pages by dragging the icon from the head section of the page to the Custom tab of the Palette, as you did for the Keywords icon.

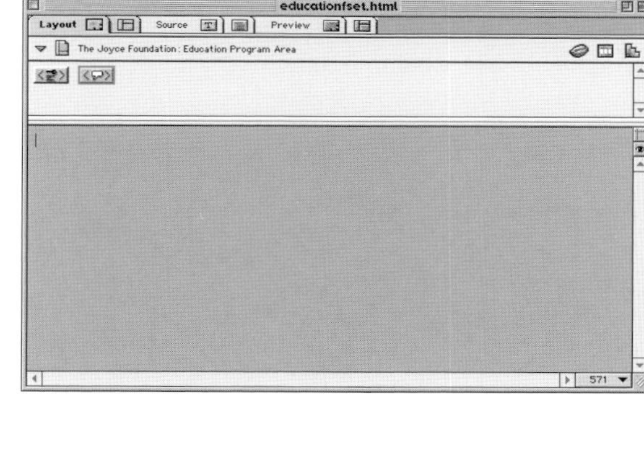

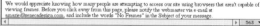

7 When visitors arrive at a framed page without a frames-capable browser, they see the contents of the <NOFRAMES> tags, which GoLive automatically inserts after the <FRAMESET> tags. By default, the <NOFRAMES> tags are initially empty, which means that visitors see a blank page—exactly what you see when you view a frameset page in Layout view in GoLive.

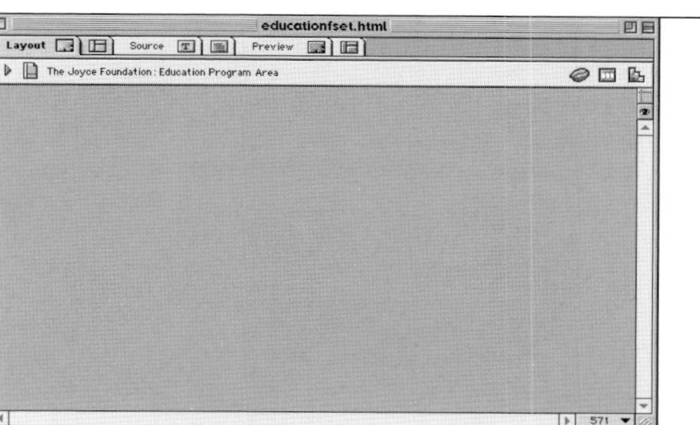

8 Any content added in the Layout view of a frameset document between the <NOFRAMES> tags will appear to visitors, so use this opportunity to offer some guidance. Typically, it's best to direct visitors to download a frames-capable browser so that they can see the site properly. Alternatively, you can add copy that describes your site (ideally using many of your metatag keywords).

Julia Hummelt
HOT
www.hotstudio.com

Designing Forms for the Web

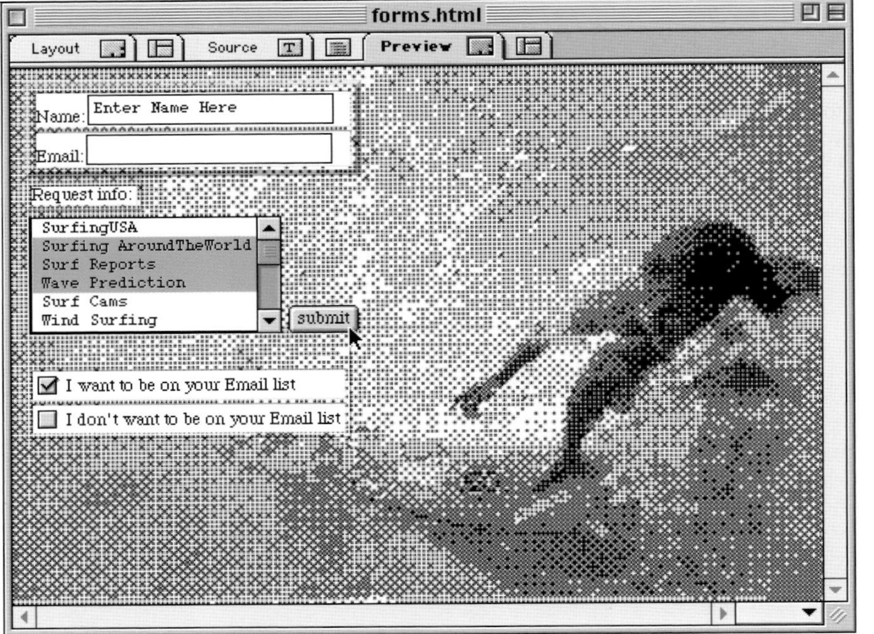

Using forms on a Web site provides myriad benefits. Whether they let you offer e-commerce, conduct surveys or register visitors, set up a complex search interface, or just let visitors e-mail the company, forms are essential. They don't have to be complicated or daunting to design, either. GoLive has a Forms palette that lets you position buttons, check boxes, list boxes, text, passwords, and more on site pages. It's wise to use tables to design forms because browsers don't display form elements at the same size, and tables help assure the alignment of objects that appear differently. Keep in mind that for forms to be processed by your server, you'll need to write a CGI script outside of GoLive. A Web server administrator can help you do that.

1 Open a new document in GoLive. In Layout view, drag a Table icon from the Basic tab of the Palette onto the page and specify the appropriate number of rows and columns. We actually created four small tables: one for the name and e-mail fields, one for the request info label, one for the scrolling list, and one for the mailing list check boxes.

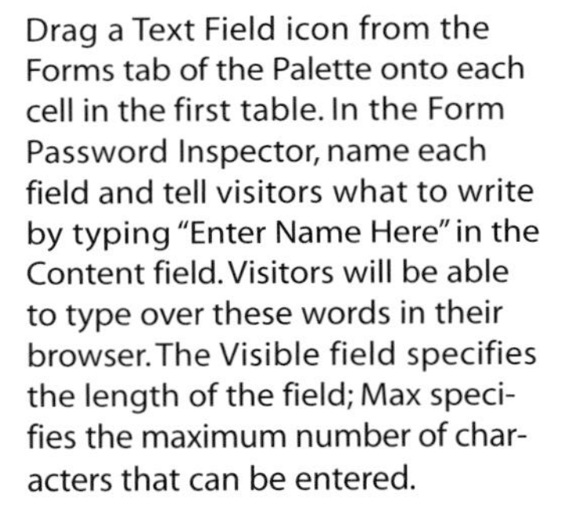

2 Drag a Text Field icon from the Forms tab of the Palette onto each cell in the first table. In the Form Password Inspector, name each field and tell visitors what to write by typing "Enter Name Here" in the Content field. Visitors will be able to type over these words in their browser. The Visible field specifies the length of the field; Max specifies the maximum number of characters that can be entered.

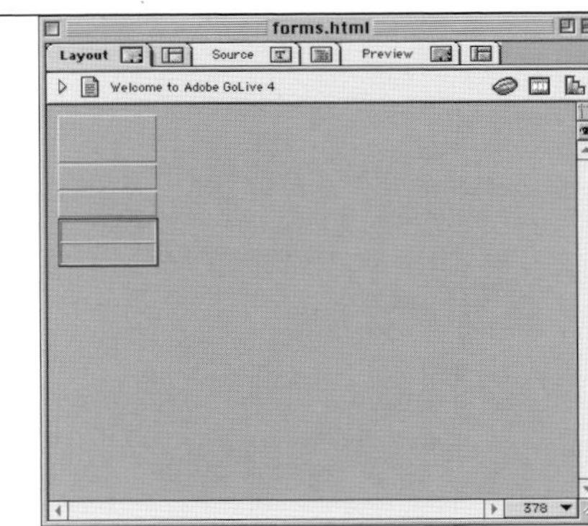

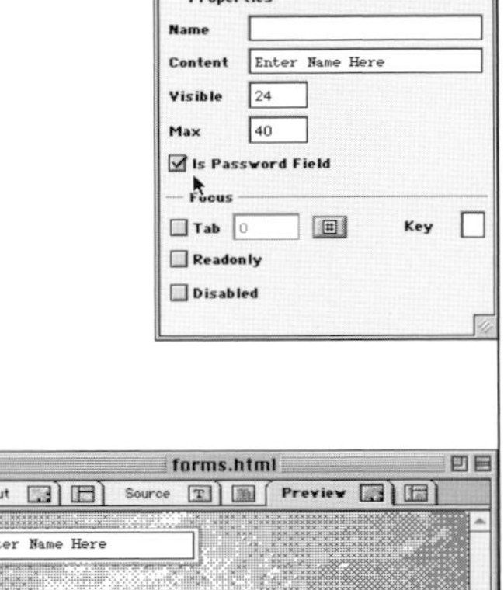

3 Label the name and e-mail text fields. Drag a Label icon into the cell in front of the text field and type to overwrite the word *label* with Name: . Then click the label with the hand cursor to view the Form Label Inspector, click the Point & Shoot button, and drag to link the label to the text field itself. Repeat for the e-mail field.

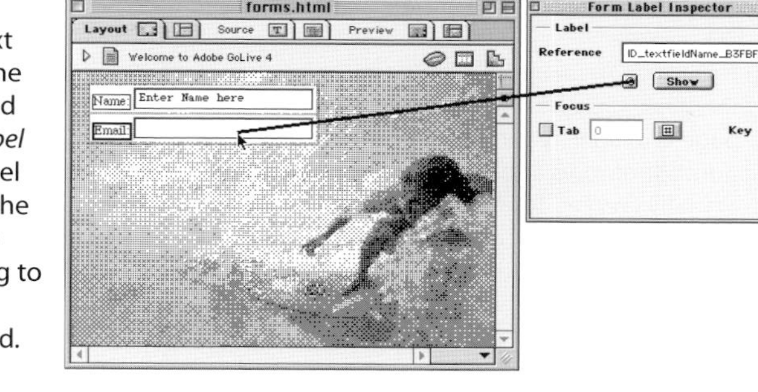

4 To create a scrolling list, drag a List Box icon from the Forms tab of the Palette to the appropriate table cell in your document. In the Form List Box Inspector, GoLive automatically displays three generic list items. Click the word *first* and edit it to say what you want, and then enter a descriptive value that will be used by the CGI script. Check the box next to the list item name to make it the default selection.

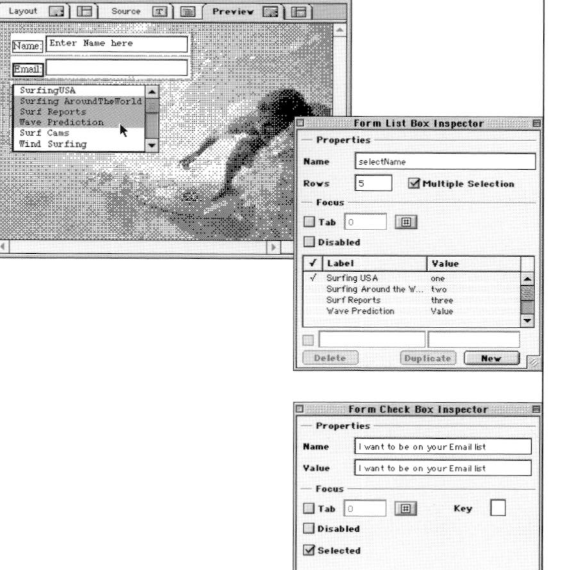

5 Drag a Check Box icon from the Forms tab of the Palette to the appropriate table cell in your document. Click to select the check box and in the Form Check Box Inspector, give it a name and a descriptive value. Indicate whether you want the default state to be Selected or not. Drag a Label icon into the cell next to the check box, give it a meaningful name, and link the label and the check box (see Step 3).

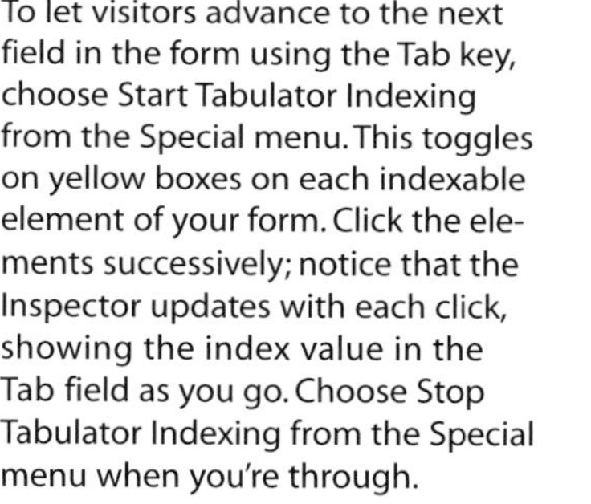

6 To create a submit button for the form, drag a Submit Button icon onto your page. Using the radio buttons in the Form Button Inspector you can designate whether the button should send info to your server or clear the form and reset it to its default state. Alternatively, you can drag an Input Image icon onto your page and designate a button graphic that you have created yourself.

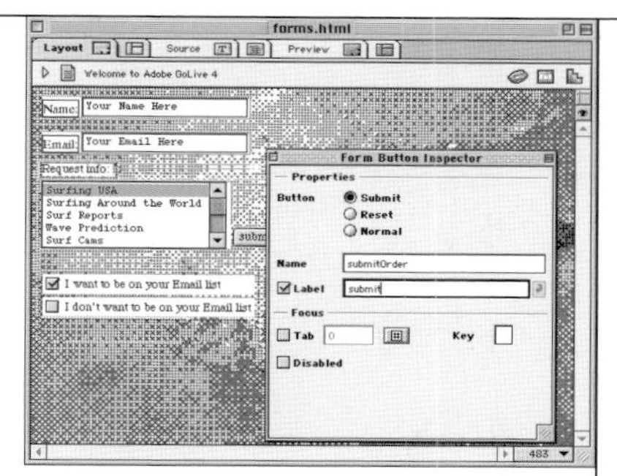

7 To let visitors advance to the next field in the form using the Tab key, choose Start Tabulator Indexing from the Special menu. This toggles on yellow boxes on each indexable element of your form. Click the elements successively; notice that the Inspector updates with each click, showing the index value in the Tab field as you go. Choose Stop Tabulator Indexing from the Special menu when you're through.

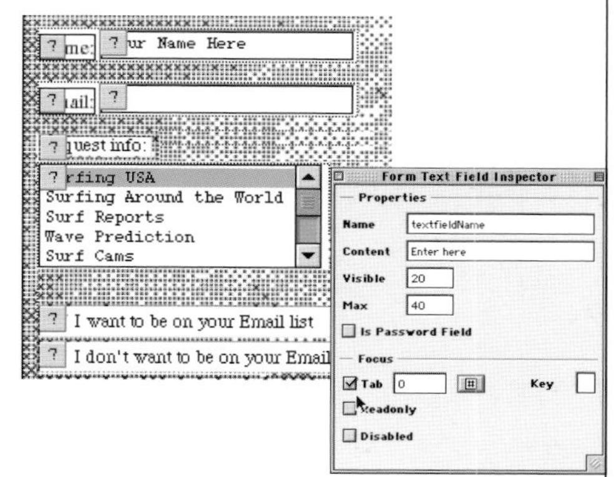

8 Finally, drag a Form icon onto your page above the first table, and drag an End Form icon onto the page below the last table. These tags are necessary for proper display of forms in Netscape Navigator. Then position any background images or other content on your page, preview in multiple browsers, and save the HTML file.

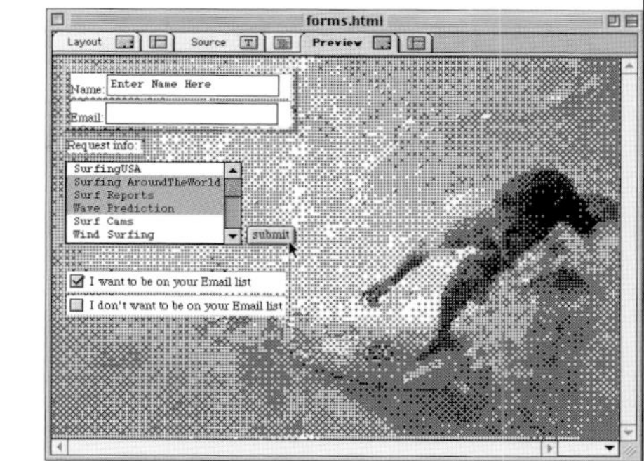

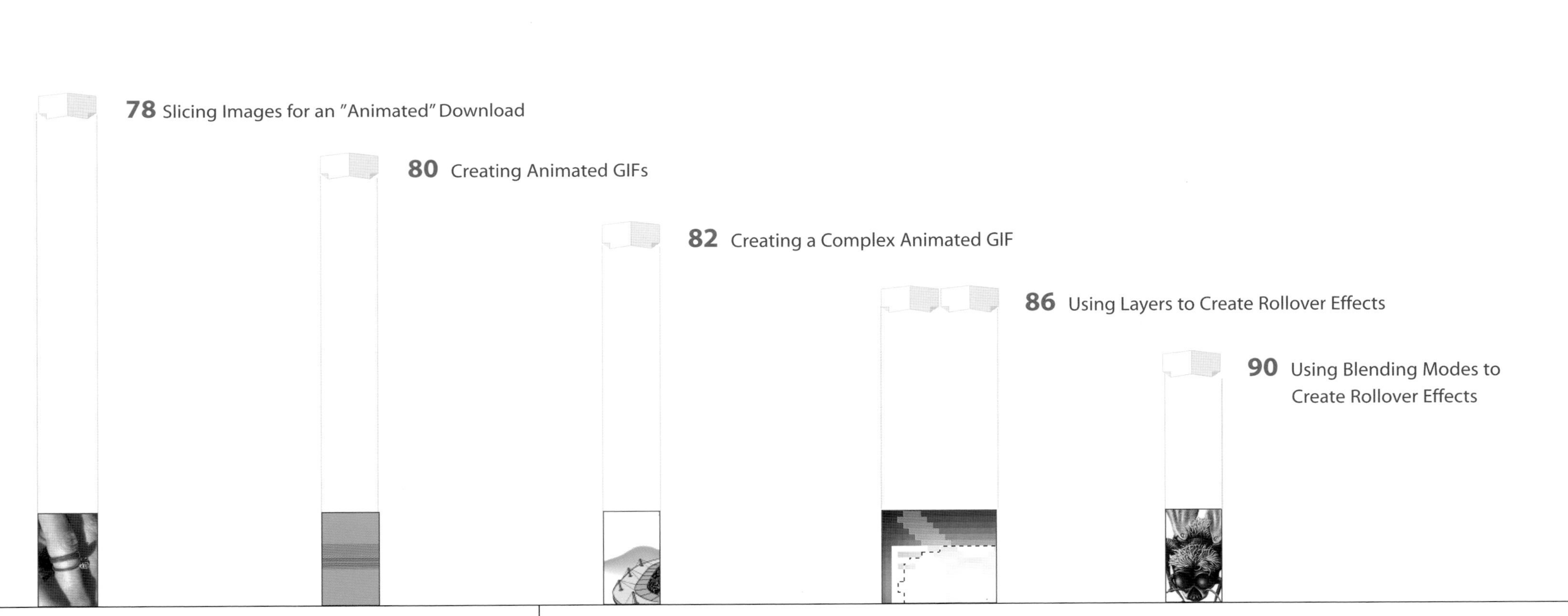

Chapter 5

Animation and Rollovers

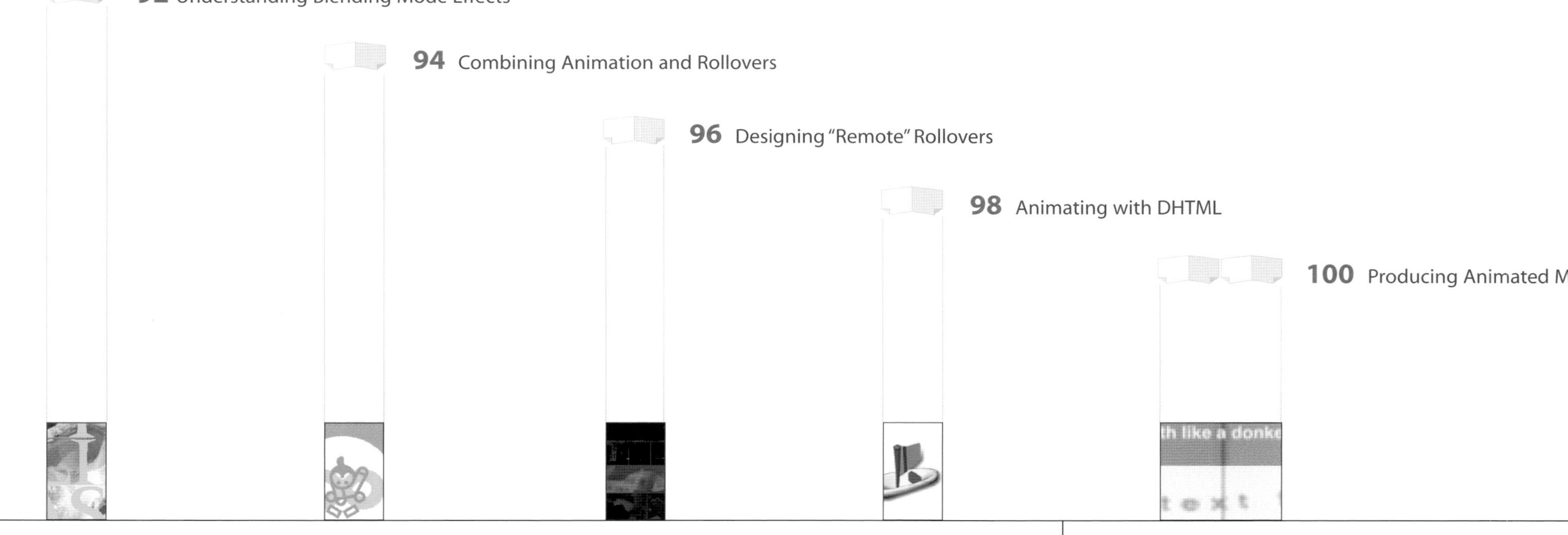

Katrin Eismann
www.photoshopdiva.com

Slicing Images for an "Animated" Download

There are myriad ways to hold visitors' interest while they wait for images to display in their browser. You can interlace your GIFs or use progressive JPEGs, for example, both of which let visitors see something of the image before it's finished downloading. Or you can use "low-source" images, which are dithered grayscale versions of slices that appear in a browser before their corresponding color slices. The flashing effect of these black-and-white and color slices will entertain visitors with slower connections until they see the composite image, but keep in mind that this technique actually makes it take longer for the final, composite image to appear in a browser.

1 Start by creating the artwork you'd like to display on your Web page. You can do this either by hand and scan it into your computer, or create it using Photoshop or Illustrator.

2 Open your artwork in ImageReady and choose Create Guides from the View menu to set the guides that will define your sliced image. In our example, we've set three evenly spaced horizontal and vertical guides.

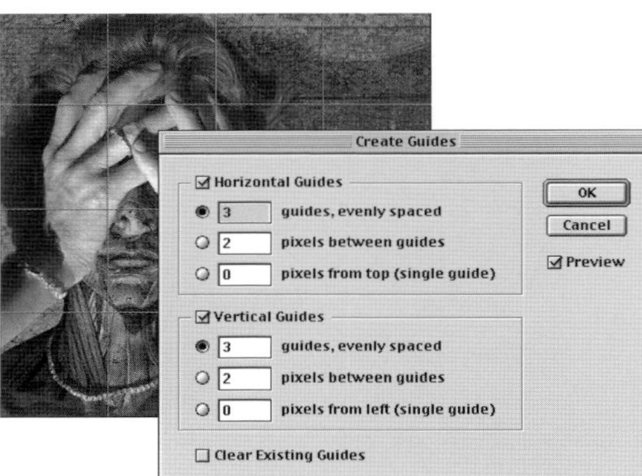

3 In the Slices menu, choose Create Slices from Guides. ImageReady gives the slices intuitive names, or you can give them new ones in the Slice palette.

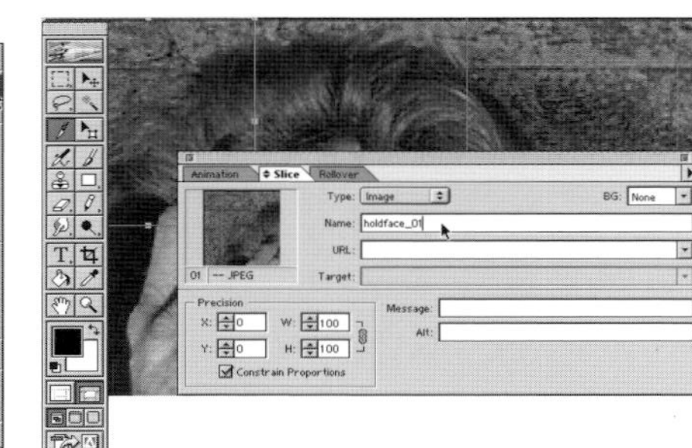

Adobe ImageReady 2.0 Adobe GoLive 4.0

4 Choose Save Optimized As from the File menu to save your slices, and check the boxes to save both the images and the HTML file. In the HTML Options dialog box, choose GoLive as the type of code you want to save.

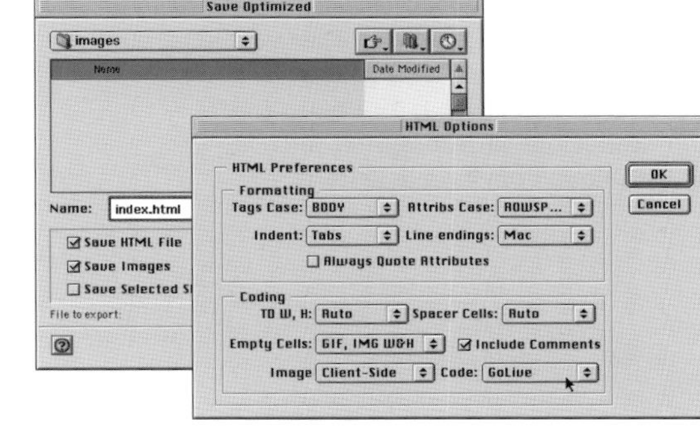

5 ImageReady creates an "images" folder that contains your slices. You should find this folder inside the folder that contains your original image.

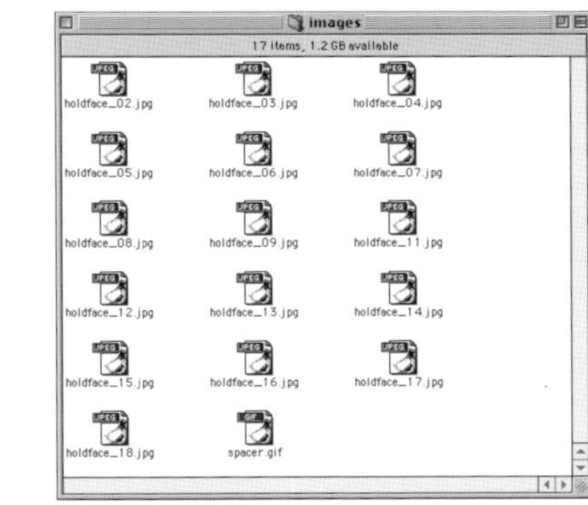

6 Launch GoLive and open the HTML file associated with your sliced image. You can see the slices positioned correctly in Layout view.

7 Click to select the upper-left slice. In the Basic tab of the Image Inspector, click the Generate button. GoLive automatically creates a dithered black-and-white GIF of the slice. Continue to generate low-source images for your other slices.

8 Check your work in the Preview tab of the page window, checking the "Show low source images" box if you want to see the dithered GIFs. Also preview in a browser: Click the Show in Browser button in the toolbar.

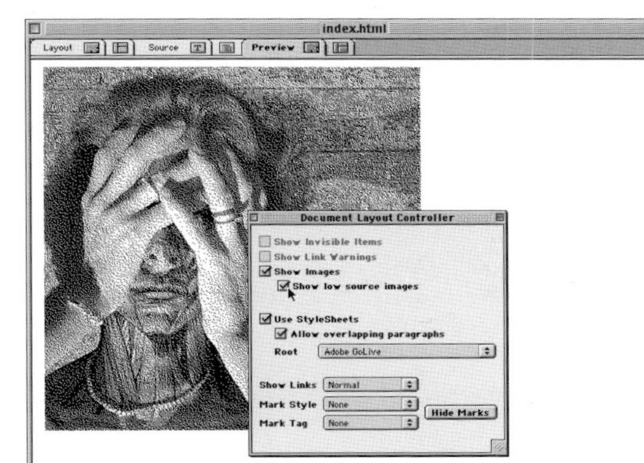

Florian Fangohr
HOT
www.hotstudio.com

Creating Animated GIFs

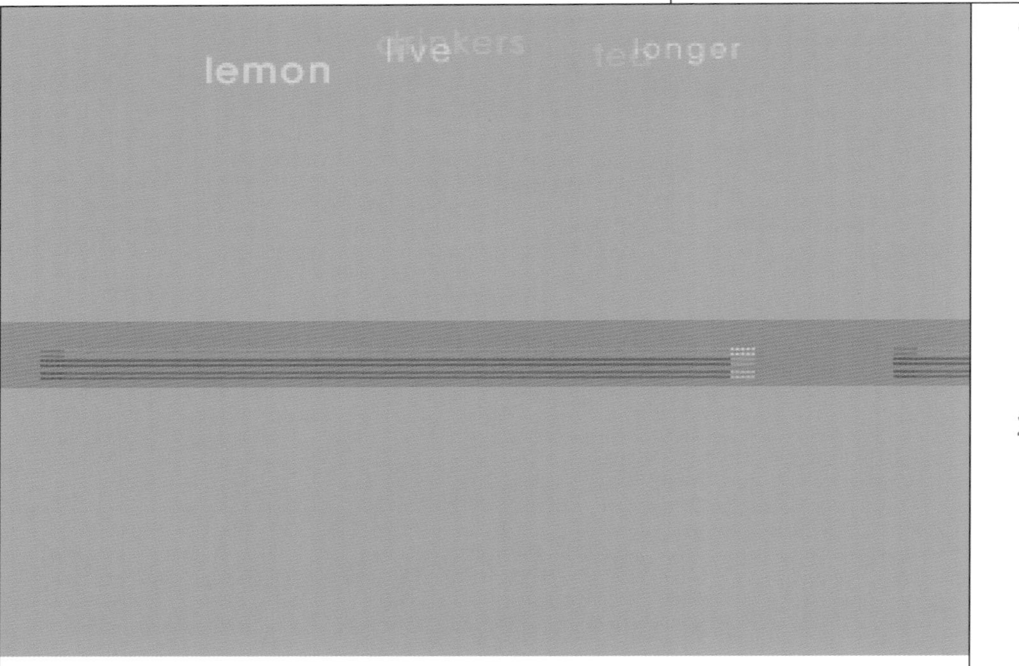

Static images and still text are for print. The Web is about activity—sound, motion, video, and animation. But you don't need to learn JavaScript or use a sophisticated 3D or video application to stimulate visitors' interest and draw them into your site. Animated GIFs do the trick nicely: They're easy to make, don't require a browser plug-in to be viewed, and make text or simple graphics dance across your pages. They're also a great way to liven up banner ads. HOT designer Florian Fangohr shows how to create an animated GIF using ImageReady's Tween feature, which automatically creates intermediate frames of motion between the start and final frame of an animation.

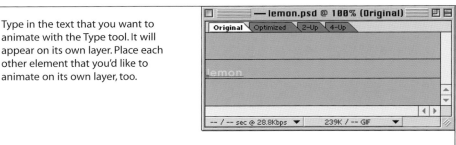

1 Type in the text that you want to animate with the Type tool. It will appear on its own layer. Place each other element that you'd like to animate on its own layer, too.

2 Create a second frame by choosing Duplicate Frame from the Animation palette's pop-up menu or clicking the button at the bottom of the palette. This will be your final frame of motion in your animation.

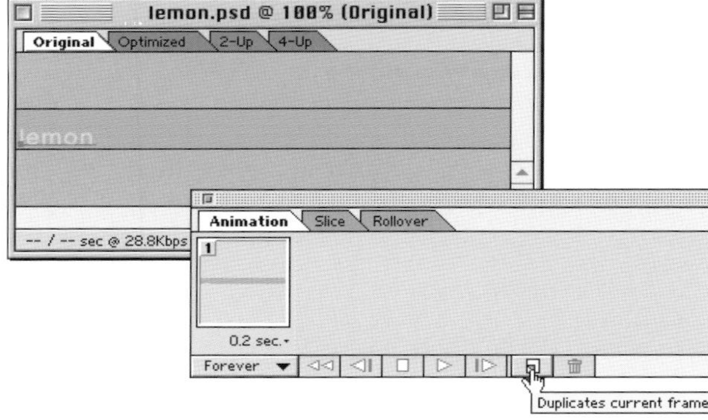

3 Drag the type or graphic to its final position using the Move tool.

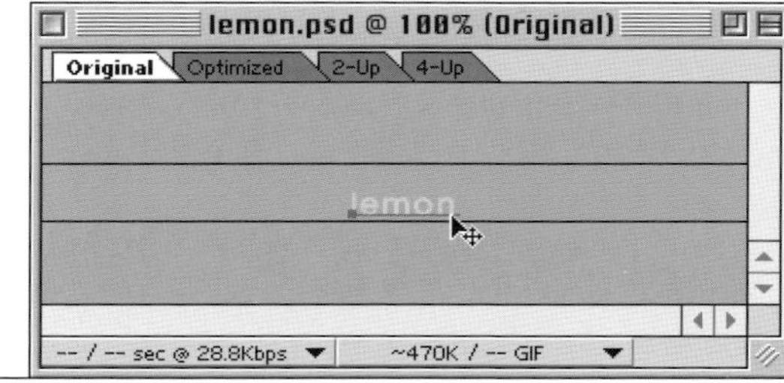

4 Press Shift and click to select the beginning and ending frames in the Animation palette, and then choose the Tween command from the palette's pop-up menu.

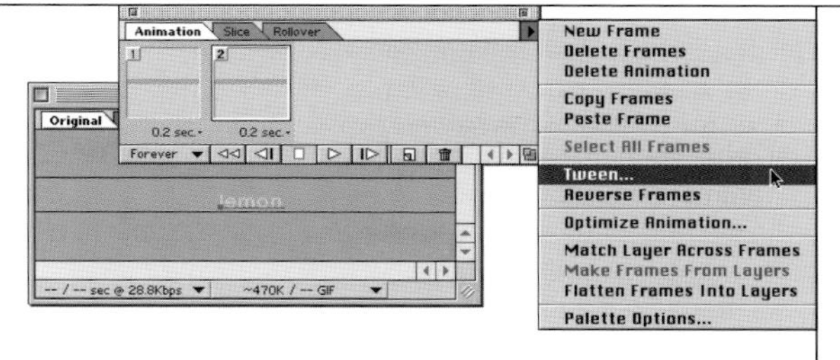

5 The "Tween with" pop-up menu should indicate Selection; specify how many frames you want to add between the two positions. You can put as many as 100 for film-quality animation, but 5 to 10 is plenty for the Web. Animate just the layer with the text or graphic you're moving, and indicate the other parameters you want to tween, including opacity and layer effects that might vary between frames.

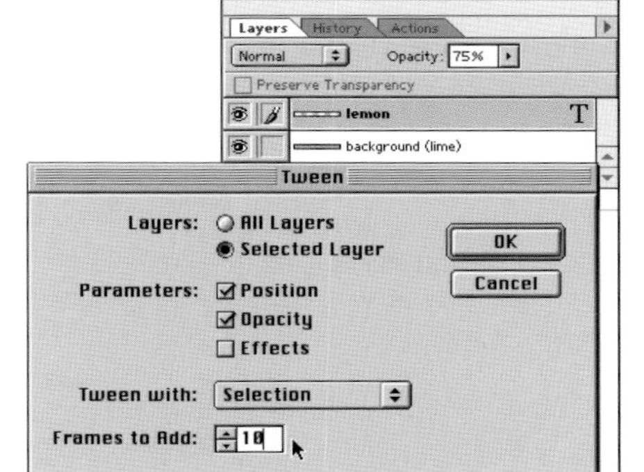

6 Select all of your frames in the Animation palette and click a downward arrow below any one of them. Select a time delay in the pop-up menu to indicate how quickly you want the frames to display. Experiment to see what works best; you can slow down and speed up individual frames as well.

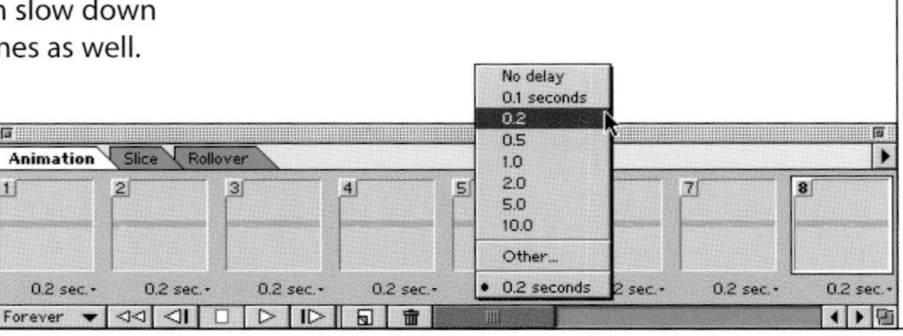

7 Indicate whether you want the animation to loop once, forever, or a specific number of times by choosing an option at the bottom of the Animation palette. Click the Play button to preview your animation.

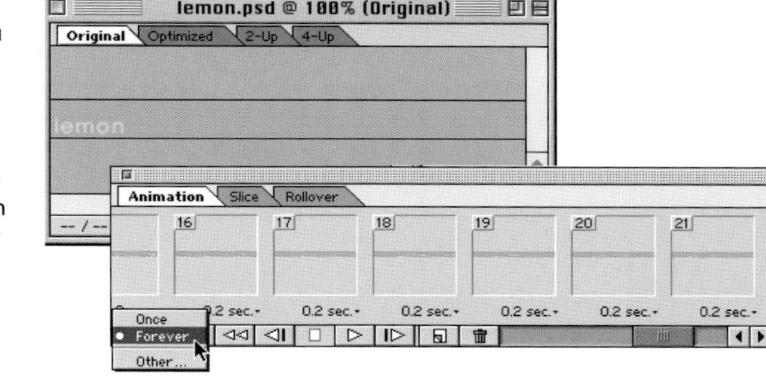

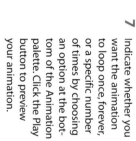

8 When you're satisfied, optimize your image. The 4-Up tab in the image window lets you see four differently optimized images at once, so you can decide which combination of file size and color choice works best. You can even click Play to preview the animation at those settings. Many sites limit animated GIF banner ads to 14K, so you might want to save your GIF at about that size.

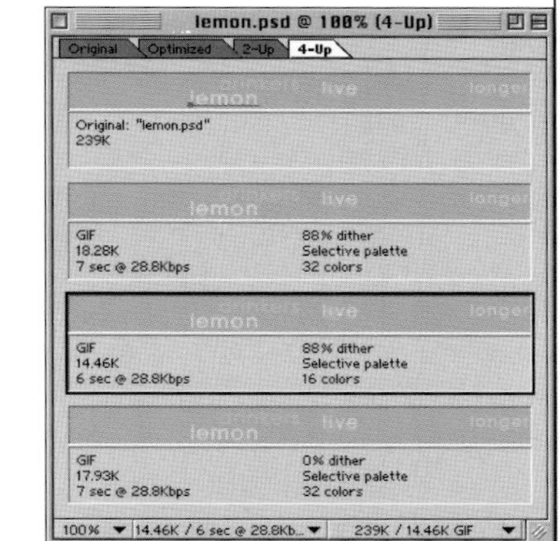

9 Save the file with a new name using the Save Optimized As command in the File menu. That way you can go back and edit your original if necessary. Be sure to preview the animation in a browser for a more accurate representation of the time delay.

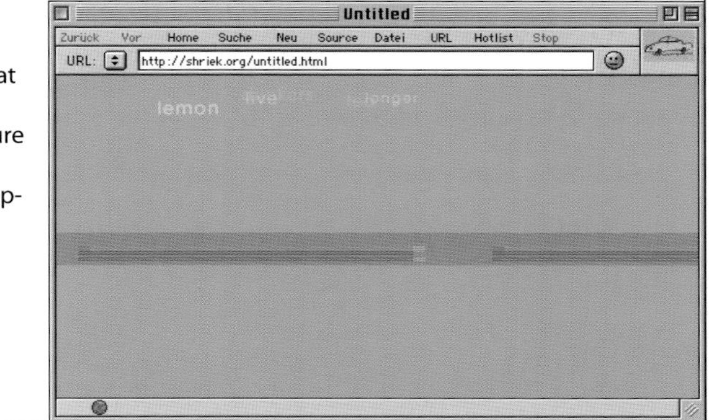

Steve McGuire
McGuire Design
www.mcguirezone.com

Creating a Complex Animated GIF

When you get comfortable with ImageReady's animation features, you can become bolder with your animated GIF creations. Freelance computer graphic artist Steve McGuire shows how to create a complex animation of a perennial favorite: fireworks. He starts by drawing the fireworks in Illustrator, adding and editing layers that represent frames of motion in Photoshop, and finally importing the layered file into ImageReady to complete the animation. This particular animation is used on Hewlett-Packard's sponsorship page for the 1998 World Cup.

1 Use the Pen or Pencil tool in Illustrator to draw the path of a single thread of a fireworks explosion. Fill it with a gradient to give the appearance of the fireworks changing color as the sparks fly outward. Be sure to use Web-safe colors: Open the Web palette by choosing Swatch Libraries from the Window menu.

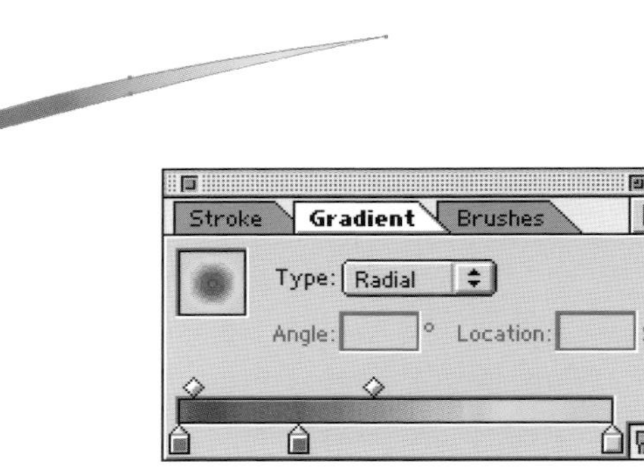

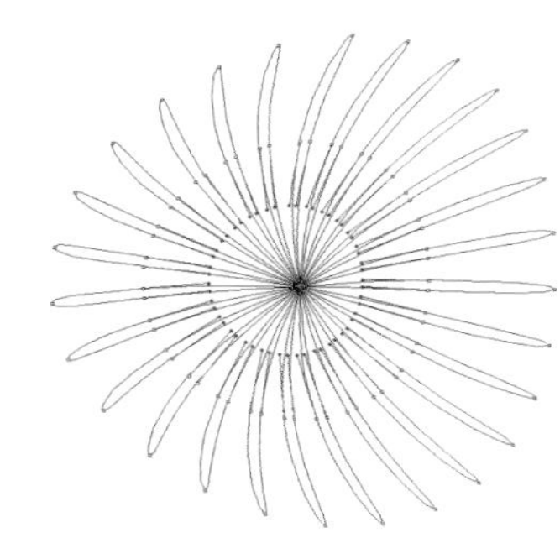

2 Switch to Artwork mode to see better detail. Use the Rotate tool to rotate and copy the path in one step: Click to set the point of origin at the end of the path, select it, and then press Option (Alt) after you drag the other end to make a copy. Then press Command-D (Control-D) to make the others in a circle.

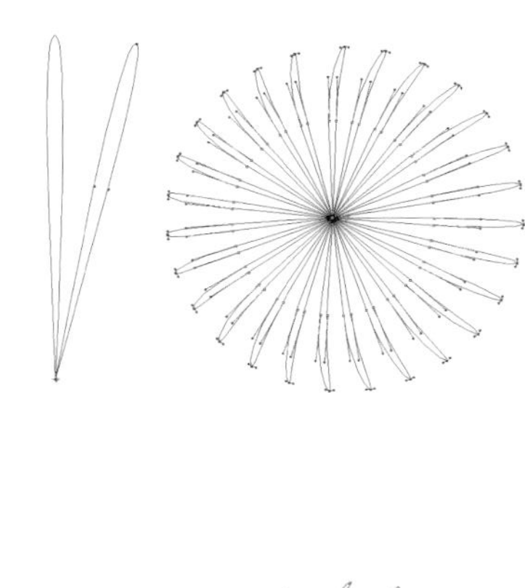

3 Use the Direct Selection tool to taper the strokes and to drag the outer node for some strokes down slightly to create a sense of gravity. Create another path to show the path of the launch of the fireworks from the stadium into the sky.

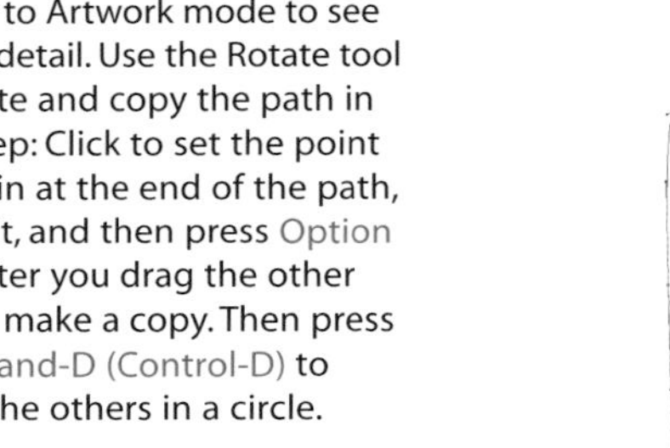

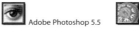

 Adobe Illustrator 8.0  Adobe Photoshop 5.5  Adobe ImageReady 2.0

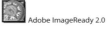

4 Make a couple of copies of your fireworks, scaling them and changing the colors to make each one unique. We made a large yellow explosion, a medium purple explosion, and a small blue one. Place each set of fireworks and each launch path on a separate layer.

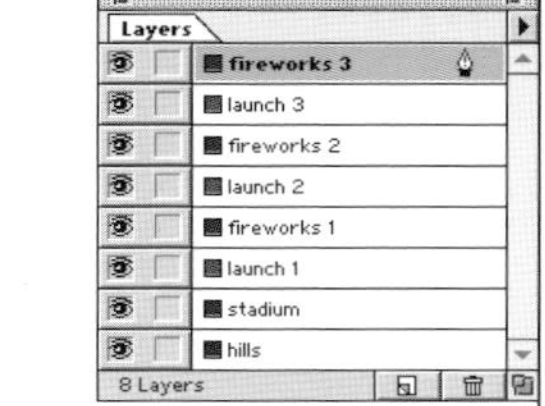

5 Export the final artwork as a Photoshop file, making sure to use the RGB color model, select Screen resolution (72 dpi), and check the Write Layers box.

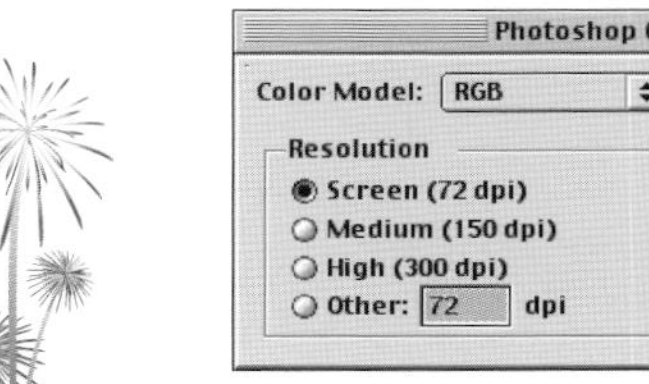

6 Open the fireworks image in Photoshop, and you'll see that your layers transferred.

7 Now you can edit the fireworks on different layers to simulate the motion of explosions. Start by duplicating the layer of the first set of fireworks and naming it "fireworks 1a."

8 Activate just fireworks 1 in the Layers palette, and then use the Eraser tool set as a soft-edged paintbrush to erase the edges of the fireworks, stroking from the outside in.

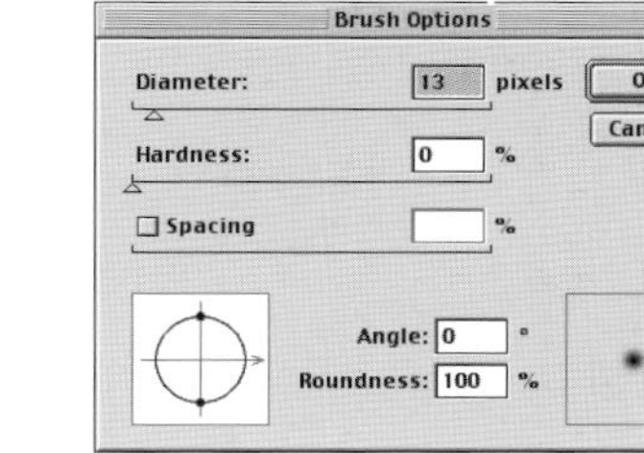

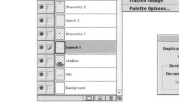

9 Now work on the fireworks 1a layer. Choose Stylize from the Filter menu and apply the Diffuse filter (specify Lighten Only) to make it look like it's exploding. Then select all and scale the layer using the Transform command in the Edit menu to make the fireworks a bit larger. Using the Eraser again, erase the middle of the fireworks, stroking outward from the center.

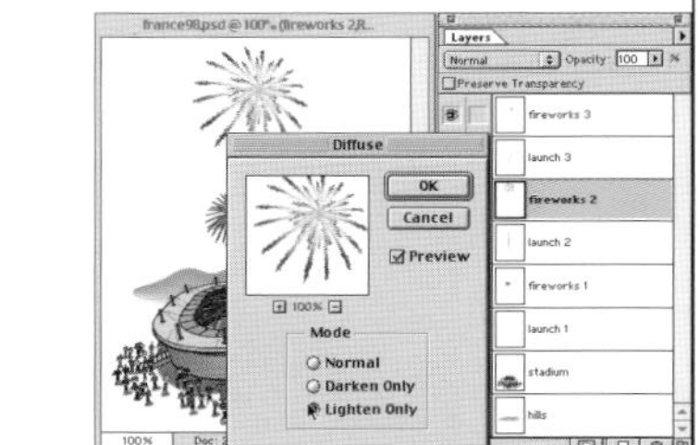

Steve McGuire
McGuire Design
www.mcguirezone.com

CONTINUED...

Creating a Complex Animated GIF

10 Duplicate this layer and name it "fireworks 1b." Set its Opacity to 50 percent; erase almost all of the fireworks except for the tips; and scale the layer a bit bigger.

11 Repeat Steps 7 to 10 for the other two sets of fireworks. The three layers will act as frames for the animation of each set of fireworks.

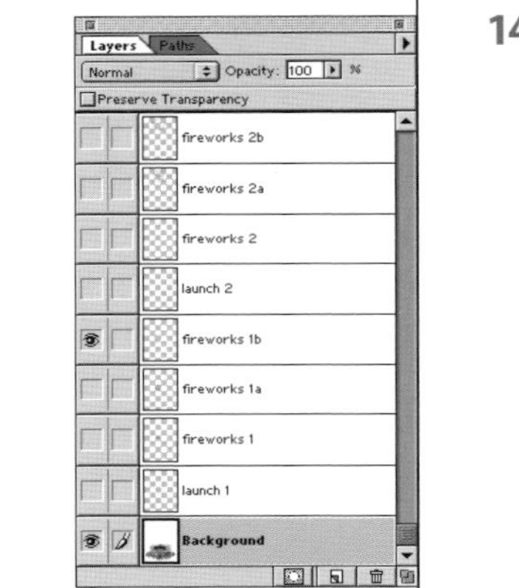

12 Duplicate each set of fireworks so that you have a total of six sets (18 fireworks layers). Name the new layers 4, 5, and 6, keeping the alphabetical convention intact.

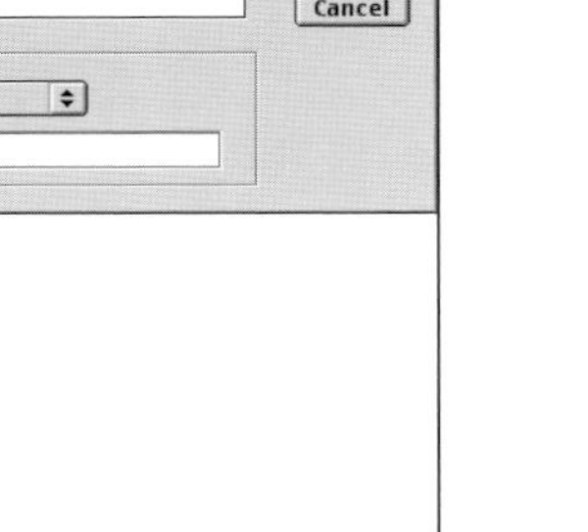

13 Select the first layer for the fourth set of fireworks and link it to fireworks layers 4a and 4b. Use the Move tool to reposition this set in the illustration; rotate and scale it so it appears unique; and then unlink the layers. Repeat the process for the fifth and sixth sets of fireworks.

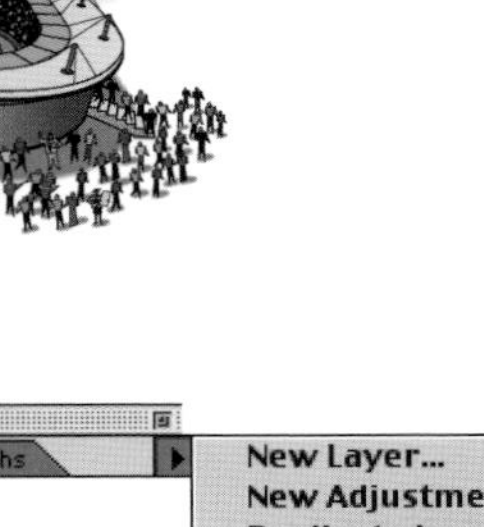

14 You're almost done in Photoshop. In the Layers palette, link all of the nonfireworks layers—all of the layers with background and other graphical elements—if they're not on one layer already. Then choose Merge Linked from the Layers palette pop-up menu. All of your fireworks will remain on their individual, unmerged layers.

15 Jump to ImageReady by clicking the button at the bottom of the tool palette, or press Command-Shift-M (Control-Shift-M). If you turn on all layers in the file, you will see all six of your fireworks, in all frames of motion.

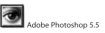

16 ImageReady automatically places each layer in its own frame, including the background, so you'll need to edit your frames to get the sequence of the explosions to your liking. To edit a frame, choose it in the Animation palette and toggle visibility of layers on and off in the Layers palette. Add new frames as necessary using the pop-up menu in the Animation palette.

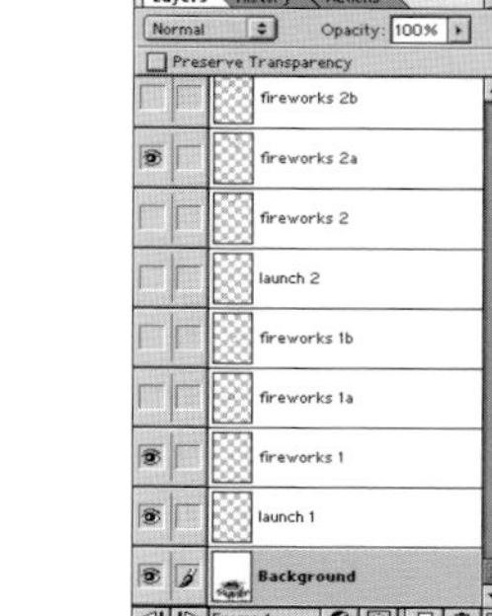

17 In the Animation palette, select the frame time delay and set the kind of looping you prefer: once, forever, or other, which lets you specify a fixed number of repeats. A time delay of zero is too fast; .2 works well for fireworks.

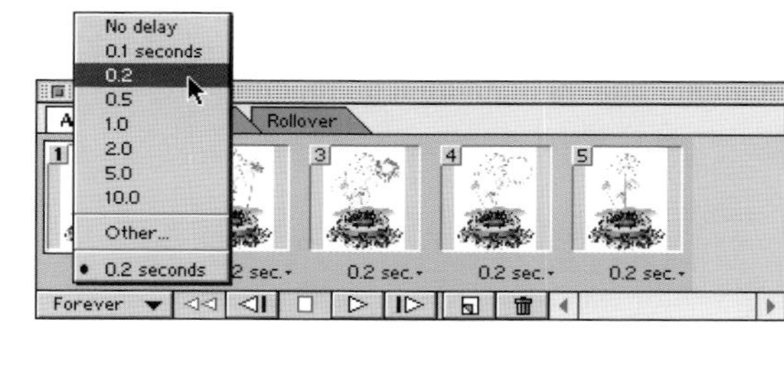

Set Loop Count

Play: 5 times

OK

Cancel

18 Preview your animation at any time by clicking the Play button on the Animation palette.

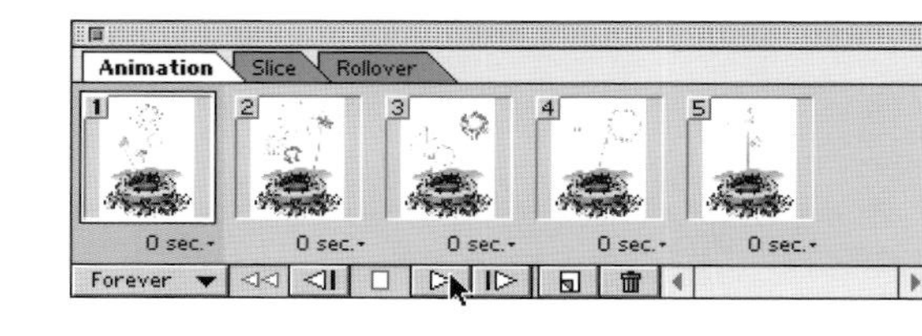

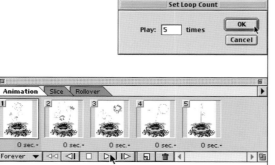

19 In the Optimize palette, make your image a GIF. For this artwork, we selected the adaptive palette using 216 colors, no transparency, no dither, no loss, and not interlaced.

Optimize | Info | Options

Settings: [Unnamed]

GIF — Lossy: 0

Adaptive — Colors: 216

No Dither — Dither:

Transparency — Matte: None

Interlaced — Web Snap: 0%

20 Finally, choose Save Optimized As from the File menu to save your animated GIF.

File

New... ⌘N
Open... ⌘O
Close ⌘W
Revert
Save Optimized ⌥⌘S
Save Optimized As... ⌥⇧⌘S
Update HTML...
Save ⌘S
Save As... ⇧⌘S
Export Original...
Place...
Import ▸
Export ▸
Image Info... ⇧⌘K
HTML Background...
Preview in ▸
Jump to ▸
Preferences ▸
Adobe Online...
Recent Files ▸
Quit ⌘Q

Michael Everitt
Informativity
www.informativity.com

Using Layers to Create Rollover Effects

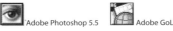

Rollovers spice up navigational buttons on the Web: When you roll the mouse cursor over the button, it changes state—lights up or glows, for example—to help the viewer see the selection. Photoshop is an excellent tool to use to prepare the "on" and "off" states of these rollover effects. Layers make it easy to sketch various effects before committing one to production: Just draw the default button state in one layer, and then experiment with rollover effects in other layers. Working with sets of buttons at once makes for visual consistency and a cohesive style. After you've designed the buttons, you can use GoLive to position them on your pages and activate them with a DHTML animation.

1 Draw the first default-state button graphic in RGB mode in Photoshop. The buttons here, for example, represent e-mail commands. To minimize surprises down the line, draw with Web-safe colors: Check the Only Web Colors box in the Color Picker, and view Web-safe colors in the ramp in the Color palette by toggling on "Make Ramp Web Safe" in the pop-up menu.

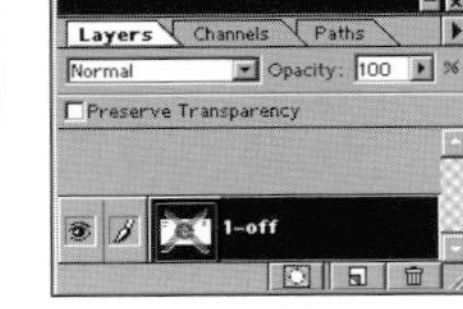

2 Continue drawing the other buttons in your interface, each on its own layer. Use the Duplicate command in the Layers palette pop-up menu to save time: It creates buttons of the same size, perfectly aligned and centered over one another.

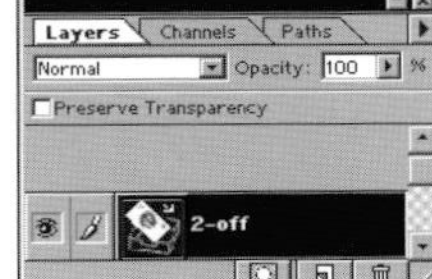

3 Once all your off-state buttons are prepared, duplicate another layer to start creating your rollover effect with Photoshop's image-editing tools and blending modes. To create the glow effect here, we selected the envelope with the elliptical Marquee tool, feathered it 5 pixels, and then filled it with white.

Adobe Photoshop 5.5 Adobe GoLive 4.0

4 Continue to experiment with visual effects by adding a layer for each "sketch" until you create the on state that you desire. For example, we tested various color glows. To see which combination of on and off states works best, toggle on visibility for the first off-state button, and then toggle on and off any single effect layer. Be sure to view the effect on each button in your navigational system.

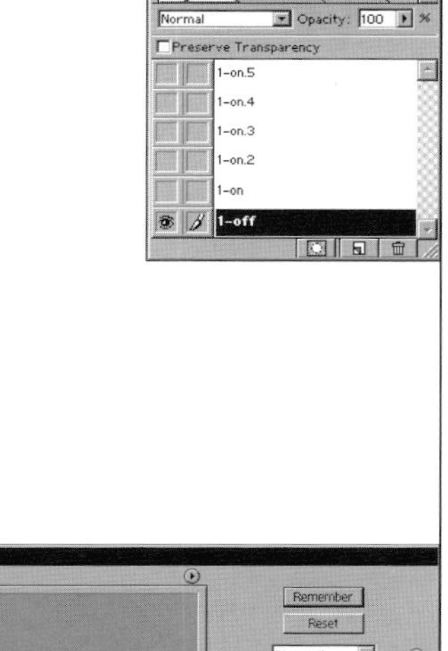

5 When you're satisfied, prepare the buttons for production. Toggle on visibility for just the first off-state button layer.

6 Choose Save for Web from the File menu and optimize the first off-state button as GIF. Experiment to see which palette and how many colors work best.

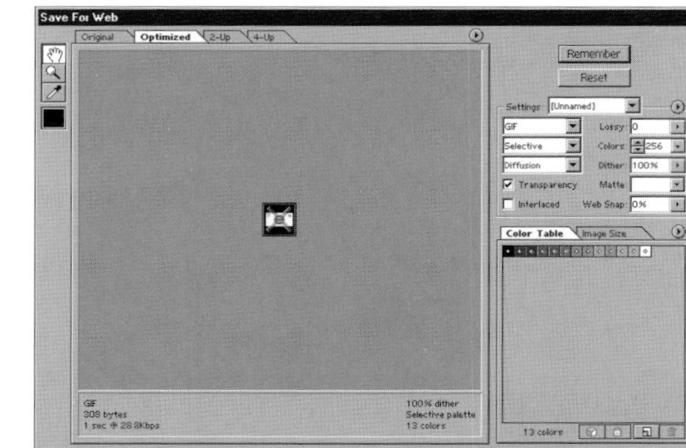

7 Make only the second off-state button layer visible, choose Save for Web, and optimize it as a GIF. Repeat the process for the other off-state buttons in your system, using intuitive filenames. We used a descriptive prefix plus "def," for default: trashdef, getdef, indef, and so forth.

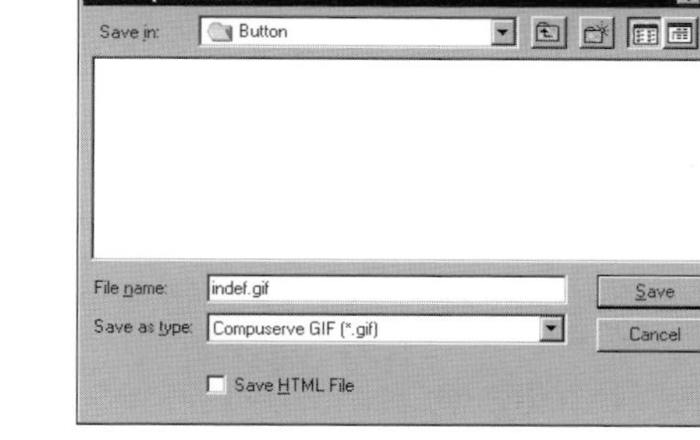

8 Now prepare the on-state buttons. Toggle on visibility for the effect layer or layers plus the first off-state button. Choose Save for Web from the File menu. Optimize the file as you did for the off-state buttons, and continue to use intuitive filenames. We added a "glow" suffix.

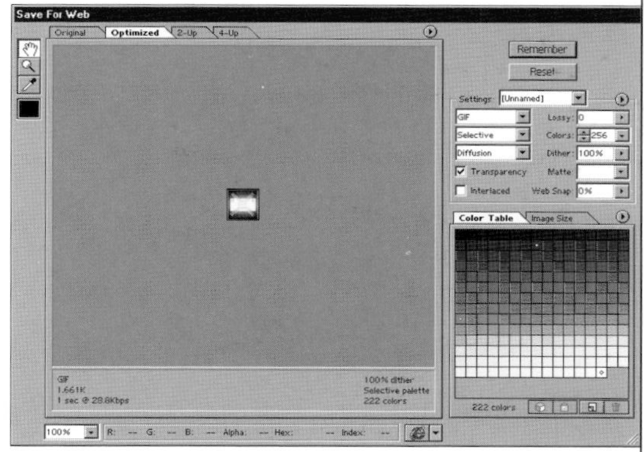

9 Repeat the process of toggling on visibility for the effect layer or layers and each button in your system, and save each for the Web.

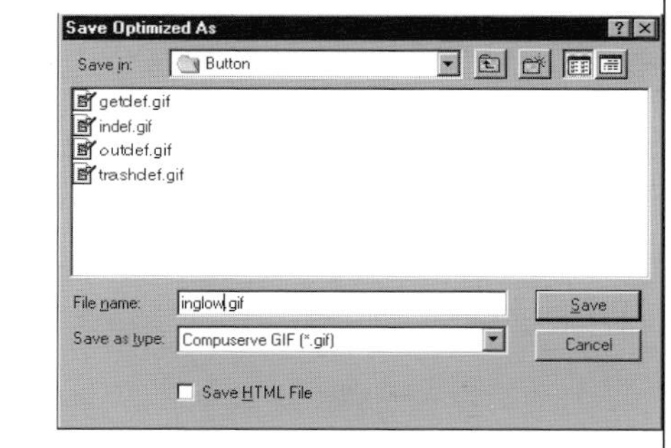

Michael Everitt
Informativity
www.informativity.com

CONTINUED...

Using Layers to Create Rollover Effects

10 When your buttons have been prepared, launch GoLive. Our page has a black background, so we set that first. Drag the RGB sliders all the way to the left in the Color Palette. Click the Page icon in the document window to view the Page Inspector. Click and drag the black sample in the Color Palette onto the Color well in the Background section of the Page Inspector.

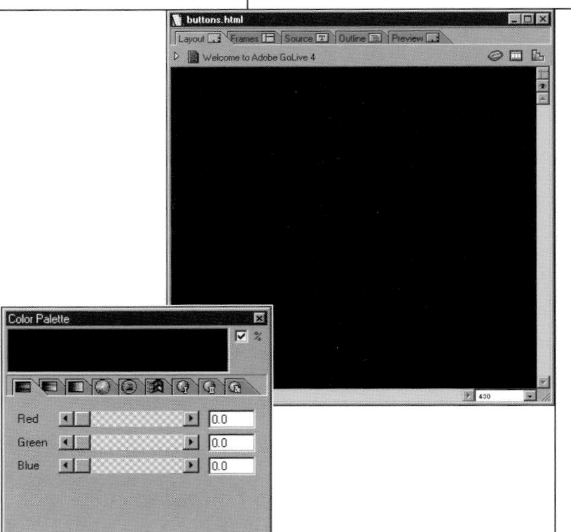

11 Now place your navigational buttons. Drag a Button Image icon from the CyberObjects tab of the palette onto the page. A green triangle appears in the upper-left corner, indicating that you are applying a DHTML animation to the button.

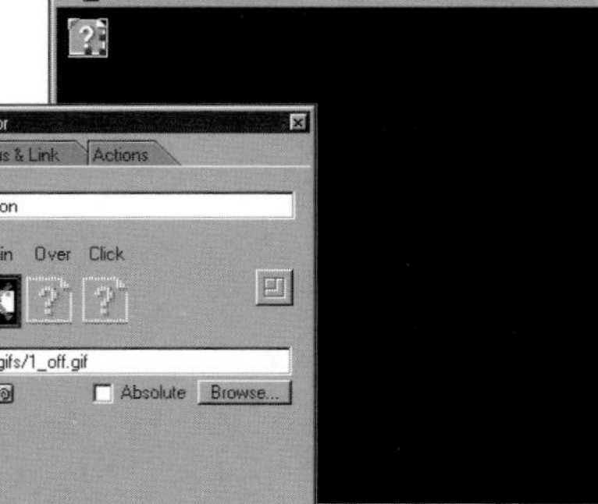

12 In the Basic tab of the Button Inspector, click the Main marker button and browse to select the first off-state button.

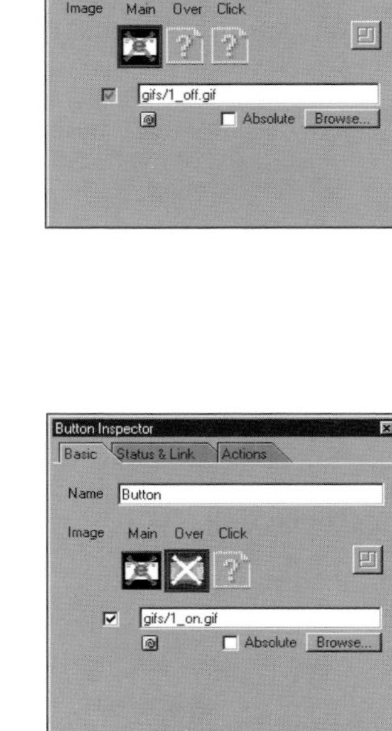

13 Click the Over marker button, and then check the box below it and browse to select the corresponding on-state button. It will swap in when the mouse cursor rolls over the off-state graphic.

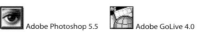

14 Drag additional Button Image icons onto the page until you have one for each navigational button. Use an HTML table, a layout grid, or just the Alignment pop-up menu in the Image Inspector to align the buttons on the page.

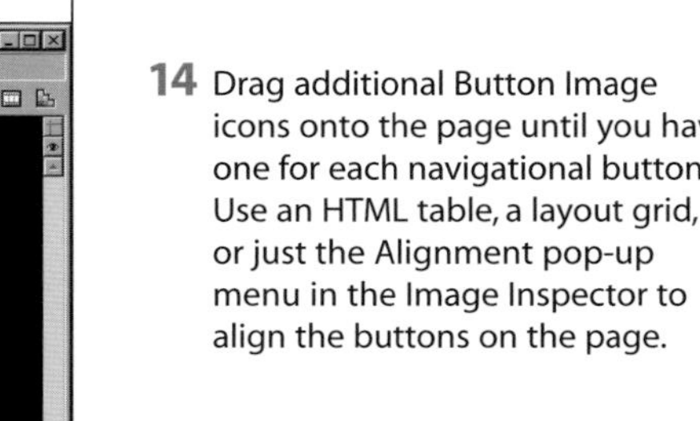

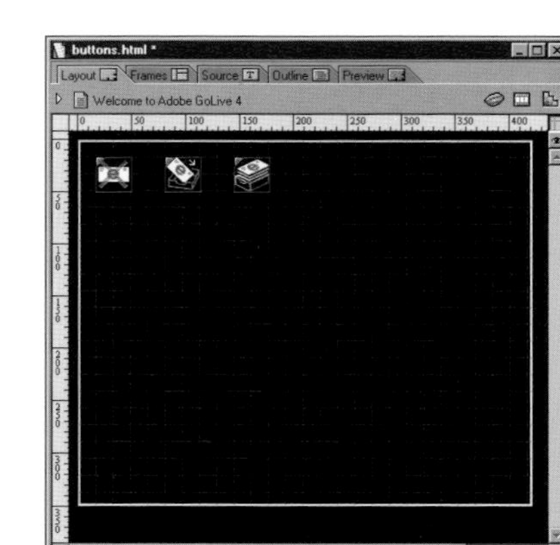

Adobe Photoshop 5.5 Adobe GoLive 4.0

15 Repeat Steps 12 and 13 for all of the other buttons in your navigational system.

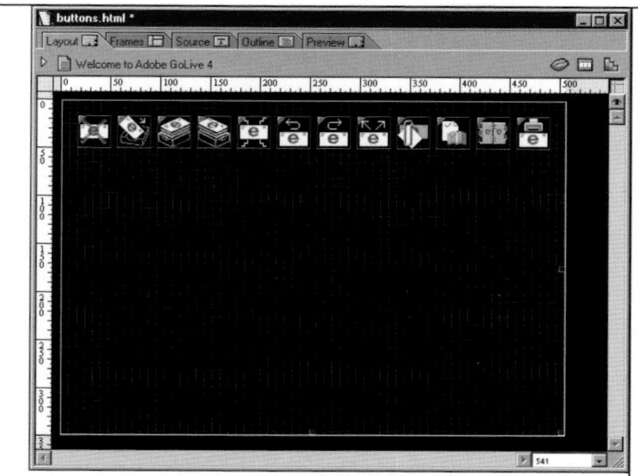

16 Test your mouse rollovers by clicking the Preview tab at the top of the document window or by viewing them in a browser.

17 To apply a link to your navigational buttons, check the URL box in the Status & Link tab of the Button Inspector and type the path in the text field or browse to select another Web page.

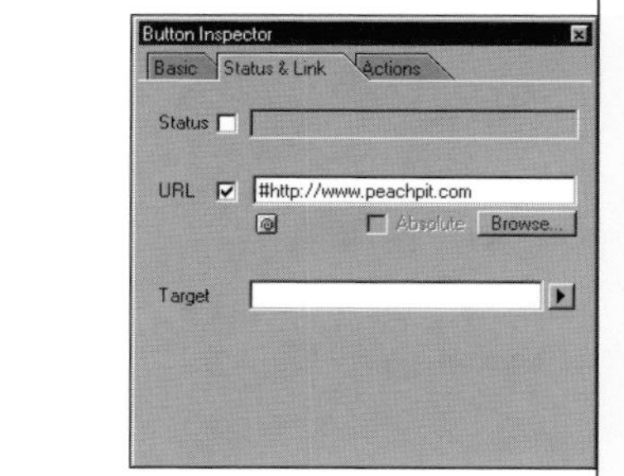

Keeping Color Consistent Between States

If for some reason you need to create your navigational buttons in multiple files, you run the risk of mistakenly using a different palette for the off and on states of the graphics. If colors shift or dithering or banding occurs between states, it can ruin the effect. To avoid this fate, arrange or create an image in Photoshop that incorporates all of the color elements you're using in each rollover state. In the Save for Web dialog box, choose a palette, and save the color table using the command in the Color Table palette pop-up menu. Then when you open each rollover state graphic in Photoshop, change the Mode to Indexed Color in the Image menu, select Custom, and load the saved color table. *—Casey Caston*

Tom Bray
Zimba
www.zimba.com
www.tombray.com

Using Blending Modes to Create Rollover Effects

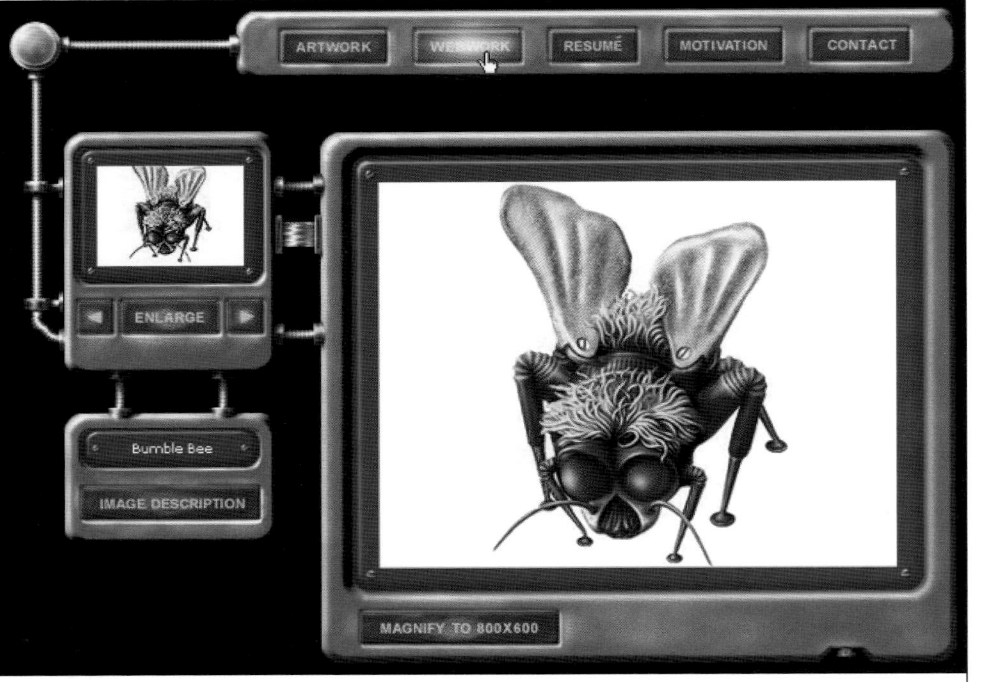

Photoshop's blending modes are fun to experiment with when designing rollover effects. When you create an effect that you like, such as a button that's lit from behind, link the layers so that the effects can be easily applied to other buttons. Since changes applied are cumulative and can be destructive to your original image data, you might want to use adjustment layers, which let you make color and tonal edits without permanently changing the pixels in the image. Once you create an effect you like, you can merge the adjustment layer with the layer below it to make the changes permanent. For a better sense of how each blending mode works, see "Understanding Blending Mode Effects," on page 92.

1 Start with the artwork that represents all of the interface buttons in their off state—as they appear by default—on a single layer in a Photoshop file.

2 Choose New Layer from the Layers palette pop-up menu and select a mode. Hard Light yields an effect similar to a spotlight, so you might start by painting with a yellow hue. Try a soft brush about 15 pixels wide.

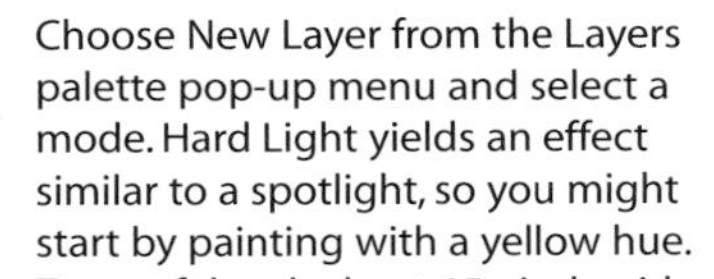

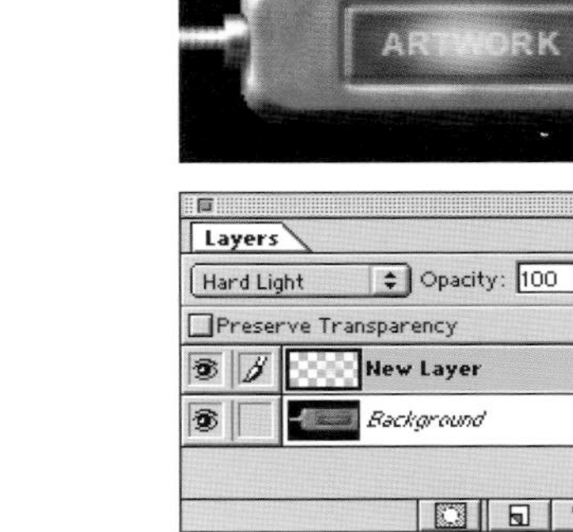

3 If the color isn't exactly to your satisfaction, blend in one of the colors from nearby pixels to make the light look more realistic. Create a new layer and change the blending mode to Color. Then select one of the colors in the interface, such as the red shown here, and start painting.

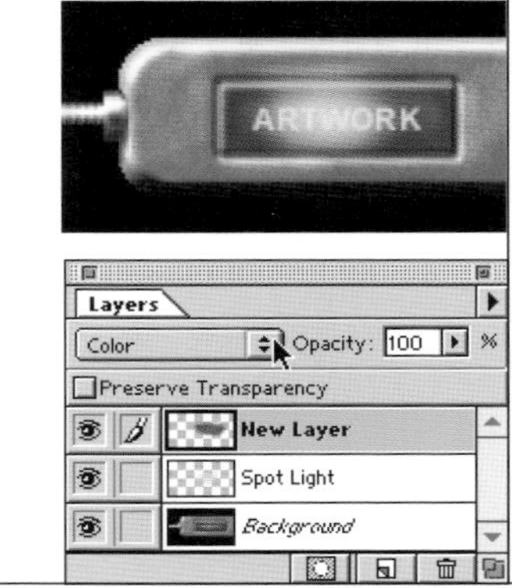

4 To play with the saturation of the color layer, choose Adjust Hue and Saturation from the Image menu and drag the sliders until you're happy.

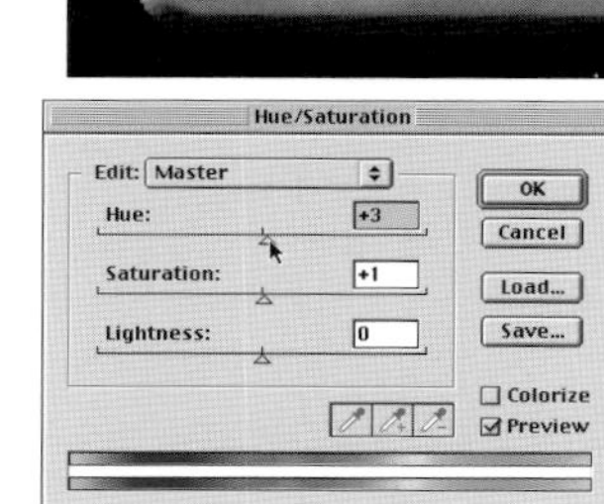

5 Since an illuminated metallic button will reflect its color beyond its border, make a new layer, set its mode to Color Dodge, and paint around the surrounding area with a darker version of the button's color—an earthy red in our example. The key is to use a fairly dark, unsaturated color to avoid making the area look washed out.

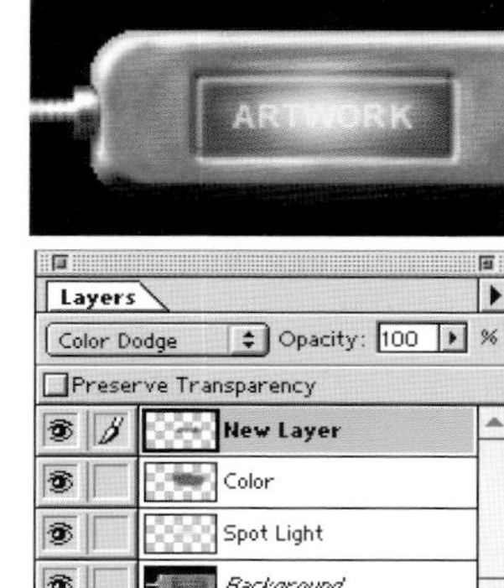

6 Continue experimenting with blending modes until you get your desired effect. The final step for this effect was to make a new layer and set its mode to Saturation. Then we picked one of the reds in the button with the Eyedropper tool and increased its saturation by launching the Color Picker (double-click the foreground color swatch), selecting the "S" radio button, and adjusting the slider. We then painted with the new color.

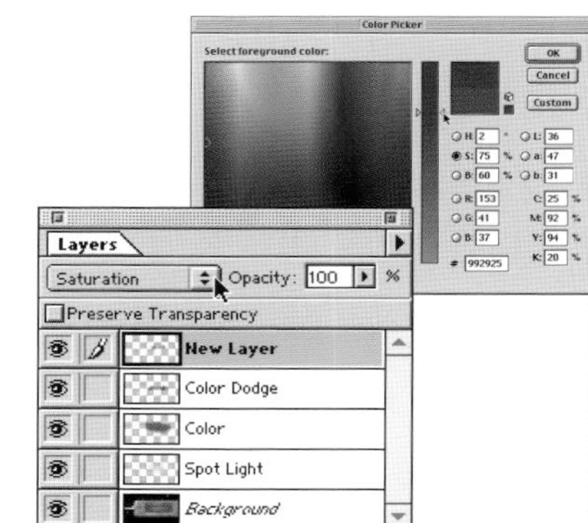

7 Once you're satisfied with the on-state effect, you need to apply it to the buttons. If the effect is on multiple layers, link them, and then choose Merge Linked from the Layers palette pop-up menu. Make the effect layer, as well as the off-state button layer, visible. Make one of those layers active. Select all and choose Copy Merged from the Edit menu. Then choose Paste Into. This creates a new layer with all of the buttons and the effect applied to the first one.

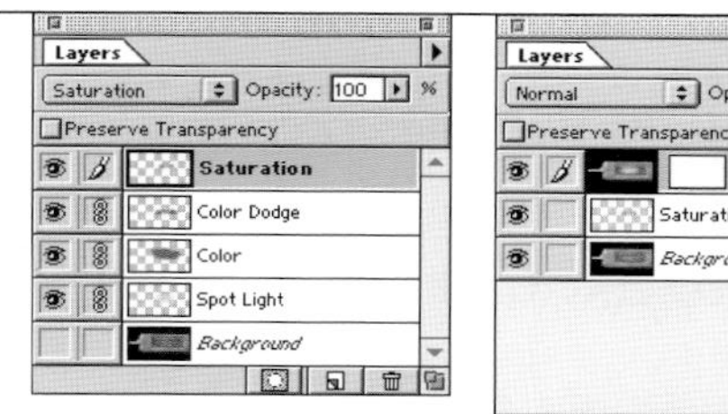

8 In the Layers palette, select the effect layer and move it above the layer with the one final on-state button. Select all, and hold down Option (Alt) while you use the Move tool to position copies of the effect over all the other buttons in the file.

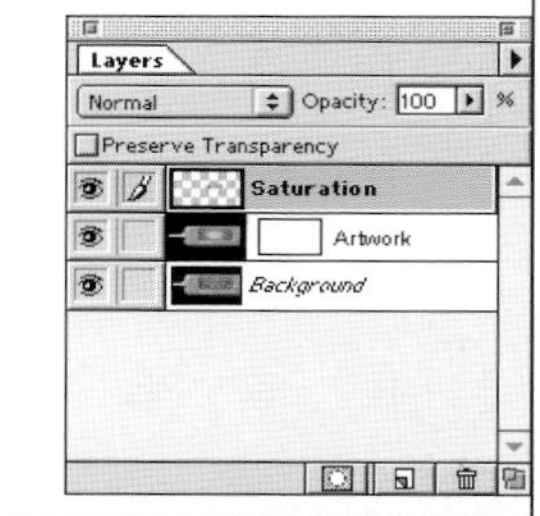

9 Finally, link and merge all on-state button layers. Now you have one layer with all the on-state buttons and one with all the off-state buttons (the background), which makes cutting up the interface a breeze.

Noreen Santini
HOT
www.hotstudio.com

Understanding Blending Mode Effects

1 **Dissolve** (right) works in much the same way as **Normal** (left), but the final color is a replacement of pixels of the base or paint color, depending on each pixel's opacity.

2 **Multiply** always produces a darker color than the original. Painting with black produces black; painting with white leaves the original color unchanged.

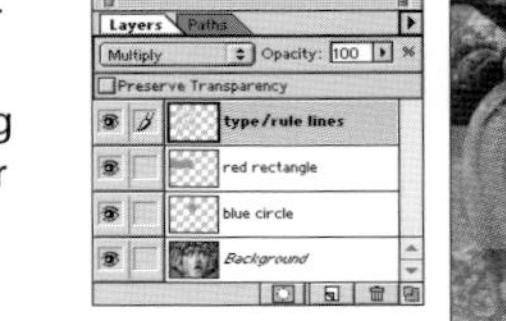

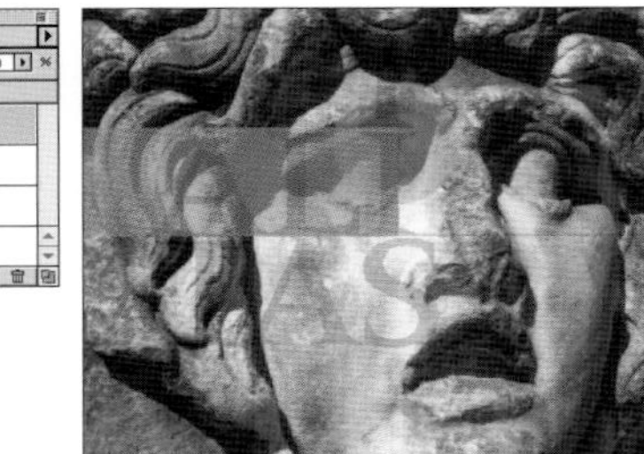

3 **Screen** is the inverse of Multiply: Painting in Screen mode always produces a lighter color, unless you paint with black, which leaves the original color unchanged.

4 **Overlay** preserves the highlights and shadows of the original color because the original color is mixed with the paint color, not replaced by it.

5 **Soft Light** produces the effect of a diffuse spotlight: If the paint color is lighter than 50 percent gray, the image is lightened. If the paint color is darker than 50 percent gray, the image is darkened.

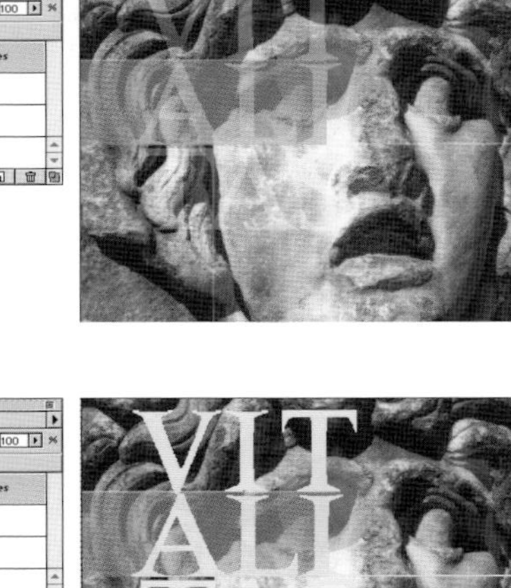

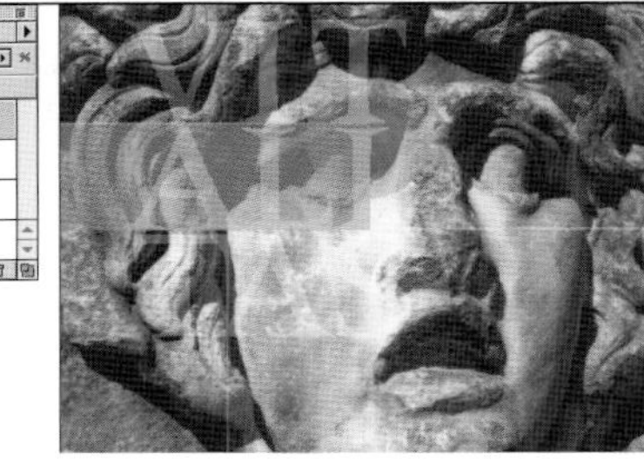

6 **Hard Light** operates like Soft Light mode, but it produces a harsher spotlight effect. Painting with pure black or white produces pure black or white, respectively.

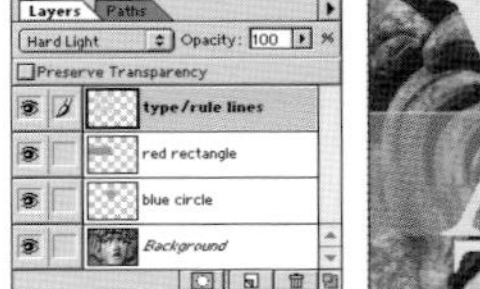

7 **Color Dodge** brightens the original color to reflect the paint color. Painting with black doesn't change the color of the original pixels.

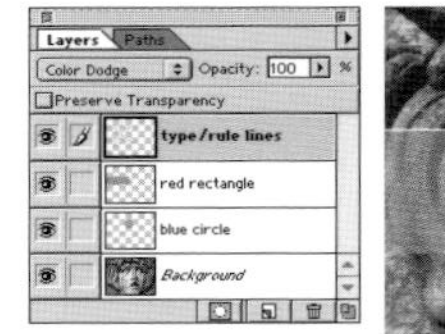

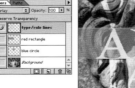

8 **Color Burn** is the inverse of Color Dodge: It darkens the original color to reflect the paint color. Painting with white leaves pixels unchanged.

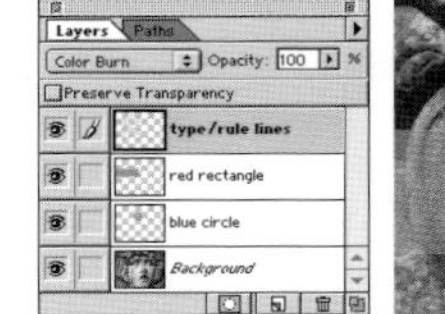

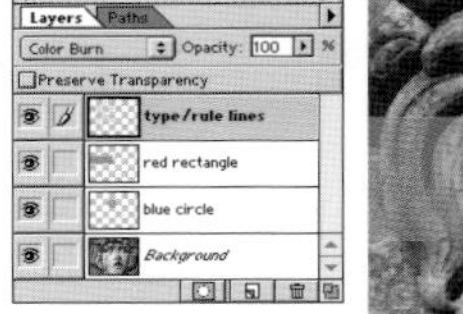

Photoshop offers more than a dozen blending modes, each of which specifies a unique way that pixels of one color are affected when painted or edited with another color. You can apply a blending mode in numerous ways, including in the Options palette when you use a brush or in the Layers palette. Before you begin mixing and matching modes, it helps to know how each works.

9 **Darken** selects whichever is darker, the original or the paint color, and changes pixels to that color. Pixels darker than the paint color do not change.

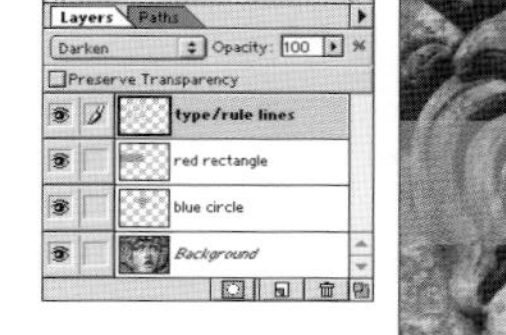

10 **Lighten** selects whichever is lighter, the original or the paint color, and changes pixels to that color. Pixels lighter than the paint color do not change.

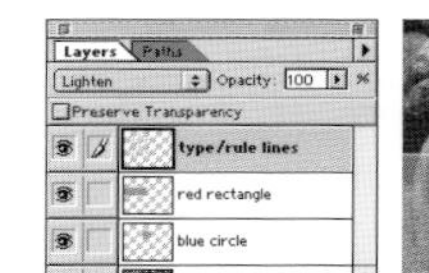

11 **Difference** subtracts the original color from the paint color or vice versa, depending on which is brighter. Blending with black leaves pixels unchanged; blending with white inverts the original pixels' color values.

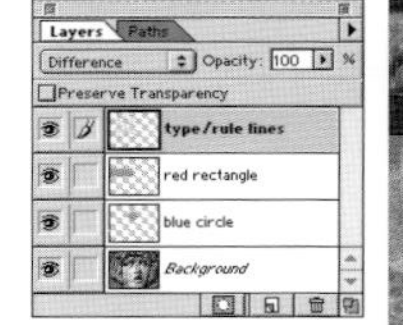

12 **Exclusion** produces an effect similar to that produced by Difference mode but with less contrast.

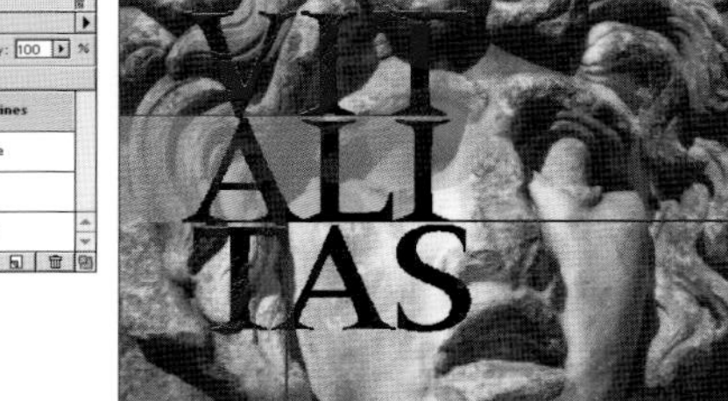

13 **Hue** produces a final color that has the hue of the paint color but the luminance and saturation of the original color.

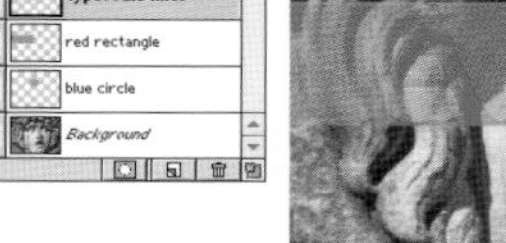

14 **Saturation** produces a final color that has the saturation of the paint color but the luminance and hue of the original color.

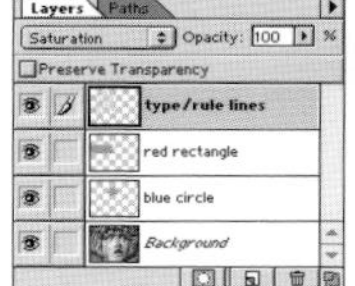
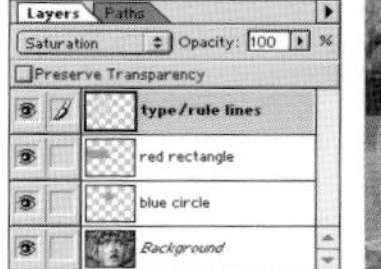

15 **Color** produces a final color that has the luminance of the original color but the hue and saturation of the paint color. It is useful for colorizing or tinting monochrome images.

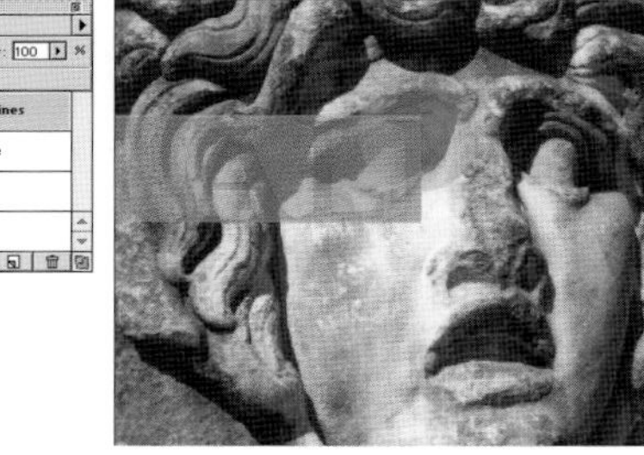

16 **Luminosity** produces a final color that has the luminance of the paint color but the hue and saturation of the original color.

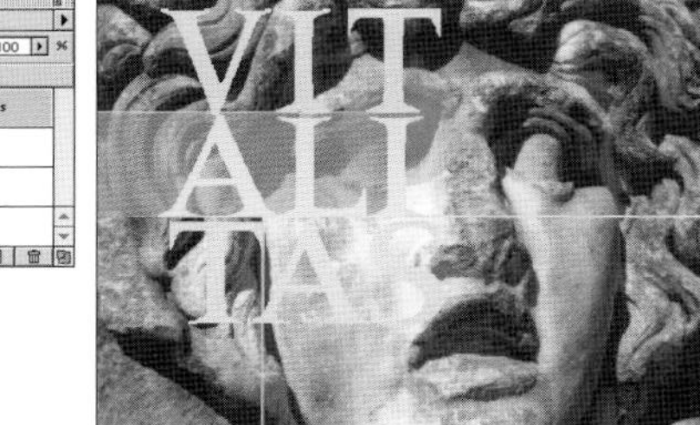

Florian Fangohr
www.hotstudio.com
artwork: ***Joachim Müller-Lancé***
www.kamedesign.com

Combining Animation and Rollovers

With a little imagination, ImageReady's animation and rollover features can be combined to create a highly graphical and animated navigational system. You can, for example, animate elements of a graphic that are triggered by mouse rollover. And when you specify a link for the slice with the rollover effect, you do double duty by making your mouseover a functional navigational system.

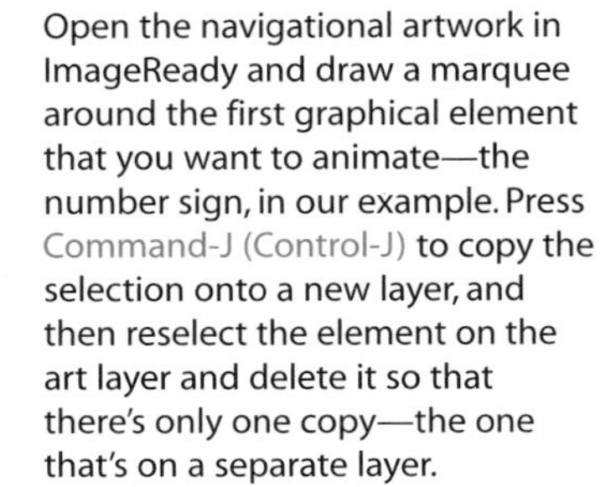

1 Open the navigational artwork in ImageReady and draw a marquee around the first graphical element that you want to animate—the number sign, in our example. Press Command-J (Control-J) to copy the selection onto a new layer, and then reselect the element on the art layer and delete it so that there's only one copy—the one that's on a separate layer.

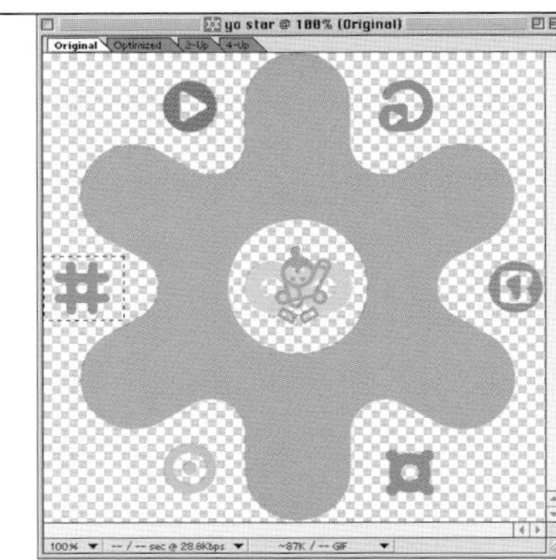

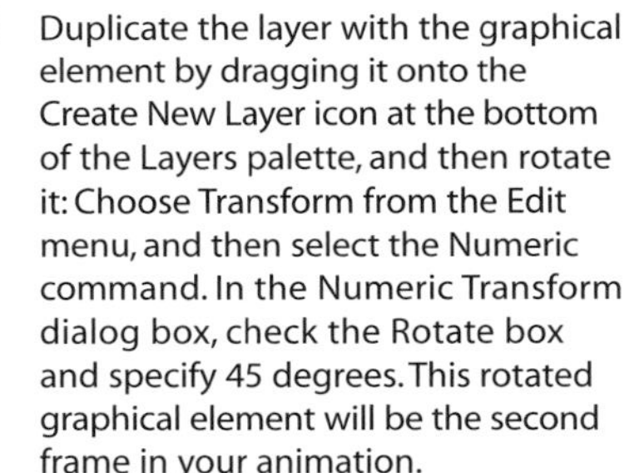

2 Duplicate the layer with the graphical element by dragging it onto the Create New Layer icon at the bottom of the Layers palette, and then rotate it: Choose Transform from the Edit menu, and then select the Numeric command. In the Numeric Transform dialog box, check the Rotate box and specify 45 degrees. This rotated graphical element will be the second frame in your animation.

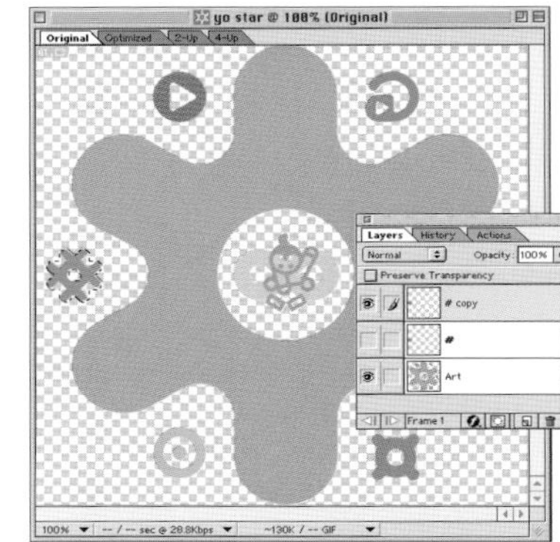

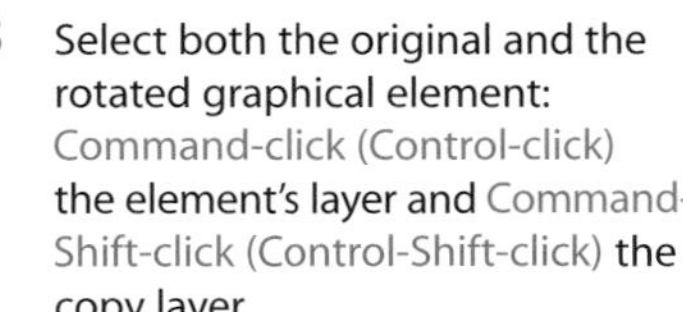

3 Select both the original and the rotated graphical element: Command-click (Control-click) the element's layer and Command-Shift-click (Control-Shift-click) the copy layer.

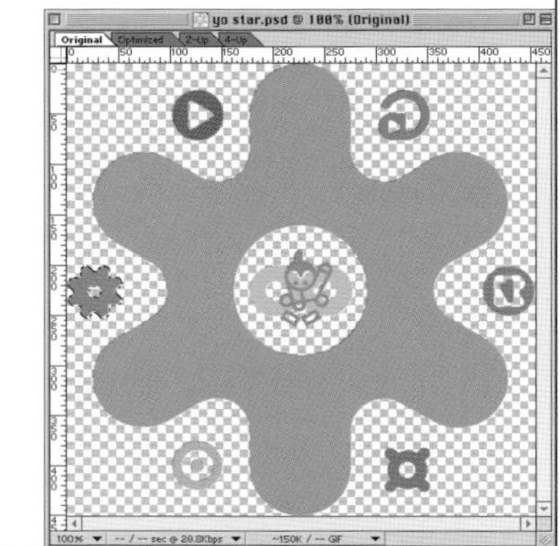

4 Choose Create Slice from Selection from the Slices menu, and then choose Trim from the Image menu to crop away all the empty pixels around the graphical element.

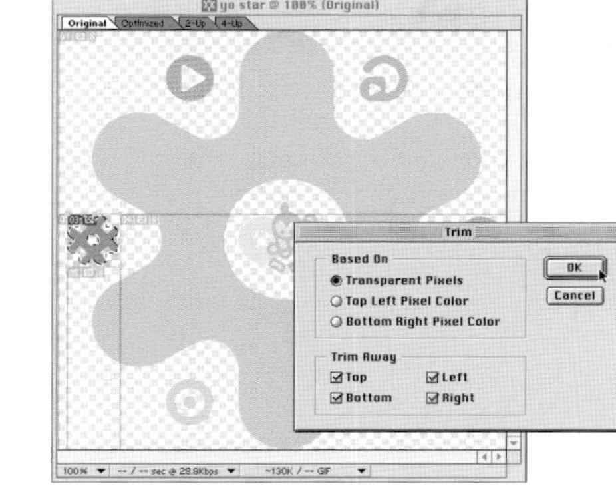

5 Now create the off and on states of the mouse rollover. Select the slice with the Slice Select tool (press "a" to get it), specify the unrotated graphic as a visible layer, and hide the rotated layer. This is the Normal (off) state of your rollover. Then click the Create New Rollover State button at the bottom of the Rollover palette.

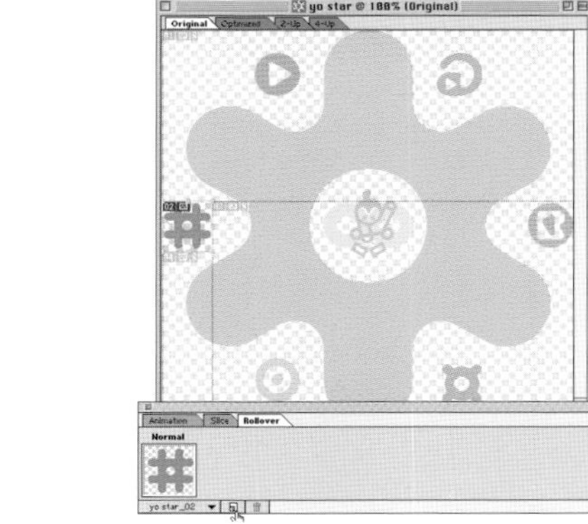

6 With the second (Over) icon selected in the Rollover palette, make the layer with the rotated element visible and hide the unrotated layer. This is your on-state graphic.

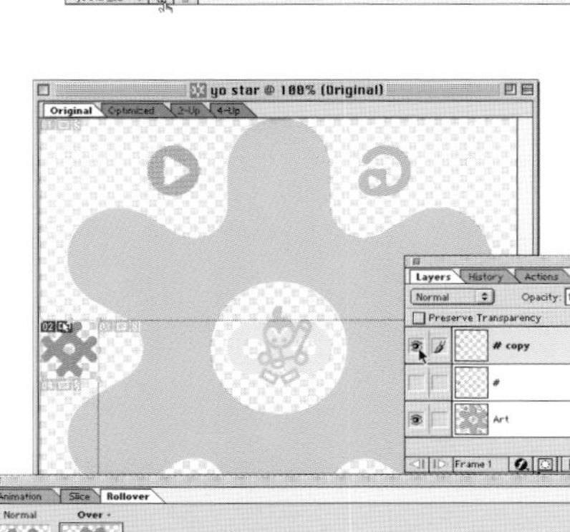

7 To animate the on state, keep the Over icon selected in the Rollover palette, and then click over to the Animation palette. In the first frame, specify the unrotated graphic and the artwork layer as the only visible layers. Create a new frame using the pop-up menu and make the rotated graphic and the artwork layer the only visible layers. Set the loop to Forever and set a time delay.

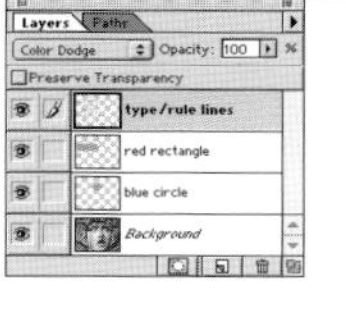

8 You can add more rollover states, such as a click state that changes the animation again when someone clicks the graphic, or you can add navigational capabilities by designating a URL link in the Slice palette.

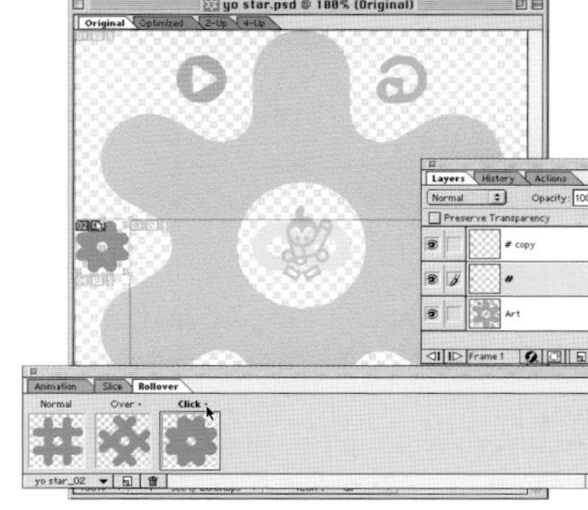

9 Repeat this process for the other icons in your image to create a fully animated navigational system. See your work in a browser at any time by choosing "Preview in" from the File menu. When satisfied, optimize the file and choose Save Optimized As from the File menu. Check the Include HTML box.

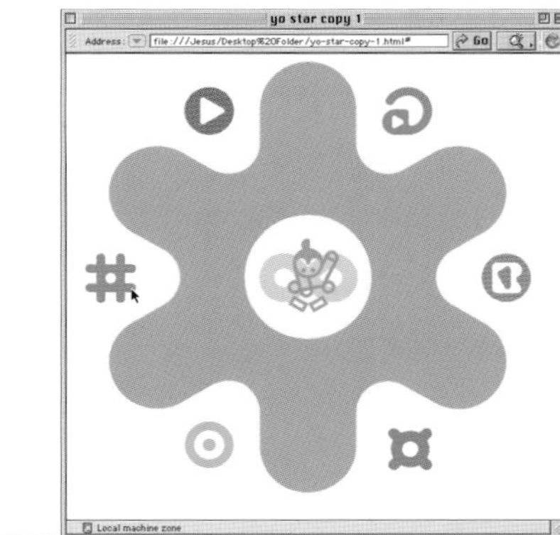

Florian Fangohr
www.untergrund.org

Designing "Remote" Rollovers

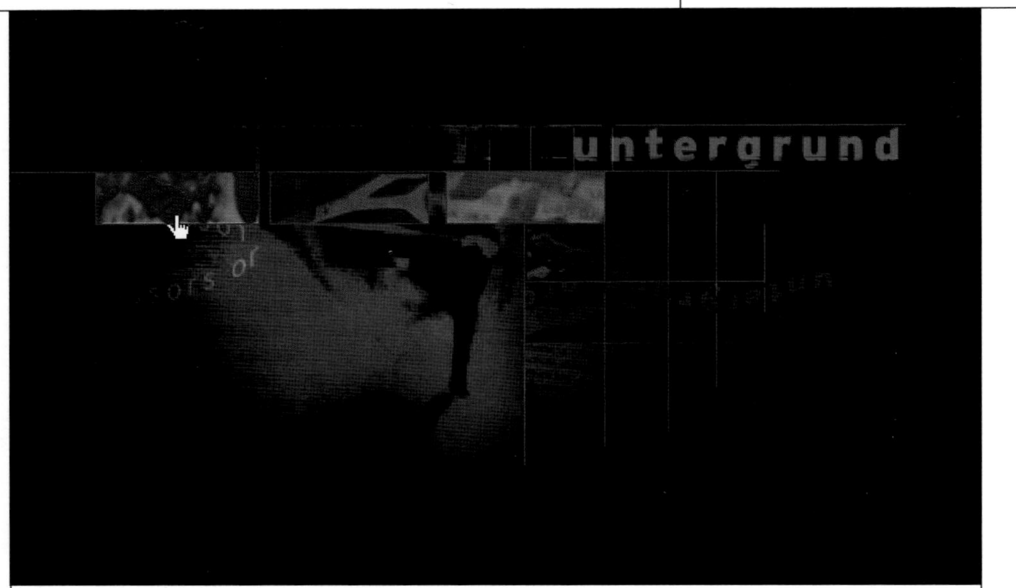

Once you get the hang of designing mouse rollovers, you can experiment with more advanced techniques. For example, you can construct a "remote" rollover—one in which the part of the image that triggers the rollover effect doesn't actually change state; rather, a slice elsewhere on the page changes state, calling attention to a link attached to that target slice. This allows you to get creative with navigation and keep visitors surprised. Start by creating the off and on state graphics for each slice that will be affected by the rollover. But don't define the rollover itself in ImageReady. Save the sliced image with HTML code, and then import them into GoLive to create your JavaScript rollover "action." HOT designer Florian Fangohr shows how he did it for his personal site, www.untergrund.org.

1 Click to select the slice that will trigger the rollover effect, the blue-tinted rock in our example, and click the Spec. tab of the Image Inspector. Set the Border to 0.

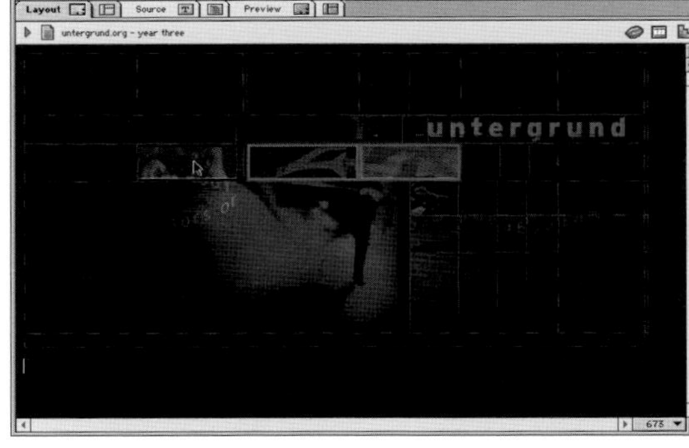

2 Name the slice that will change state during the rollover. Click that target slice, to the right of the trigger slice in our example, and type in a name in the Spec. tab in the Image Inspector.

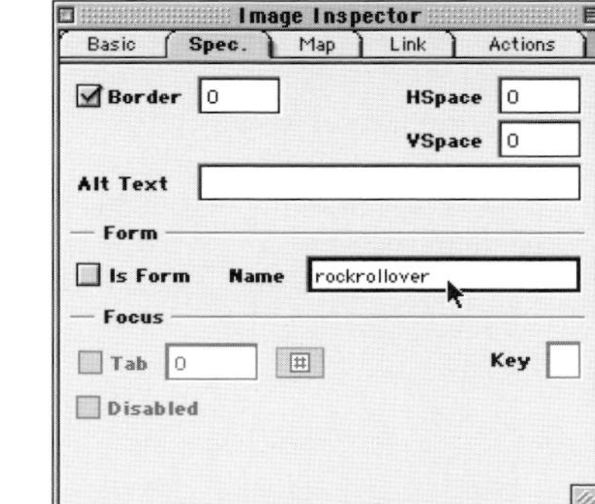

3 Click your trigger slice again, and then click the Actions tab of the Image Inspector. In the Events list, select Mouse Enter to trigger the action when a mouse pointer is moved over the blue rock slice. Then click the plus-sign button, and an action placeholder appears called None. In the Action pop-up menu, select Image, Set Image URL.

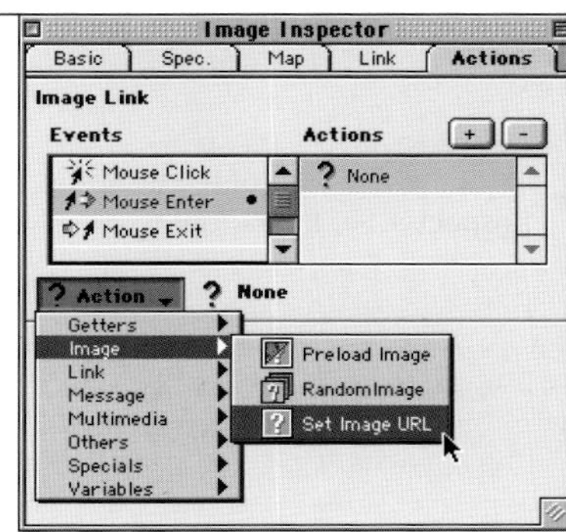

4 Click the Image pop-up menu and choose your target slice, rockrollover in our example. Finally, in the Link field, browse to select the slice that you want to be swapped during the action, the one that constitutes the on state of the rollover.

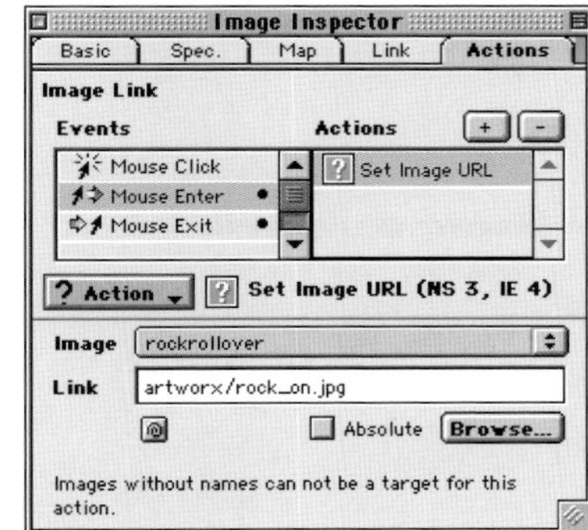

5 Finish the action by selecting Mouse Exit so that when the pointer is moved away from the trigger slice, the target slice returns to its normal state. In the Actions tab, click Mouse Exit, click the plus-sign button, and select Image, Set Image URL in the Action pop-up menu. Choose rock-rollover from the Image pop-up menu, and in the Link box, choose the file for this target slice's off state.

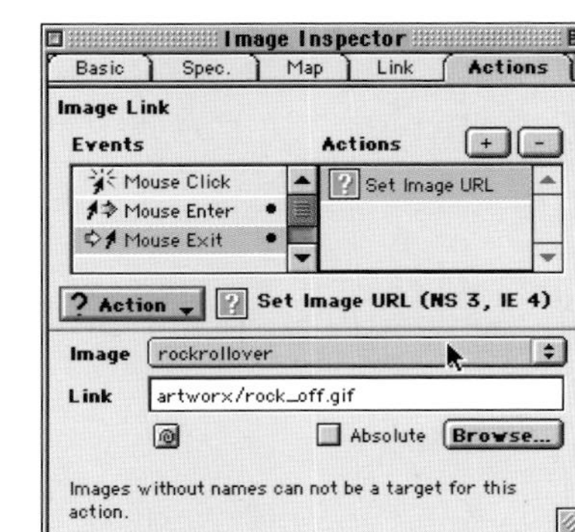

6 Repeat the process for any other remote rollovers you want to create, giving them new action names appropriately. For example, we created remote rollovers for the red-tinted scissors slice and for the yellow-tinted paper slice.

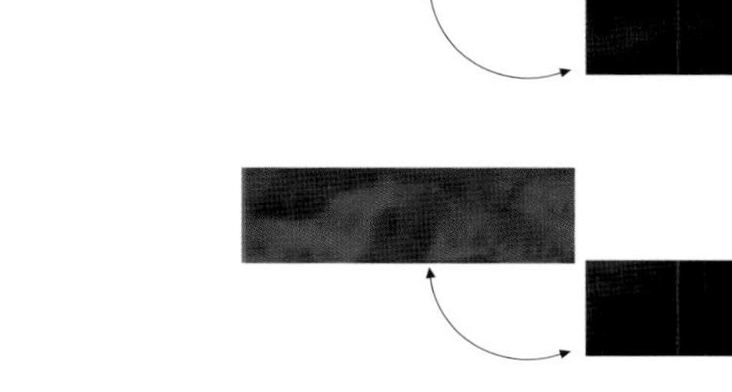

7 To add a hyperlink to the target slice, select it, click the Link tab of the Image Inspector, and enter the URL.

8 To preview your remote JavaScript rollovers in a browser, click the Show in Browser button in the toolbar.

Amy Franceschini
Futurefarmers
www.futurefarmers.com

Animating with DHTML

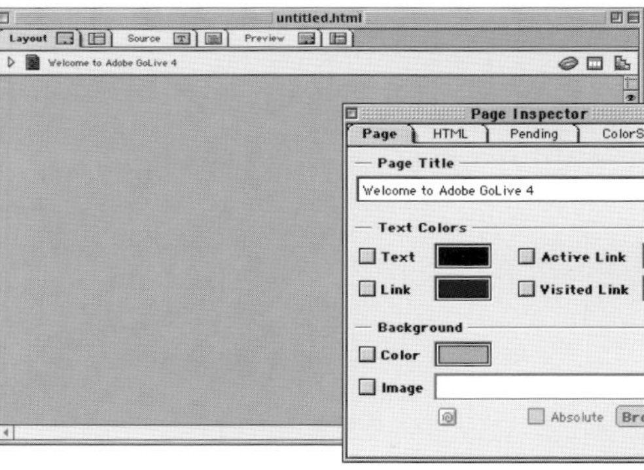

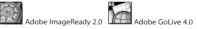

Another technique for adding animation to your Web page is to use DHTML. DHTML animations, which are supported by Netscape Navigator and Internet Explorer in versions 4.*x* and later, can be produced without programming in GoLive. The software's "floating boxes" hold images that can move along a path you specify by simply dragging the box across the page. You can use the following technique with any object you've created in a 2D or 3D application and saved in a Web-friendly format. Amy Franceschini shows how to do it using a 3D image of a boat that she created for an online game.

1 Bring your object into ImageReady and optimize it. Because we wanted the outline of our boat to be silhouetted against the other graphics on the page, we saved it in GIF format with the Transparency box checked (you could also use a JPEG graphic for this example, but you would not be able to make any part of it transparent). We deselected the Interlaced check box, and specified a Matte of None.

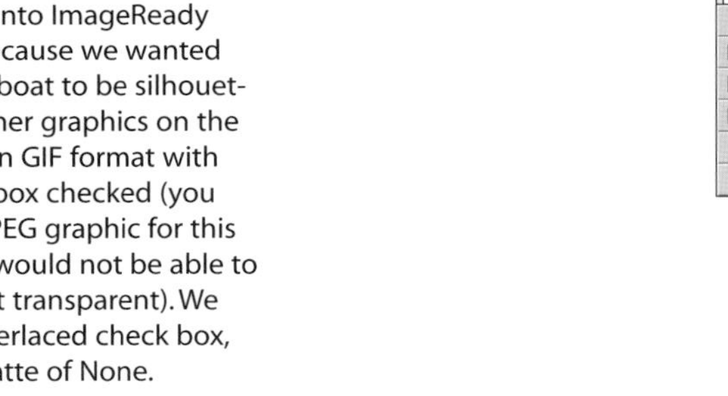

2 Prepare the page for your animation, including specifying a background color. Launch GoLive and click the Page icon in the upper-left corner of the untitled document window to view the Page Inspector.

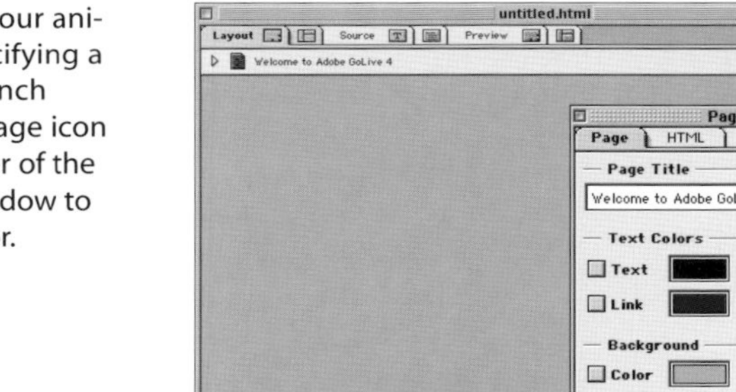

3 Check the Color box, click the well next to it, and select white (or another color if you prefer) in the Color Palette for your background. Then click and drag the swatch in the palette to the background color well in the Page Inspector. Your untitled page will turn white. You can also use a background graphic.

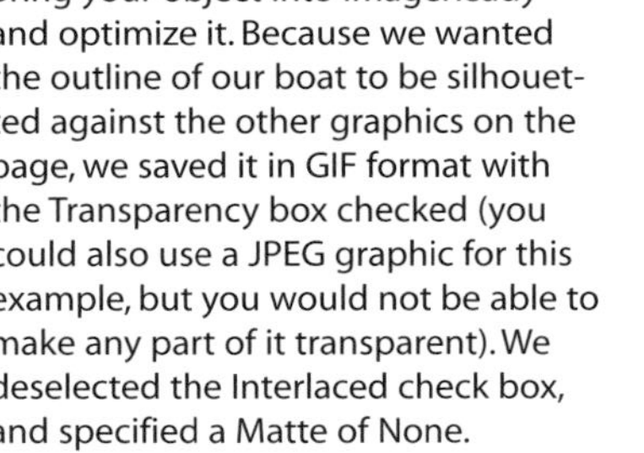

 Adobe ImageReady 2.0  Adobe GoLive 4.0

4 If you want your animated image to move over or around other images or text, import the elements you want to serve as the background. GoLive automatically places floating box graphics in a layer above other elements on the page.

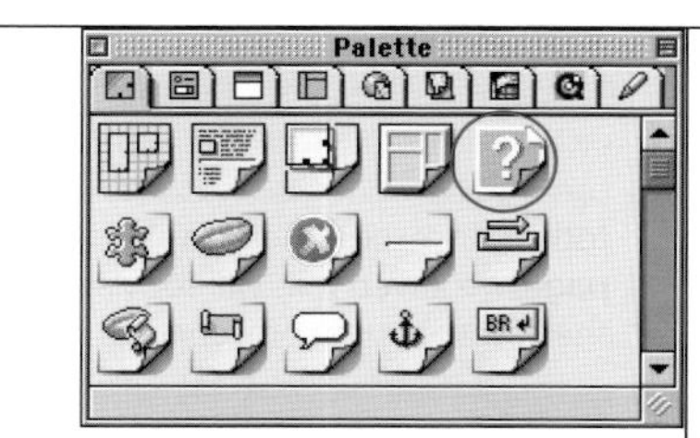

5 Now you're ready for your animated graphic, in our case, the boat. In the Basic tab of the palette, select the Floating Box icon and drag it onto the document so that the "SB" icon is at the top of the page.

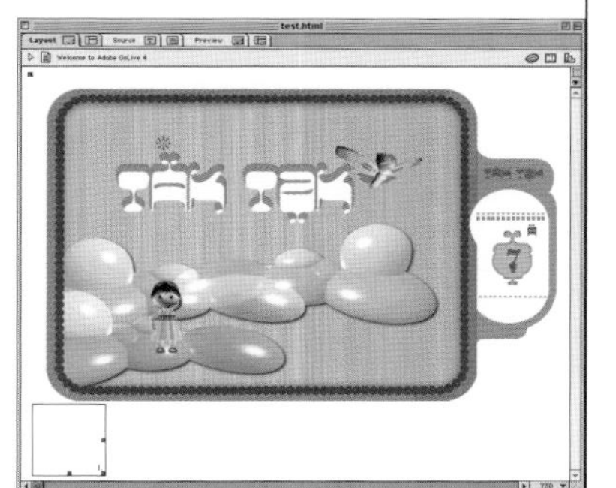

6 Drag an Image icon onto the floating box. In the Image Inspector, click the Browse button and select the source graphic object from your directory.

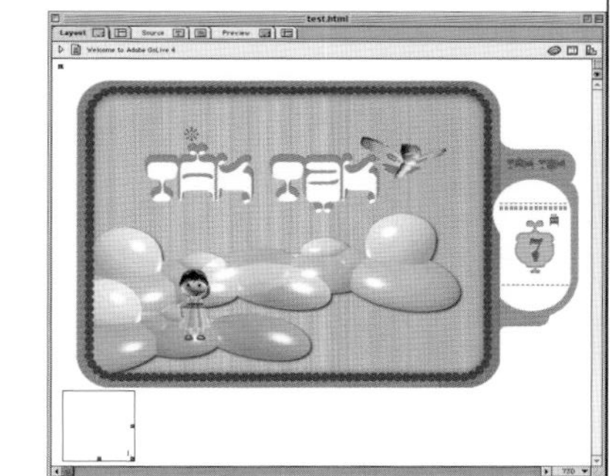

7 Deselect the graphic and click the edge of the floating box to select it instead. Move the mouse over the floating box until a left-pointing glove appears. Drag the floating box to the starting point for your animation. At the bottom of the Floating Box Inspector, click the Record button.

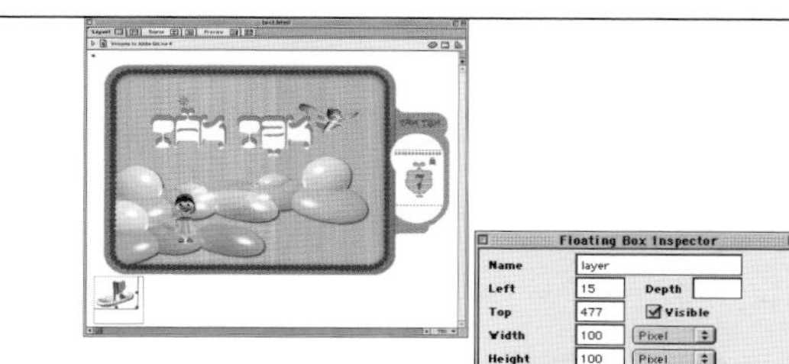

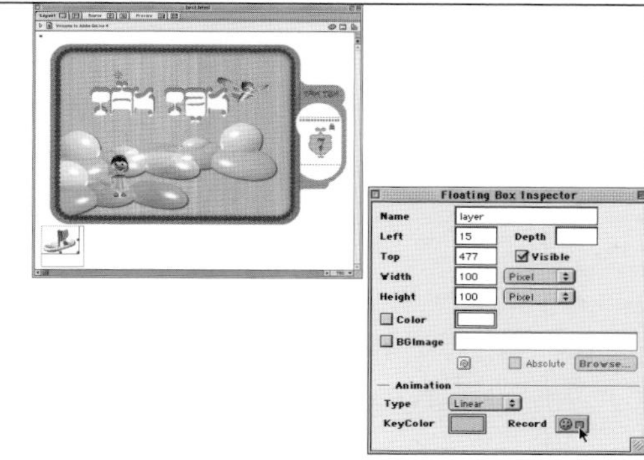

8 Back in the document window, drag the floating box along the path you wish your animated graphic to follow. Make sure that the cursor changes to the left-pointing glove before you start to drag; otherwise, you're dragging the image around within the floating box. The recording stops when you release the mouse button.

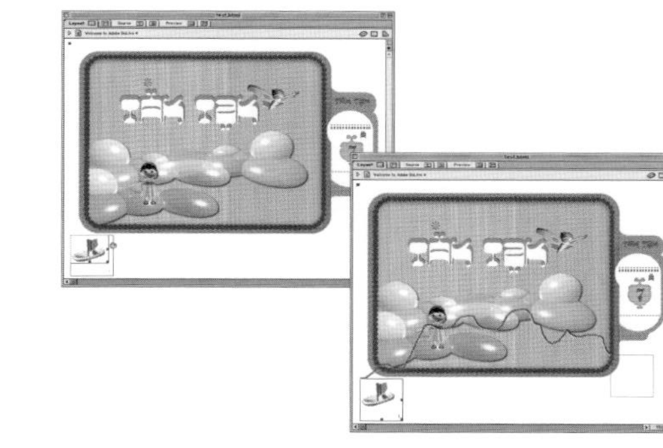

9 Before saving the animation, test it in a browser by choosing Show in Browser from the Special menu.

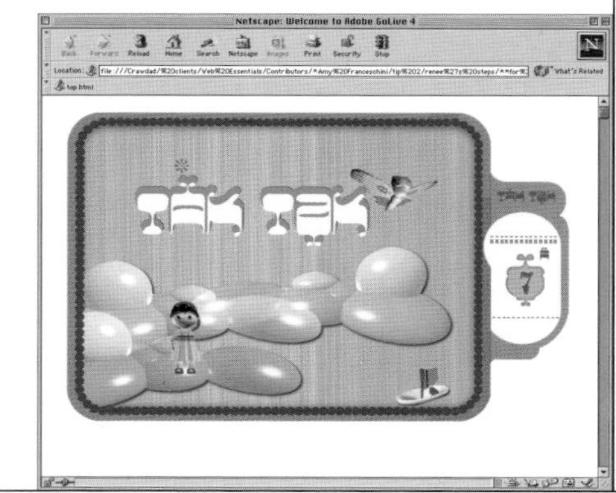

Florian Fangohr
HOT
www.hotstudio.com

Producing Animated Movies

In this tip, you will use Adobe After Effects 4.1 to animate text along a path, and render the animation as a QuickTime movie using some background scene elements that were created in Photoshop. Although Apple QuickTime is commonly used for video content, you can design animations for the Web with this format as well. QuickTime movies can be viewed by browsers on both the Macintosh and the PC, and the latest version (4.0.2) supports streaming video so browsers can begin playing the movie even before the whole file is downloaded. QuickTime gives site visitors control over the playback: They can adjust volume and playback controls, and (if the site designer allows it) they can download QuickTime movies to their hard drives to watch as frequently as they like.

1 In an open After Effects project, choose New Composition from the Composition menu. We created a composition that is 480x60 pixels, with a duration of 4 seconds, at 30fps. Name the composition, "Path Text Comp."

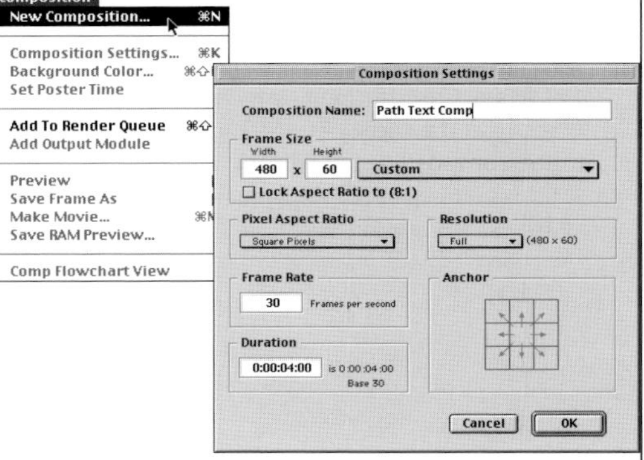

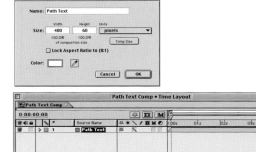

2 In your composition, choose New Solid from the Layer menu; this layer will contain text that will move along a simple path. In the Solid Settings dialog box, choose a color for the solid layer (we chose white), name the layer "Path Text," and click OK. The layer appears in the Time Layout window and the Composition window.

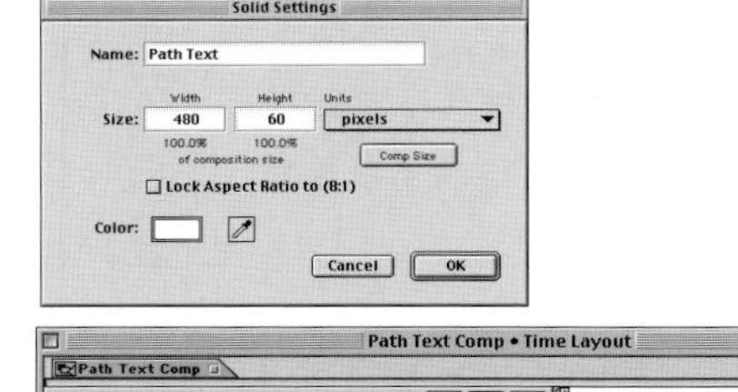

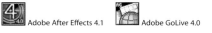

3 To import the other graphic elements, choose Import Footage Files from the File menu, and select the files you want to use. Click Done when you have imported all of the files. In our example, we used three files (which were created in Adobe Photoshop): background colors, vertical lines, and type.

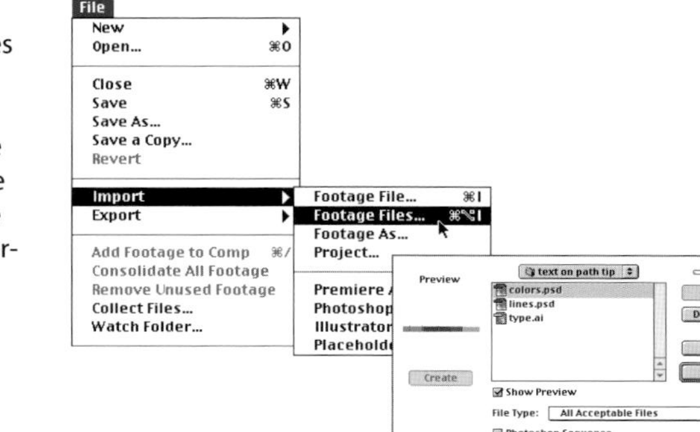

Adobe After Effects 4.1 Adobe GoLive 4.0

4 After you import the footage files, they appear in the Project window. Drag each file name to the Time Layout window to make them layers in the composition.

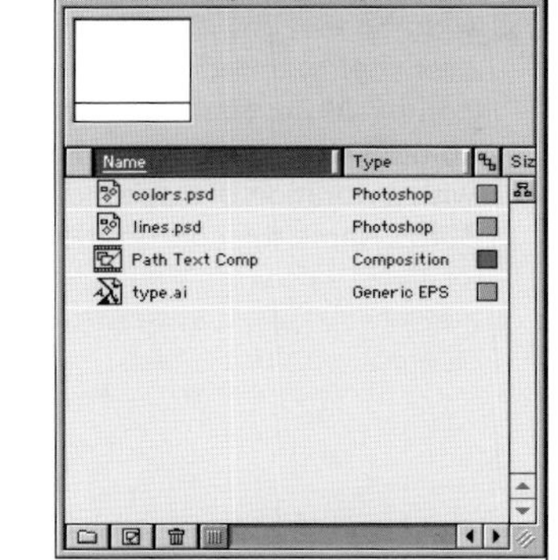

5 In the Time Layout window, arrange the order of the layers, so that the top layer appears at the top of the list. Click a layer to select it; when a layer is selected you can display and change any of its properties, such as position or scale.

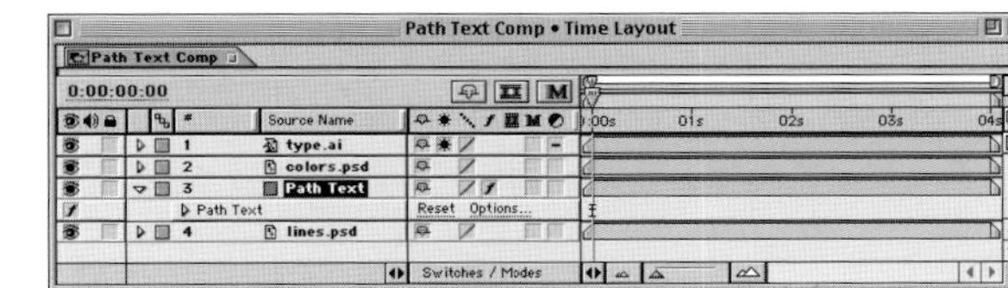

6 Now you are ready to place path text in the Path Text layer. Select the Path Text layer in the Time Layout window and choose Path Text from the Effect menu.

7 In the dialog box that appears, choose a font and style from the pulldown menus, and type the text you want in the text box. Click OK to close the dialog box. The Path Text attributes appear within the Effect Controls window.

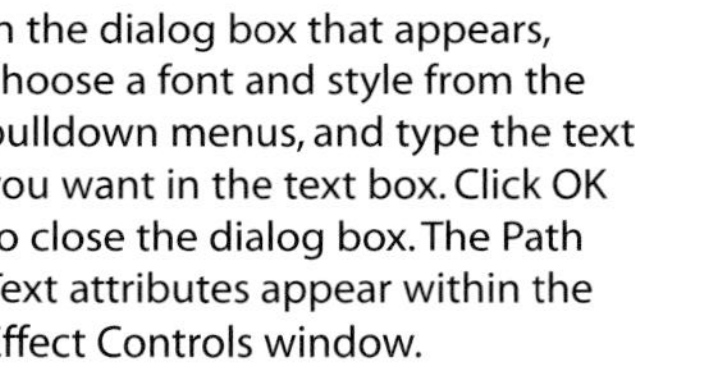

8 In the Path Text section of the Effect Controls window, customize the attributes of your text, such as font size, fill, and stroke color. In the Shape Type pulldown menu of the Path Text Effect Controls, choose Bezier.

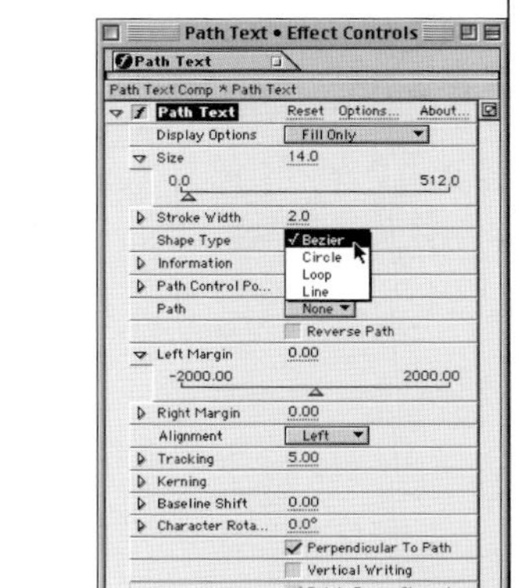

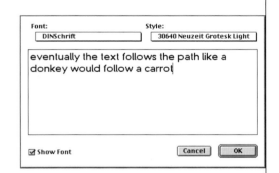

Florian Fangohr
HOT
www.hotstudio.com

CONTINUED...

Producing Animated Movies

9 In the Composition window, drag the control handles and anchor points of the Path Text to create the path you want.

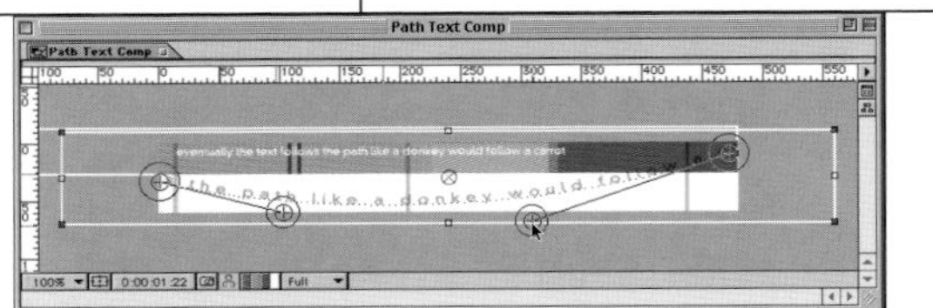

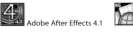

10 Now you are ready to make the text move along the path. In the Time Layout window, position the Current Time Marker at the beginning of the composition. Display the effect properties for the Path Text Layer. Click the Stopwatch icon next to the Left Margin setting of the Path Text Effect to create a keyframe, and click the number next to the setting to change its value. In the Slider Control dialog box, enter a number like –900 to place the text to the far left side of the path.

11 Reposition the Current Time Marker later in the composition. (For example, set the current time to 4:00, at the end of the composition.) Click the number next to Left Margin setting to set its value for this frame of the composition.

12 In the Slider Control dialog box, enter a number, such as 500, to place the text on the far right side of the path. After Effects creates a new keyframe for this value at this point in time. After Effects will also interpolate (or tween) the Left Margin values be-tween the first keyframe you created and the second.

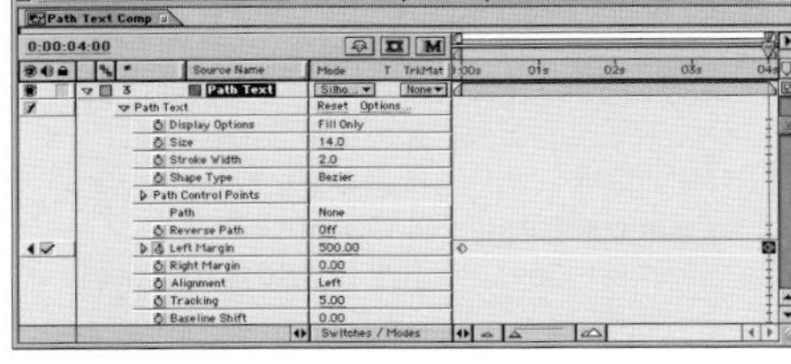

13 Check the animation by choosing a type of Preview from the Composition menu, or click the RAM Preview button in the Time Controls window. You can use the Quality Switches of a layer to change its display quality, or use the Resolution pulldown menu of the Composition window to change the overall display quality.

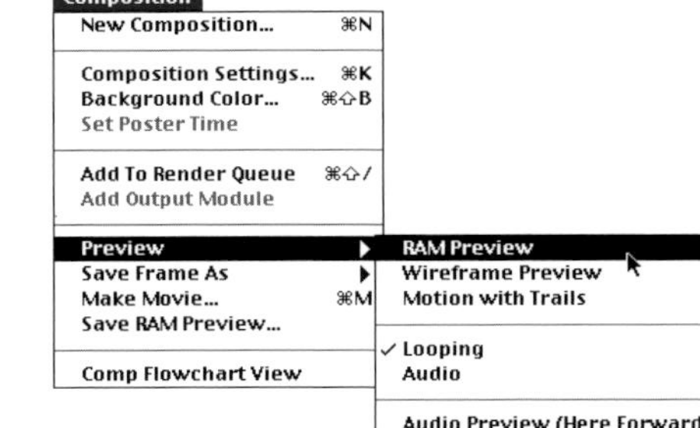

14 Animate and adjust other layers as you like. Preview your progress, as explained in the previous step. When you are satisfied with the results, render the composition by choosing Make Movie from the Composition menu. In the Save dialog box, choose a name and destination for the movie, and click Save.

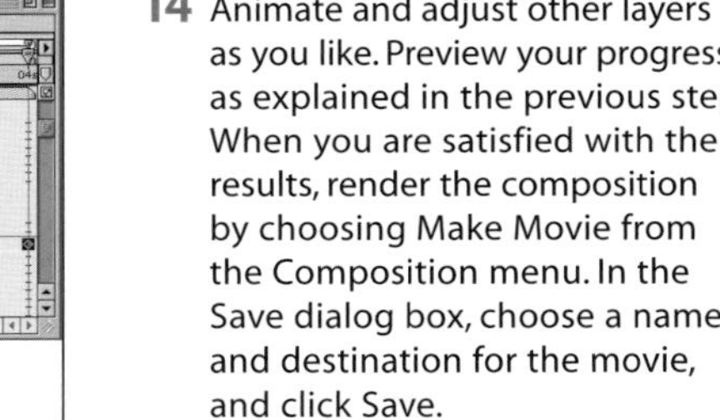

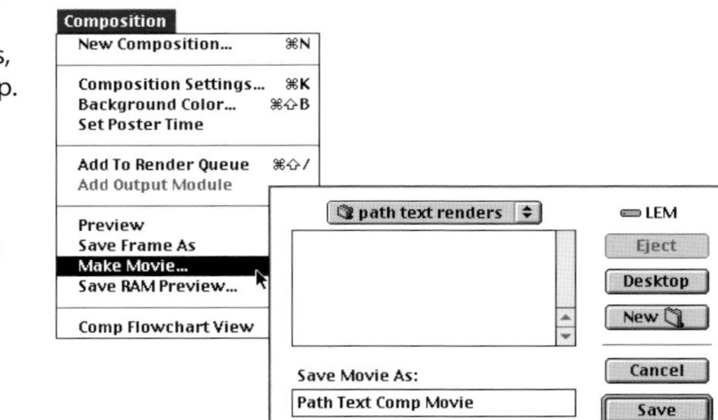

 Adobe After Effects 4.1  Adobe GoLive 4.0

15 In the Render Queue dialog box, choose output settings. For Render Settings, choose Best, or click Best to open the Output Module dialog box and choose specific settings. For Output Module, select Lossless, or click Lossless to open the Output Module dialog box and choose specific settings.

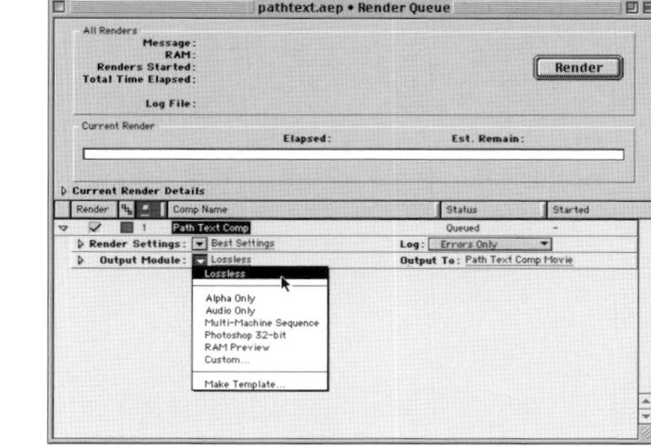

16 You can add other versions to the Render Queue by choosing Add to Render Queue in the Composition menu. When you are ready to render, click the Render button. To create a Fast Start or Streaming video, you will have to recompress the rendered movie using a program such as QuickTime Player or Media Cleaner Pro.

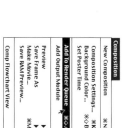

17 You can include a QuickTime movie in a HTML page in Adobe GoLive. In a GoLive site, drag a Plug-in icon from the Basic palette onto a page. In the Plug-In inspector, check the File box and browse to select the movie. Preview the page in a browser.

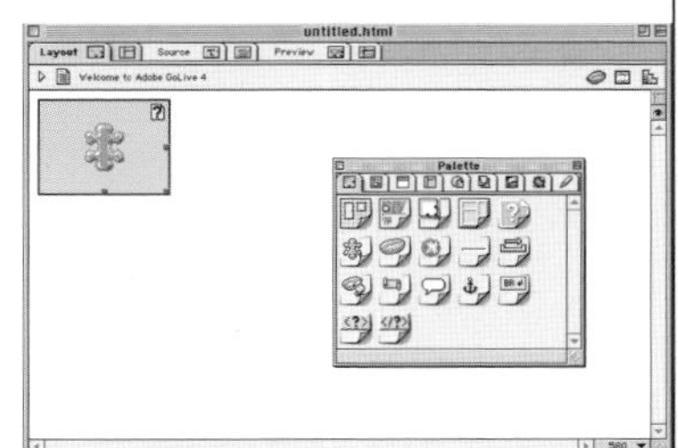

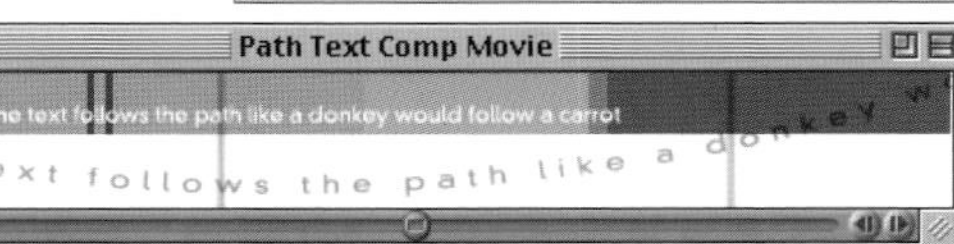

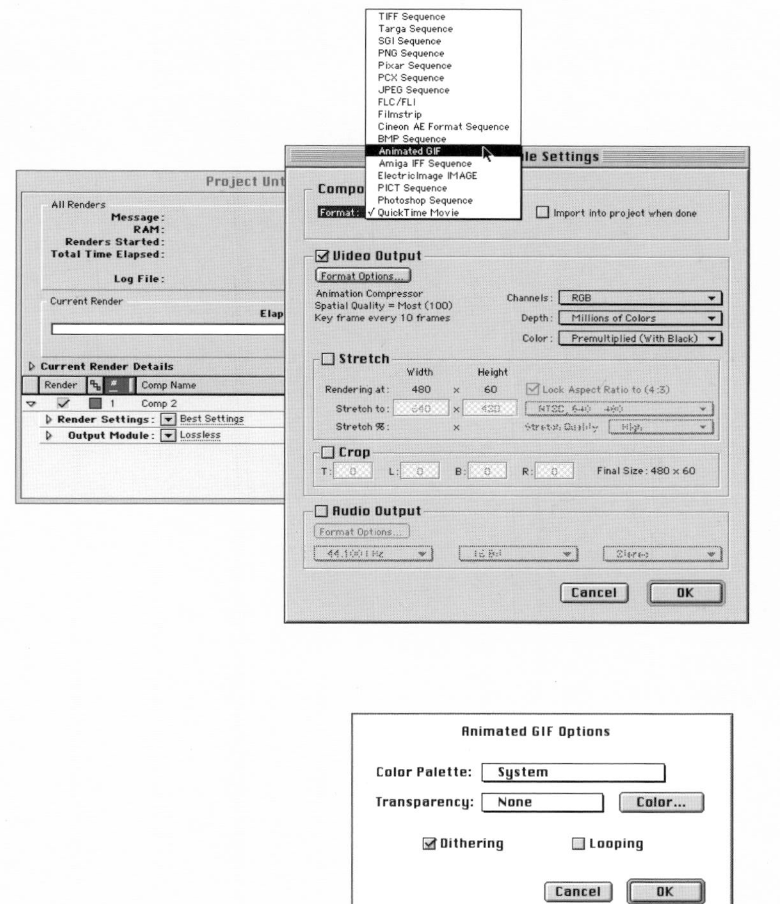

Exporting GIF Animations

You can also export animations from After Effects as animated GIFs. Click the Output Module menu and select Custom in the Render Settings dialog box. Choose Animated GIF as the format, and specify the palette and whether you want transparency.*—*Florian Fangohr

Chapter 6

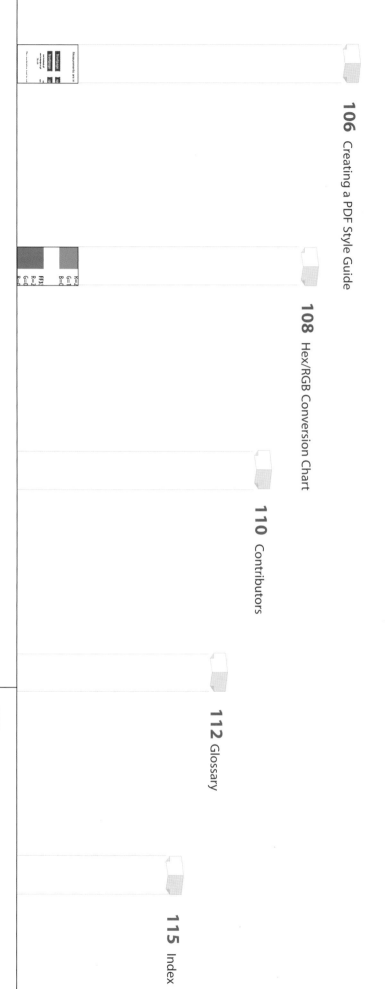

Appendices

Renee Anderson
HOT
www.hotstudio.com

Creating a PDF Style Guide

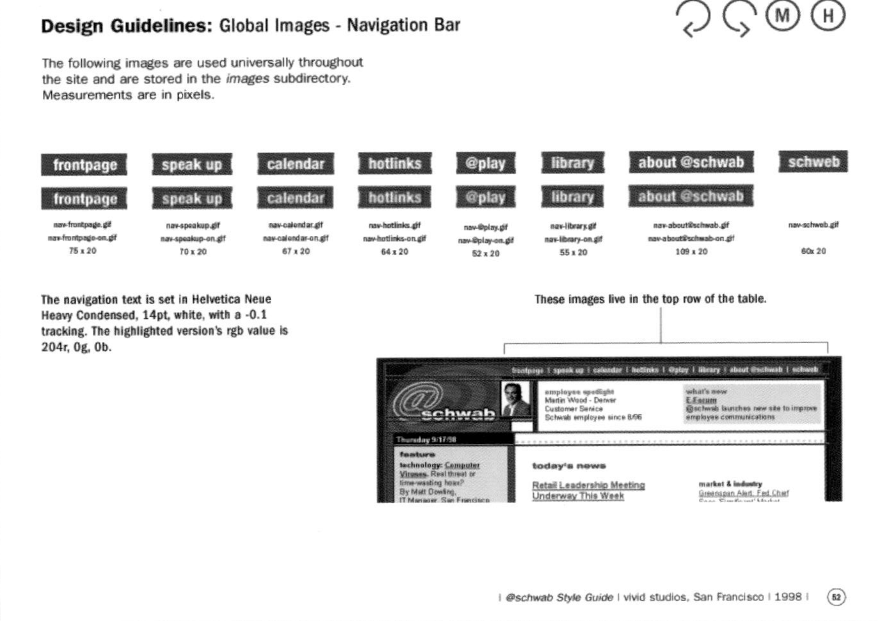

Design Guidelines: Global Images - Navigation Bar
The following images are used universally throughout the site and are stored in the images subdirectory. Measurements are in pixels.
frontpage
speak up
calendar
hotlinks
@play
library
about @schwab
schweb
75 x 20
70 x 20
67 x 20
64 x 20
52 x 20
55 x 20
109 x 20
60x 20
The navigation text is set in Helvetica Neue Heavy Condensed, 14pt, white, with a -0.1 tracking. The highlighted version's rgb value is 204r, 0g, 0b.
These images live in the top row of the table.
today's news
Retail Leadership Meeting Underway This Week
| @schwab Style Guide | vivid studios, San Francisco | 1998 |

Just because you've launched the site doesn't mean you can cash the client's check. If you're not responsible for the day-to-day upkeep of the site, you have to document the interface so that clients can publish content themselves. The best way to do that is to produce a style guide that includes information about the use and storage of graphics, fonts, colors, and other elements of the design, which the client can use to develop the site consistently. HOT uses Acrobat for client style guides because PDF is cross-platform, its compressed file size is easy to send over networks, and it allows a wide variety of links between pages and to external graphics and Web pages.

1 Take advantage of Illustrator's capability to save PDF files and design your style guide in Illustrator. It's a nice idea to include navigational icons on each page, which can be made into links in Acrobat. And be sure to draw an invisible bounding box to hold all page elements. Otherwise, the software will only save to the corners of the graphical elements.

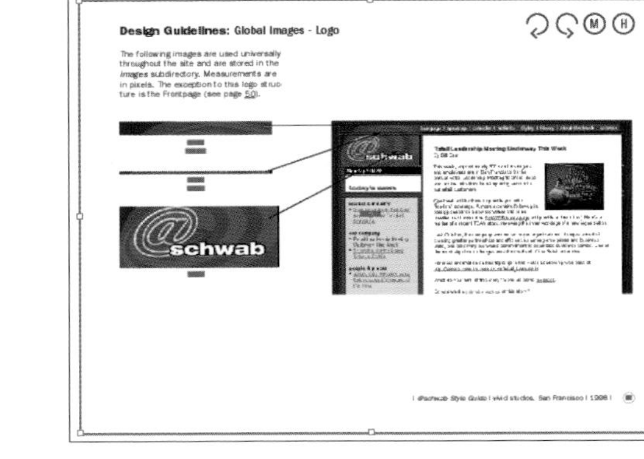

2 Lay out each page in a separate file, and save each as Acrobat PDF. Specify Web Ready as your options set in the PDF Format dialog box and indicate how you want to embed fonts and whether you want compatibility with Acrobat 3.0 or 4.0. Choose RGB as your color conversion option.

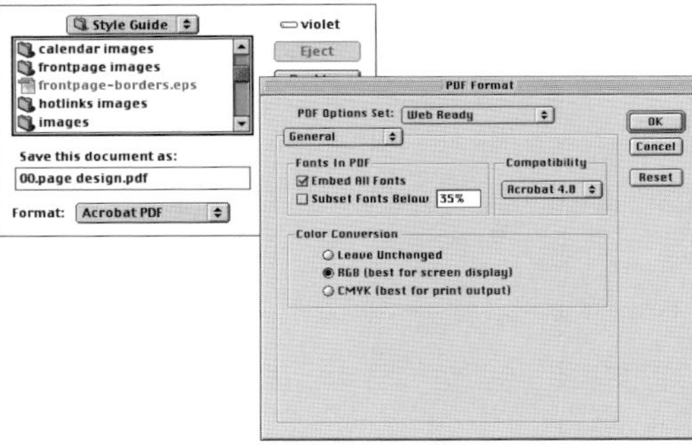

3 Open your first page in Acrobat. Choose Insert Pages from the Document menu, and select the second page in the guide. Continue to add all the other pages to your file.

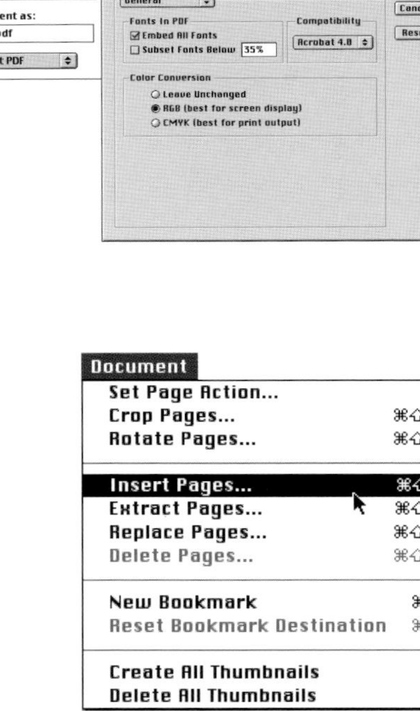

Adobe Illustrator 8.0 Adobe Acrobat 4.0

4 To link the pages by the navigational icons, click the Link tool and drag to create a box around the first icon. Specify the type of link you want in the Create Link dialog box, which appears when you release the mouse button.

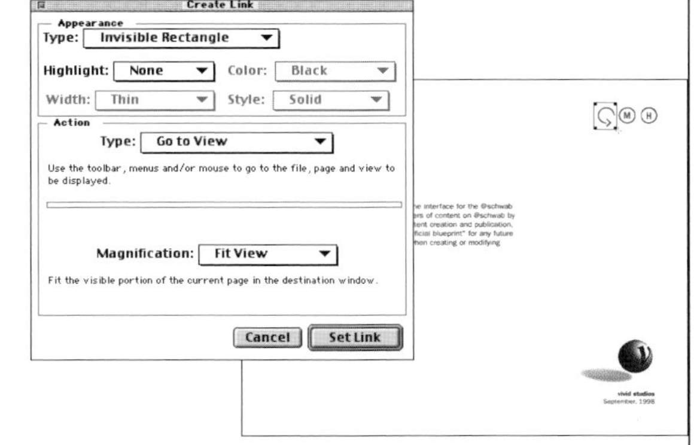

5 Before clicking the Set Link button, specify the page to which you want to link. Either advance through the document using the arrow buttons at the bottom of the window, or press Command-N (Control-N) to bring up the Go To Page dialog box.

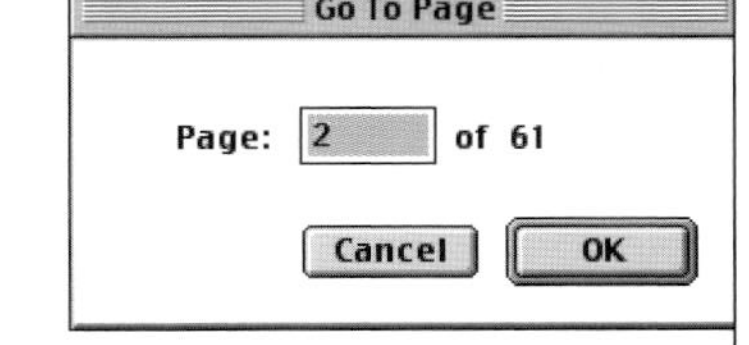

6 Make sure you're viewing both the link-from and link-to pages at the same magnification, ideally 100 percent. Otherwise, your viewers will jump between different magnifications as they click through the links. Then click Set Link. Make links for the table of contents as well.

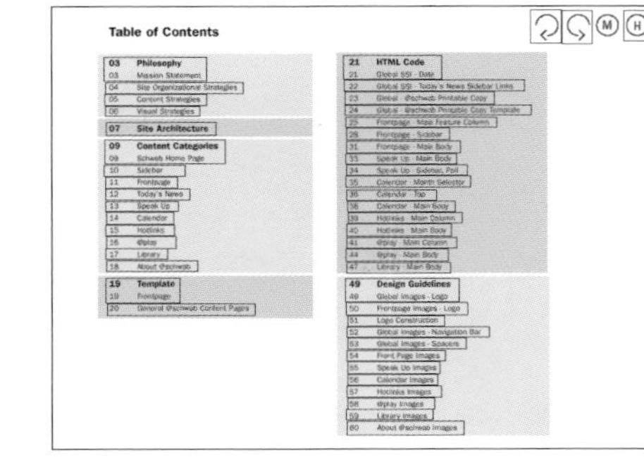

7 You can enhance links by labeling flowchart boxes in your Illustrator documents with colored, underlined type (simulating a text hyperlink) and then making the actual links for those boxes in Acrobat; by linking from your company's logo to your company's Web site; and by linking each graphic reference to its actual file so that clicking the link automatically opens the file in the creative application.

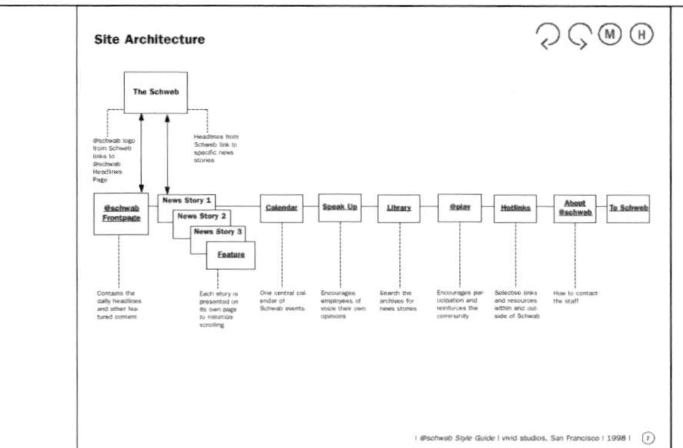

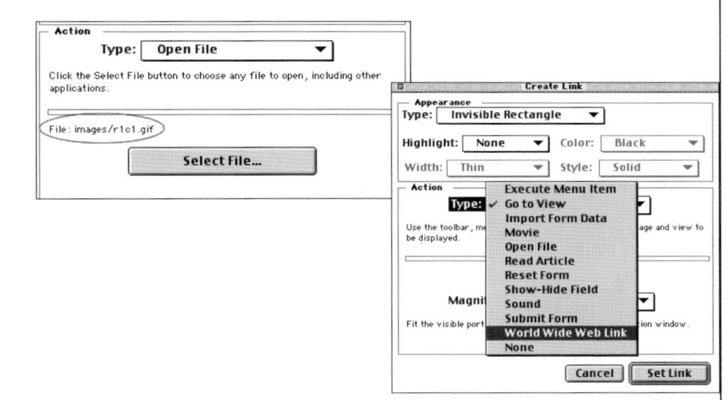

8 When you're done, choose Save As from the File menu. Check the Optimize box to compress the file.

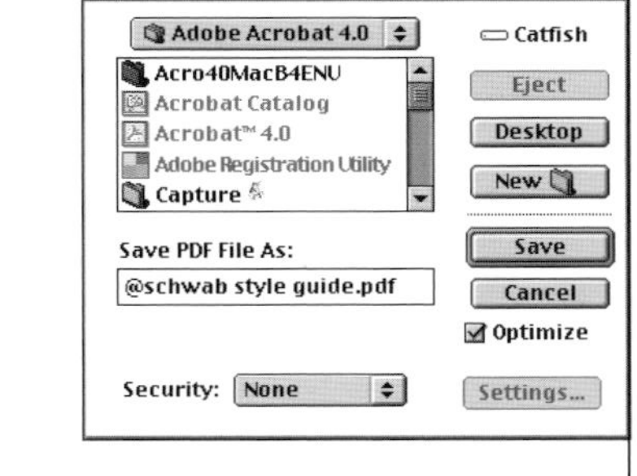

Hex/RGB Conversion Chart

FFFFCC R=255 G=255 B=204	CC6600 R=204 G=102 B=000	CC3333 R=204 G=051 B=051	FF6699 R=255 G=102 B=153	CC6699 R=204 G=102 B=153	660066 R=102 G=000 B=102	9966CC R=153 G=102 B=204	660099 R=102 G=000 B=153	6666FF R=102 G=102 B=255	3333CC R=051 G=051 B=204
FFFF99 R=255 G=255 B=153	FF9966 R=255 G=153 B=102	CC0000 R=204 G=000 B=000	FF3399 R=255 G=051 B=153	CC3399 R=204 G=051 B=153	663366 R=102 G=051 B=102	9933FF R=153 G=051 B=255	663399 R=102 G=051 B=153	003366 R=000 G=051 B=102	3300FF R=051 G=000 B=255
FFFF66 R=255 G=255 B=102	FF6633 R=255 G=102 B=051	660000 R=102 G=000 B=000	FF0099 R=255 G=000 B=153	CC0099 R=204 G=000 B=153	990099 R=153 G=000 B=153	9900FF R=153 G=000 B=255	666699 R=102 G=102 B=153	333366 R=051 G=051 B=102	0000FF R=000 G=000 B=255
FFFF33 R=255 G=255 B=051	FF6600 R=255 G=102 B=000	990000 R=153 G=000 B=000	FF3366 R=255 G=051 B=102	FF66CC R=255 G=102 B=204	993399 R=153 G=051 B=153	9966FF R=153 G=102 B=255	9999CC R=153 G=153 B=204	000066 R=000 G=000 B=102	0033FF R=000 G=051 B=255
FFFF00 R=255 G=255 B=000	FF3300 R=255 G=051 B=000	993333 R=153 G=051 B=051	FF0066 R=255 G=000 B=102	FF33CC R=255 G=051 B=204	996699 R=153 G=102 B=153	CC00FF R=204 G=000 B=255	6666CC R=102 G=102 B=204	000099 R=000 G=000 B=153	3333FF R=051 G=051 B=255
FFCC33 R=255 G=204 B=051	CC3300 R=204 G=051 B=000	990033 R=153 G=000 B=051	CC3366 R=204 G=051 B=102	FF00CC R=255 G=000 B=204	CC00CC R=204 G=000 B=204	CC33FF R=204 G=051 B=255	6633CC R=102 G=051 B=204	330099 R=051 G=000 B=153	0066FF R=000 G=102 B=255
FFCC00 R=255 G=204 B=000	FF6666 R=255 G=102 B=102	996666 R=153 G=102 B=102	CC0066 R=204 G=000 B=102	FF33FF R=255 G=051 B=255	CC33CC R=204 G=051 B=204	CC66FF R=204 G=102 B=255	6600CC R=102 G=000 B=204	333399 R=051 G=051 B=153	3366FF R=051 G=102 B=255
FFCC99 R=255 G=204 B=153	FF3333 R=255 G=051 B=051	CC6666 R=204 G=102 B=102	993366 R=153 G=051 B=102	FF00FF R=255 G=000 B=255	CC66CC R=204 G=102 B=204	CC99FF R=204 G=153 B=255	9999FF R=153 G=153 B=255	003399 R=000 G=051 B=153	6699FF R=102 G=153 B=255
FFCC66 R=255 G=204 B=102	FF0033 R=255 G=000 B=051	CC9999 R=204 G=153 B=153	990066 R=153 G=000 B=102	FF66FF R=255 G=102 B=255	CC99CC R=204 G=153 B=204	000033 R=000 G=000 B=051	CCCCFF R=204 G=204 B=255	0000CC R=000 G=000 B=204	0099FF R=000 G=153 B=255
FF9900 R=255 G=153 B=000	FF0000 R=255 G=000 B=000	FF9999 R=255 G=153 B=153	660033 R=102 G=000 B=051	FF99FF R=255 G=153 B=255	9900CC R=153 G=000 B=204	330033 R=051 G=000 B=051	6600FF R=102 G=000 B=255	3300CC R=051 G=000 B=204	3399FF R=051 G=153 B=255
FF9933 R=255 G=153 B=051	CC0033 R=204 G=000 B=051	FFCCCC R=255 G=204 B=204	FF99CC R=255 G=153 B=204	FFCCFF R=255 G=204 B=255	9933CC R=153 G=051 B=204	330066 R=051 G=000 B=102	6633FF R=102 G=051 B=255	0033CC R=000 G=051 B=204	99CCFF R=153 G=204 B=255

The chart below shows the 216 Web-safe colors with both their RGB and hexadecimal values specified. Note that while all of the numeric values are accurate, some of these colors fall outside of the CMYK spectrum rendered by the offset printing process. Therefore, the color swatches that appear here aren't necessarily representative of how they look onscreen.

Hexadecimal/RGB Value	
FF = 255	66 = 102
CC = 204	33 = 051
99 = 153	00 = 000

3366CC R=051 G=102 B=204	99FFFF R=153 G=255 B=255	336666 R=051 G=102 B=102	66CC99 R=102 G=204 B=153	66FF99 R=102 G=255 B=153	33CC66 R=051 G=204 B=102	66FF00 R=102 G=255 B=000	99CC66 R=153 G=204 B=102	666633 R=102 G=102 B=051	000000 R=000 G=000 B=000
0066CC R=000 G=102 B=204	33FFFF R=051 G=255 B=255	006666 R=000 G=102 B=102	33CC99 R=051 G=204 B=153	339900 R=051 G=153 B=000	00CC66 R=000 G=204 B=102	99FF33 R=153 G=255 B=051	99CC33 R=153 G=204 B=051	666600 R=102 G=102 B=000	333333 R=051 G=051 B=051
006699 R=000 G=102 B=153	66FFFF R=102 G=255 B=255	003333 R=000 G=051 B=051	00CC99 R=000 G=204 B=153	339933 R=051 G=153 B=051	66CC66 R=102 G=204 B=102	99FF00 R=153 G=255 B=000	99CC00 R=153 G=204 B=000	CC9966 R=204 G=153 B=102	666666 R=102 G=102 B=102
336699 R=051 G=102 B=153	00FFFF R=000 G=255 B=255	003300 R=000 G=051 B=000	00FFCC R=000 G=255 B=204	009933 R=000 G=153 B=051	00FF00 R=000 G=255 B=000	99FF66 R=153 G=255 B=102	99CC99 R=153 G=204 B=153	CC9933 R=204 G=153 B=051	999999 R=153 G=153 B=153
6699CC R=102 G=153 B=204	00CCCC R=000 G=204 B=204	333300 R=051 G=051 B=000	66FFCC R=102 G=255 B=204	009900 R=000 G=153 B=000	33FF33 R=051 G=255 B=051	CCFF00 R=204 G=255 B=000	CCCC99 R=204 G=204 B=153	CC9900 R=204 G=153 B=000	CCCCCC R=204 G=204 B=204
3399CC R=051 G=153 B=204	33CCCC R=051 G=204 B=204	336633 R=051 G=102 B=051	33FFCC R=051 G=255 B=204	66CC33 R=102 G=204 B=051	66FF66 R=102 G=255 B=102	CCFF33 R=204 G=255 B=051	CCCC66 R=204 G=204 B=102	993300 R=153 G=051 B=000	FFFFFF R=255 G=255 B=255
0099CC R=000 G=153 B=204	66CCCC R=102 G=204 B=204	336600 R=051 G=102 B=000	99FFCC R=153 G=255 B=204	66CC00 R=102 G=204 B=000	33FF66 R=051 G=255 B=102	CCFF66 R=204 G=255 B=102	CCCC00 R=204 G=204 B=000	996600 R=153 G=102 B=000	
00CCFF R=000 G=204 B=255	99CCCC R=153 G=204 B=204	006633 R=000 G=102 B=051	CCFFCC R=204 G=255 B=204	33CC00 R=051 G=204 B=000	00FF66 R=000 G=255 B=102	CCFF99 R=204 G=255 B=153	CCCC33 R=204 G=204 B=051	996633 R=153 G=102 B=051	
33CCFF R=051 G=204 B=255	009999 R=000 G=153 B=153	006600 R=000 G=102 B=000	99FF99 R=153 G=255 B=153	33CC33 R=051 G=204 B=051	00FF33 R=000 G=255 B=051	669966 R=102 G=153 B=102	999966 R=153 G=153 B=102	663300 R=102 G=051 B=000	
66CCFF R=102 G=204 B=255	339999 R=051 G=153 B=153	339966 R=051 G=153 B=102	33FF99 R=051 G=255 B=153	00CC33 R=000 G=204 B=051	33FF00 R=051 G=255 B=000	669900 R=102 G=153 B=000	999933 R=153 G=153 B=051	663333 R=102 G=051 B=051	
CCFFFF R=204 G=255 B=255	669999 R=102 G=153 B=153	009966 R=000 G=153 B=102	00FF99 R=000 G=255 B=153	00CC00 R=000 G=204 B=000	66FF33 R=102 G=255 B=051	669933 R=102 G=153 B=051	999900 R=153 G=153 B=000	330000 R=051 G=000 B=000	

Contributors

Maria Giudice is founder and creative director of HOT Studio, Inc., a San Francisco-based design agency committed to making information accessible and understandable across multiple media. With a design career spanning more than a decade, Maria is an established speaker, educator, and author. *Web Design Essentials* is Maria's third book on Web design and technology, having also coauthored the award-winning first and second editions of *Elements of Web Design*. Maria teaches part-time at City College of San Francisco and lives in the city with her husband, Scott Allen.

Anita Dennis is a freelance writer and editor in San Francisco who has covered electronic publishing, including Web design and digital printing and prepress, since 1993. Her work has appeared in *Publish*, *eMediaweekly*, the *Seybold Report on Internet Publishing*, the *Seybold Report on Publishing Systems*, *i/o*, *PC/Computing*, the *San Francisco Examiner*, the *New York Daily News*, and *Penthouse*. Anita has a masters in journalism from Columbia University and spent two years as a police and political reporter at a daily newspaper before becoming a technology journalist.

Amy Franceschini founded Futurefarmers, a San Francisco-based multimedia design company, in 1995. Futurefarmers has an award-winning Web site (www.futurefarmers.com) and has developed projects for a wide variety of clients, including Weiden & Kennedy (Nike), NEC, Autodesk, MSNBC, Dreamworks, and Levi Strauss. Amy also cofounded Atlas (www.atlasmagazine.com), an online magazine that was the first Web site to become part of the permanent collection of the San Francisco Museum of Modern Art. Amy is currently working on a traveling multimedia installation that can be accessed at www.nutrishnia.com.

Jeremy Tai Abbett was born in Vinh Long, Vietnam, and grew up in the Midwest, Texas, and Minneapolis. He attended the University of Wisconsin-Stout and spent 1994 as an exchange student at the Fachhochschule Hildesheim/Holzminden in Germany. In 1996 he cofounded Fork Unstable Media in Hamburg, Germany, with an American friend, David Linderman.

Renee Anderson has been a graphic designer since 1995, specializing in design, production, project management, and art direction for print- and Web-based projects. She earned a masters in graphic design from San Francisco State University in 1999 while working at HOT. She is a painter, dreams about urban renovation, and fights for a car-free society.

Hyland Baron joined HOT as director of operations in March 1999. Previously, she led the *East Bay Express* newspaper's transition from mechanical to digital production. She has a degree in communication design from Parsons School of Design and spends her free time designing affordable, community-oriented housing for artists in Oakland.

Tom Bray is an experience designer for www.zimba.com, an online contact management service. A San Francisco resident, Tom was previously senior Web developer at Addictive Media, where he produced design documentation, created Web interfaces, programmed interactivity, and implemented e-commerce sites.

Geoffrey Brown has been designing Web pages since 1994. His designs have been featured by Netscape, Microsoft Network, Projectcool, and Cool Site of the Day, as well as in a number of design publications. He is director of Web and new media development at deerfield.com, and he is lead designer for the Web zine ZeroZine (www.zerozine.com).

Casey Caston is a graphic designer and production specialist at CNET, where he specializes in Web marketing design and GIF animation. Casey also produces the Web zine Fear Not Drowning (www.drowning.com) and has lectured about Photoshop at the Web Builder Live conference. His production advice has been featured in several design books.

Anne-Marie Concepción founded Chicago-based Seneca Design & Consulting in 1987. She has been a systems consultant, software trainer, and Mac therapist; and she teaches courses in Photoshop, Illustrator, GoLive, and Web site design, production, and marketing. She is a frequent lecturer and has written articles for many graphic arts publications.

Melissa Crowley is art director at Fluid Design + Development in San Francisco. She is also the creator of www.redbean.com, an award-winning explorative design site. She began her career in Sydney, Australia, focusing on print media and typography. Her studies have spanned multiple facets of art and design.

Katrin Eismann is a digital artist, author, and educator. She is coauthor of *Photoshop Studio Secrets, 2nd edition*, and *Web Design Studio Secrets* (IDG Books) as well as *Real World Digital Photography* (Peachpit Press).

In 1999, Katrin was named a Vanguard of Visual Computing by SGI, and she chaired two Thunder Lizard Productions conferences on Photoshop.

Michael Everitt is president of Informativity, an interface and graphic design company that has been knee-deep in form and content since 1991. Informativity is one of those little dots in Venn circle diagrams where interactivity, information, and creativity overlap.

Florian Fangohr began Web design in 1996 in Hamburg, Germany. His areas of expertise include information architecture and interface, usability, and motion design. In 1998, he joined HOT, where his talents have inspired projects for Bank of America and Agfa.

David Herman is Adobe product pupport engineer for Photoshop, ImageReady, and ImageStyler. He is the creator of the PhotoBooks Web site (www.jetcity.com/~davidh/psbooks/photobooks.html), a comprehensive source of reviews and information on books about Photoshop and Web graphics, and he is the founder and webmaster of The Photoshop Zone (www.photoshopzone.com). He lives in Seattle.

Susan Horovitz is an instructional design manager for Adobe. She managed the design and content for *Adobe GoLive Classroom in a Book*, *Adobe Illustrator Classroom in a Book*, and *Adobe Acrobat Classroom in a Book*. Susan contributes regularly to the Adobe Web site and has a degree in design from the University of California, Davis.

Julia Hummelt was born in Stuttgart, Germany, grew up in Bavaria and Austria, and has a BFA from the Academy of Art College in San Francisco. Her expertise and focus is in Web design, animation, and motion graphics, and she designs for and consults with a variety of U.S. and international clients.

Irv Kanode, an Adobe GoLive product support engineer, started working on the Web in the days of Netscape Navigator 1.0. His first project was a high-school textbook created using HTML and plug-ins delivered via CD-ROM and the Web. He joined GoLive technical support in June 1997 and has helped many graphic designers get their first pages "live" on the Web.

Sandra Kelch is a San Francisco Bay Area illustrator and graphic designer. She was educated at The Cooper Union School of Art and the Cranbrook Academy of Art. Although her background is mainly in design, these days Sandra focuses on editorial illustration, which is her passion.

Frank Kolodziej wanted to draw comic books but instead taught himself JavaScript, Perl, Flash, and DHTML. The creative director of spyplane, a new media design firm in San Francisco, hired Frank in 1998 after seeing his personal Web site, www.cacophony.com. Since then Frank has been working with such clients as match.com, Novell, and Sony.

Jason Kottke is a Web designer for B-Swing in Minneapolis. He produces www.0sil8.com, which has received a number of accolades: It is reviewed in the book *Web Design 100*, which features the best 100 sites chosen by the Japanese design firm Kinotrope, and it won the Best Personal Site award at the 1999 SXSW Interactive Festival.

Steve McGuire has been a freelance computer graphic artist since 1989. A San Francisco Bay Area resident, he specializes in illustration, information graphics, and 2D animation for agencies, designers, publishers, and high-tech corporations. He has also taught Photoshop and Illustrator in corporate environments and at professional training centers.

Joachim Müller-Lancé, a graduate of the Basel School of Design in Switzerland and student of fine arts at The Cooper Union School of Art in New York, received the 1993 Gold Prize in the Morisawa typeface competition for his Lancé typeface family. He is the principal of Kame Design in San Francisco, which specializes in graphic design, typography, cartooning, and animation.

Macky Pamintuan was born in Davao City, Philippines. He moved to the United States in 1997 and is currently studying illustration and 2D animation at the Academy of Art in San Francisco. He is also a freelance illustrator.

Steve Piasecki has four years' experience developing online content and user interfaces. A San Francisco resident, he is also a portrait photographer, a writer who develops educational materials for Web technologies, and a teacher of HTML theory and design.

Gregory Ramsperger is from Crestline, a community nestled in the San Bernardino mountains of Southern California. He studied physics at Oregon State University, where he worked with the university's central Web services department writing HTML and JavaScript, and doing Web design. He began working at HOT in August 1999.

Noreen Santini designs print- and Web-based infographics and site architecture at HOT. She has also designed navigational signage for spaces such as hospitals and museums, and she has won several design awards, including the American Corporate Identity Environmental Graphic Design award and the IIDA Interior Design Best of Competition award.

Ben Seibel, a freelance designer in the San Francisco Bay Area, has created Web sites and print brochures, advertisements, and ID collateral. Ben has also worked at design and advertising agencies and was art director of the literary magazine *The Fugue*. He contributed to *Elements of Web Design* (Peachpit Press) and has a BFA from the University of Kansas.

André Sjøberg is an information designer for Razorfish in Oslo, Norway. He was a freelance designer from 1995 to 1997 before joining Spray Network, which merged with Razorfish in 1998. Clients include KPMG and NATWEST in England. He shares his living space with some turntables and a hefty number of 12-inch vinyl discs.

Glossary

a

adaptive palette A palette of colors that is weighted toward the most commonly used colors in the image.

animated GIF A GIF graphic file that includes multiple frames of motion that can be played back as an animation.

anti-alias A method of smoothing the jagged edges of type or line art on computer screens by adding pixels of intermediate color values along the object's edge.

attribute A value in an HTML tag that specifies additional information about how the tagged element should be treated, such as height or color.

autotrace To convert a raster image into a vector graphic so that you can work with editable lines instead of pixels.

b

banding Noticeable steps in a graduated tonal image.

bit depth The number of bits of color information per pixel. For example, an 8-bit RGB image consists of as many as 256 colors.

bitmap A type of graphic file, most often used for continuous-tone photographic images, composed of an array of pixels. See *vector graphic*.

bot Short for "robot." Software bots search the Web for new and updated HTML documents to add to search engine indexes. Bots are also sometimes called worms or spiders.

browser Software that communicates with Web servers and displays content on a computer screen. Netscape Navigator and Microsoft Internet Explorer are the two most common browsers.

c

Cascading Style Sheets Sets of rules that can be applied to HTML documents and govern the placement, positioning, size, and other aspects of HTML text and graphical elements.

CGI Common Gateway Interface. A set of rules that allows browsers and servers to exchange information based on requests from the browser.

CGI script A program on a Web server that allows a browser to access another program on the server, such as a database. Can be used to process forms.

class A group of HTML elements, selected by the designer, that can have the same layout attributes applied through a Cascading Style Sheet.

color table The values of all colors in a particular image file, used by image-editing software to convert between color models and by browsers to display images. Also called a color lookup table, CLUT, or color palette.

comment tag Contains reference information in an HTML document that isn't displayed by a browser. See *metatag*.

common gateway interface See *CGI*.

CSS See *Cascading Style Sheets*.

d

DHTML Dynamic HTML. A version of HTML that supports such technologies as Cascading Style Sheets and JavaScript, so pages can contain animation and interactivity.

dithering A process of interpolating the values of adjacent pixels in an image to simulate intermediate colors and create smoother edges. The most common method applies an error-diffusion calculation.

dpi Dots per inch. A measure of resolution for an output device such as a laser printer or imagesetter. See *ppi*.

dynamic HTML. See *DHTML*.

e

EPS Encapsulated PostScript. A format for saving and exchanging PostScript graphic files between applications, whether they contain bitmap or vector elements.

f

font A complete set of uppercase and lowercase characters and punctuation marks in a typeface of a specific size, weight, and style.

frame One image in a sequence of motion in a video, movie, or animation file.

frames A feature of HTML that allows multiple documents to appear in separate areas of one browser window. The documents can interrelate but each can be updated and scrolled independently.

frameset The HTML tag that defines the number and positioning of the frames that appear in a browser window.

FTP File transfer protocol. A way for computers to transfer files to an Internet server, and how a computer can download files from a server.

g

GIF Graphics Interchange Format. A cross-platform bitmap file format that contains as many as 256 colors. The GIF89a format supports transparency, interlacing, and animation and is the most common format for graphics on the Web. See *animated GIF* and *JPEG*.

h

hexadecimal A base-16 numbering system used to define colors on the Web. It includes the digits 0 through 9 and the letters A through F (for 10 though 16). RGB colors expressed in hex triplets include three two-character pairs, such as #6A5ACD.

hotspot An area of an image map defined by pixel coordinates that contains a link to another HTML document.

HTML Hypertext Markup Language. Uses tags to define structural elements of documents published on the Web, including links to other documents.

hyperlink. See *link*.

i

image map An image used for navigation on the Web. Different areas of the image contain links to other HTML pages. See *hotspot*.

indexed color An image mode that restricts the total number of colors in a file to no more than 256, based on a specified palette.

interlacing The capability of a GIF image to appear gradually in a browser so that visitors can watch the image appear in successively higher resolution versions as it downloads.

Internet A decentralized, global computer network originally financed by the U.S. government to facilitate communication between academics and scientists.

j

JavaScript A scripting language developed by Netscape allowing HTML authors to put interactivity and dynamic content—animation, sound, and rollover effects, for example—in their pages.

JPEG A compressed bitmap file format designed for photographic images or images with many subtle color transitions. The name stands for Joint Photographic Experts Group, which developed the format for the International Standards Organization. See *GIF*.

k

keyword Describes the content of an HTML page and can be used by search engines to locate relevant documents.

l

link Short for hyperlink. An element in an HTML document that lets the visitor click with the mouse to jump to another part of the document or to another page entirely.

loop The number of times an animation or video file is played: once, a specific number of times, or forever.

low-source image An image that appears in a browser before a source image. It is usually a lower resolution version of the source file, giving visitors a preview of the final graphic.

m

metatag Includes information about the HTML document, such as keywords that can be used by search engines. See *comments tag*.

moiré A pattern of interference in a printed halftone image caused by conflicting screen angles. Moiré can also be created when a halftone image is scanned into a computer.

n

navigational system A graphical interface to a Web site that lets visitors find their way through contents and pages.

o

opacity The degree of transparency of pixels in an image.

optimize To save graphic files for the Web with the most appropriate file format, color palette and the smallest possible file size.

p

page An HTML document containing text, images, and other elements.

palette A set of colors that can be applied to indexed color images for the Web. An Exact palette, for example, includes the exact colors in an RGB image of 256 or fewer colors. See *adaptive palette* and *Web-safe palette*.

PDF Portable Document Format. An electronic file format developed by Adobe Systems based on a compressed form of PostScript. PDF files can be published to the Web and display documents with their original formatting intact.

Glossary

pixel Short for "picture element". The smallest unit of measure in a scanner or monitor.

ppi Pixels per inch. A measure of resolution for onscreen images. See *dpi*.

q

QuickTime A video format developed by Apple Computer and supported by both Apple Macintosh computers and Windows PCs.

r

raster See *bitmap*.

resolution The degree of detail contained in a digital image, determined by the number of dots per inch or pixels per inch. Images created for the Web are generally 72 pixels per inch. See *dpi* and *ppi*.

RGB The additive model used by computer monitors that blends red, green, and blue light to create a full spectrum of color.

rollover An effect that can be triggered when a mouse cursor interacts with an HTML element. Effects are usually triggered by a mouse rolling over a specific area of an image and may include animation or sound. When an effect is applied to another area of the image, it is called a remote or secondary rollover.

s

search engine Software that lets someone search for content on the Web or within a site using keywords. See *bot*.

site A collection of related and linked Web pages with a cohesive navigational system that resides on one or more servers.

slice A portion of an image cut to fit into an HTML table cell. Each slice of a large image can be optimized independently, contain a link, and support animation and rollover effects.

source image A graphic file that displays in an HTML page in a browser. See *low-source image*.

state The image or file that appears in a browser before a rollover is triggered (the "off" state) or when it is activated (the "on" state).

streaming A method of transferring multimedia content over the Web so that it is processed by the client's system in a continuous stream and can begin to be displayed or played before the whole file has been transmitted.

style sheet A document that defines rules for the layout of an HTML file. The rules can be applied by style tags or style classes. See *Cascading Style Sheets*.

t

tables A set of tags and attributes that allow HTML content to be displayed in cells, rows, and columns, giving greater control over the placement of elements on the page.

tags Codes used to define content in an HTML document. A structural tag describes a document element, such as body text or an image; a style tag describes the layout.

tile To arrange and repeat a graphic in an HTML page so that it appears as a single contiguous background image in a browser.

time delay The time, in seconds, that elapses between the display of frames in an animation.

tolerance The range from 0 to 255 that an image-editing tool uses when selecting or filling pixels. A low tolerance selects or fills pixels similar in color; a high tolerance selects or fills a broader range of colors.

transparency Pixels with no color values, allowing a background color or pattern to show through. See *opacity*.

tween To automatically create intermediate frames of motion in an animation. The term comes from *in betweening*, used in traditional animation.

u

URL Uniform Resource Locator. The address of documents on the World Wide Web.

v

vector graphic An image whose content is defined by lines and curves and measured by mathematical vectors. The alternative is bitmap. See *bitmap*.

w

Web-safe palette A set of 216 colors common to both the Windows and Macintosh operating systems that won't dither when displayed in a browser in 8-bit color.

World Wide Web The computers on the Internet that serve linked, formatted HTML documents. These documents can be accessed and viewed by any computer platform through a graphical browser.

Index

Index

j

k

l

m

n

o

p

Index